How to Rehearse a Play

Based on interviews with over forty award-winning artists, *How to Rehearse a Play* offers multiple solutions to the challenges that directors face from first rehearsal to opening night.

The book provides a wealth of information on how to run a rehearsal room, suggesting different paths and encouraging directors to shape their own process. It is divided into four sections:

- lessons from the past: a brief survey of influential directors, including Stanislavski's acting methods and Anne Bogart's theories on movement;
- a survey of current practices: practical advice on launching a process, analyzing scripts, crafting staging, detailing scene work, collaborating in technical rehearsals and previews, and opening the play to the public;
- rehearsing without a script: suggestions, advice, and exercises for devising plays through collaborative company creation;
- rehearsal workbook: prompts and exercises to help directors discover their own process.

How to Rehearse a Play is the perfect guide for any artist leading their first rehearsal, heading to graduate school for intense study, or just looking for ways to refresh and reinvigorate their artistry.

Damon Kiely is the author of *How to Read a Play* (Routledge 2016) and is a director, playwright, and professor of directing and acting. He is the chair of performance for the Theatre School of DePaul University, USA.

How to Rehearse a Play

A Practical Guide for Directors

Damon Kiely

Routledge
Taylor & Francis Group
NEW YORK AND LONDON

First published 2021
by Routledge
52 Vanderbilt Avenue, New York, NY 10017

and by Routledge
2 Park Square, Milton Park, Abingdon, Oxon, OX14 4RN

Routledge is an imprint of the Taylor & Francis Group, an informa business

© 2021 Taylor & Francis

The right of Damon Kiely to be identified as author of this work has been asserted by him in accordance with sections 77 and 78 of the Copyright, Designs and Patents Act 1988.

All rights reserved. No part of this book may be reprinted or reproduced or utilised in any form or by any electronic, mechanical, or other means, now known or hereafter invented, including photocopying and recording, or in any information storage or retrieval system, without permission in writing from the publishers.

Trademark notice: Product or corporate names may be trademarks or registered trademarks, and are used only for identification and explanation without intent to infringe.

Library of Congress Cataloging-in-Publication Data
Names: Kiely, Damon, author.
Title: How to rehearse a play: a practical guide for directors / Damon Kiely.
Description: New York, NY: Routledge, 2020. | Includes bibliographical references and index.
Identifiers: LCCN 2020005448 (print) | LCCN 2020005449 (ebook) | ISBN 9781138299474 (hardback) | ISBN 9781138483811 (paperback) | ISBN 9781351053778 (ebook)
Subjects: LCSH: Theater rehearsals. | Theater–Production and direction.
Classification: LCC PN2071.R45 K54 2020 (print) |
LCC PN2071.R45 (ebook) | DDC 792.02/8–dc23
LC record available at https://lccn.loc.gov/2020005448
LC ebook record available at https://lccn.loc.gov/2020005449

ISBN: 978-1-138-29947-4 (hbk)
ISBN: 978-1-138-48381-1 (pbk)
ISBN: 978-1-351-05377-8 (ebk)

Typeset in Sabon
by Deanta Global Publishing Services, Chennai, India

For my brother, Colin.

Contents

List of Figures		*viii*
Foreword		*ix*
Acknowledgments		*xii*
1	Introduction	1
2	Lessons from the Past	4
3	A Survey of Current Practices	29
4	Rehearsing a Play Without a Script: Notes on Devising	137
5	Rehearsal Workbook	165
	Appendices	*193*
	Bibliography	*202*
	List of Interviews	*204*
	Biographies of Interviewees	*206*
	Index	*222*

Figures

2.1	*Boy* by Anna Ziegler	20
2.2	*Black Mask* by Damon Kiely and Frank Bradley	26
3.1	*The Glass Menagerie* by Tennessee Williams	36
3.2	*Macbeth* by William Shakespeare	41
3.3	*She Kills Monsters* by Qui Nguyen	58
3.4	*A Streetcar Named Desire* by Tennessee Williams	65
3.5	Areas of the Stage, Proscenium	68
3.6	Areas of the Stage, Thrust	69
3.7	*Macbeth* by William Shakespeare	81
3.8	*Miracle* Music and Lyrics by Michael Mahler, Book by Jason Brett	112
4.1	*The Revel* by Damon Kiely	138
4.2	*Rooming House* co-created by Julia Rhoads and Leslie Buxbaum Danzig	147
4.3	*The Hunter and the Bear* Created and performed by PigPen Theatre Co.	153
4.4	*The Revel* by Damon Kiely	162

Foreword

Kimberly Senior

It's a basement. Or a classroom. Or a loft. Or someone's living room. Maybe it's above a Mexican restaurant. Likely there's no natural light. And you probably can't control the temperature. There might be inconvenient architectural details to navigate—a pillar, an odd jog in the wall. A mug filled with highlighters and pencils. A stack of post-it notes. A table taped off into squares with facsimiles of production props. A wall lined with research, costume renderings. The floor taped out like a crime scene. This is a door. A window. The bedroom. And the ghosts. Don't forget the ghosts. All the practitioners who came before you. The souls of characters from the mind of Euripides to the heart of the next best emerging playwright. There's only one place you can be. Rehearsal.

As defined by Merriam Webster, rehearsal is "something recounted or told again." Or "a private performance or practice session preparatory to a public appearance". Or "a practice exercise: trial." The French call it *répétition*. All of these definitions are apt, yet none of them begin to describe the alchemy (Merriam Webster, again: a power or process that changes or transforms something in a mysterious or impressive way) of the most sacred of spaces, REHEARSAL.

Rehearsal is a place of transformation. The play, previously in one dimension on the page, begins to live a vibrant, multidimensional life. Not only does the play transform, but also its makers. Everyone who touches it—stage manager, actors, directors, designers—shapeshifts to accommodate and prioritize the story. When we enter rehearsal, we are in service of something larger than ourselves.

When making film or television, we prepare in order to attain perfection. We create take after take to then capture it, edit it, and lock it in for history. No matter which moment in history or which audience watches, the work remains unchanged. We may change as a result of our viewing, but the work is permanent. So, what exactly are we preparing for in the theatre? How do we prepare for something so ephemeral? Perhaps we prepare in order to remain available and awake in the work as it happens. To build confidence in our story, our scene partners, our scaffolding so that no matter what happens in live performance, the play, bigger than all of us, will survive. We rehearse as if our story depended on it. We rehearse in order to save our play's life. Because our work, in essence, is a world premiere every night. No two performances and audiences are alike. The unique combination of the barometric pressure, events on the world's stage, and the last phone call you had with your mom create a one night only event. How do we prepare for that? What rehearsal can get us ready for that? On the opening night of my production of Ayad Akhtar's *Disgraced* at Berkeley Repertory Theatre, the six coordinated terrorist attacks devastated Paris. How could we have rehearsed our play to prepare for the climate that particular day, that unique performance? So the art and craft of rehearsing, this practice exercise, is a private opportunity to do something that will one day be public. Instead of making the work perfect, we are making ourselves ready to be imperfect. We are in the process of uncovering, rather than covering. It is a room dominated by questions, rather than answers. What if we tried it this way? What if I move left instead of right? What if it's a kiss instead of a slap? One draft after another. Always beginning.

Rehearsal is a space of infinite possibilities but even in the most collaborative rooms, someone needs to lead, to help harness these possibilities and to unlock others. There is a Buddhist philosophy that applies to leading—the idea of being big and small at the same time. Knowing when is the moment to stand in the front of the room with big answers and big questions and when is the moment to sit on the floor among your people. This delicate navigation is never more present than in a rehearsal process where we are working toward the eventual public consumption of our art. And in a place where our fear and vulnerability want to take the wheel.

What if there was a book that gave some shape to the ephemeral practice that is rehearsal? A book that could build one's confidence to lead in the infinite landscape of a rehearsal room? A gentle guide full of suggestions and anecdotes. Nutrient rich with questions and answers. A book that provides a broad perspective and many different options. A book written by someone who is always beginning, always asking questions. A book that is imminently read-able, use-able, and love-able.

Over the past fifteen years when I've hit a stumbling block in my work—whether it is the diagnosis of what's not working in a scene, or finding the right words with which to collaborate with an actor, or clarifying the given events over the course of an act—I've been fortunate enough to have a "phone-a-friend" option. That friend is Damon Kiely—a remarkable director, actor, teacher, and writer. We have spent hours over tupperwared salads in his office debating the merits of one approach or another, posing solutions, playing out scenarios. This significant book is chapters full of lunchtime chats, fertile with insights from a myriad of directors, encountering multiple texts, in a vast array of circumstances.

Acknowledgments

Many thanks to my editors, Lucia Accorsi and Stacey Walker, who supported me at every turn and helped me navigate the editing process during a challenging period in my life. This book could not have been possible without the backing of DePaul University—the Theatre Department supported me with an academic leave, research support, and administrative help.

Thanks to all the directors who sat down with me to share their insights on rehearsals and production and to the theatre companies and photographers who allowed me to use their lovely images. I'm grateful to all my early readers including Rachel Walshe, Michael Osinski, Jason Gerace, and Lavina Jadhwani. I can't thank my students enough for their tireless work assisting on this project, including Tiff Abreu, Ryan Kirby, Stephanie LeBolt, Mallory Metoxen, Eamon Hurd, Madi Delk, Mikael Burke, and Jennie Russianoff. You should all thank April Cleveland for mercilessly hounding me to clarify and simplify my writing. Big thanks to Bob Willems for helping me with the cover!

I'm honored to call Kimberly Senior my friend and colleague. She's encouraged me in so many ways throughout the years and graced me with an eloquent forward.

I'm blessed to have a mother I see every day who always believed I could do more than I thought possible. Finally, I have to thank my wife, Jennifer Tanaka, and our two kids, Isabella and Finn. They've supported me in all of my creative endeavors and put up with my moods as I cranked out draft after draft of this book.

Chapter 1

Introduction

I love rehearsal rooms: groups of artists trying to unlock a mystery together.

Long before everyone gathers to work on the play, a director sits alone with a script, dreaming on the production. In my first book, *How to Read a Play*, I outline the many ways directors prepare for rehearsals and design meetings. Some read the play from beginning to end over and over, while others dissect the script beat by beat, cataloging events and given circumstances. Directors research the world of the play and the writing style of the playwright. They search for answers to the riddle: How does this play work?

Once a director develops some ideas, they gather designers and start a new discovery process. Teams of artists make sketches, craft models, test cues, and write casebooks. The group pores over research, maps the action of the script, and seeks inspirational images and music. As a team, they imagine how this particular production will play. The director casts a group of actors they believe will match an evolving vision for the production.

In this book, I focus on rehearsal: the electric moment all the artists come together.

As soon as the cast meets for the first time, a clock starts ticking down to opening night. With a limited amount of time, the director communicates a shared vision to the actors and seeks their input on how the play works. The director coordinates the vision for the production, helps analyze the text, guides staging, and delves into the details of scenes. When technical rehearsals begin, the director facilitates the synthesis of actors and designers in a short creative period before spectators arrive. Lastly, they listen to audience reactions and steer the entire team toward opening the production.

A director offers direction: a way forward, a line of thought, guidance. But how?

I wrote this book for anyone approaching directing for the first time. How do directors launch an exploration? How can you work on text with actors? What methods create dynamic and clear staging? What tools unlock the mysteries of a complex scene? Rather than outlining one way to accomplish these tasks, this book challenges directors to discover their own methods. Take this book into a scene study class to deepen your process or keep it in your bag as you head into rehearsals for your first play.

I also wrote this book for any directors entering graduate school. Artists who've experienced challenges while running their own rehearsal rooms may want to take a moment to examine their proces deeply. You've directed actors—do you always have the language you need? You've crafted scenes; Do you want a fresh look at how to create truthful moments? Is it time to shake up your thinking?

Finally, I wrote this book for my colleagues in the field. We're in a lonely business. Actors watch each other work all the time. Designers collaborate with their colleagues show to show. Directors almost never have a chance to observe how a colleague gives notes, listens to preview audiences, or works with a playwright. This book offers a peek behind the curtain.

The heart of this book is the **Workbook** chapter. These twenty-one exercises and prompts won't tell you how to direct a play but rather provoke crucial questions: What is a rehearsal? Why do we conduct them? How do we start with some words on a page, or a group of actors, or an idea—and end with a thrilling, live performance.? The workbook starts with preproduction, moves into the first day of rehearsal, and covers text work, staging, and scene work.

The other chapters provide context and stories to flesh out those practical exercises.

The **Survey of Current Practices** delivers ideas from my interviews with forty working directors. I talked to Tony Award–winning artists, radical experimentalists, university professors, and storefront theatre warriors. I spoke to directors on the West Coast, those working regionally, New York based directors, and those working in my hometown of Chicago. I traveled to Russia and England to gather more perspectives. I asked each director practical questions: What is your first day like? Do you spend time at the table analyzing the script? How do you stage a physical moment? What does scene work look like for you? How do you collaborate with actors?

The Survey of Current Practices takes readers through all the common tasks directors tackle in a rehearsal process, from the first read through to opening night. In each section I lay out competing ideas, encouraging you to find your own path. Some directors like to spend at least a week sitting at a table, poring through the script with their cast, learning the rhythms of the play. Others immediately jump on their feet, staging the first day. One director will run their play up to a dozen times in a three-week rehearsal process, while another will still be crafting the last scene just before technical rehearsals begin. What methods work for you?

Where I think it will help, I offer my own experiences from twenty years working as a professional director as well as my current position as the Chair of Performance at DePaul University in Chicago. I've observed thousands of hours of rehearsals by MFA Directing students, learning from their trial and error.

In the chapter on **Rehearsing a Play without a Script**, I offer **Notes on Devising**. I interviewed a diverse group of artists who create their projects with an ensemble in a room rather than starting with a written play. How do they develop ideas? What methods do they use to generate material? How do they refine and focus their projects? What role does audience feedback have in the final product? This chapter should inspire artists interested in company created work, while offering new ideas to those who work on established plays.

In **Lessons from the Past**, I highlight six representative thinkers, writers, and directors from throughout history. Their ideas echo throughout the book, providing context for my interviews with directors working now.

What are some lessons from the past we can use today? Let's take a look.

Chapter 2

Lessons from the Past

I teach a class called Directing Theories with a reading list that is measured in feet.

I challenge student directors to read stacks of classic texts penned by influential directors and thinkers. Once a week we dissect the theories of thought leaders such as Russian acting teacher Konstantin Stanislavski, German revolutionary Bertolt Brecht, and American experimentalist Anne Bogart. One student engages us with the director's biography, and another will illuminate important historical and artistic movements of the time.

Then we probe: Why did they make theatre? How did they make theatre? What did their theatre look like? What ideas did they reject? What new ideas did they foster?

Why did Stanislavski create what he called a grammar of acting? What was he reacting to in Russian Theatre at the turn of the 20th century? How did Brecht create what he called Epic Theatre, art that actively criticized the political corruption in Germany post World War I? What is Anne Bogart's theory of stimulating actors through movement exercises?

During the weekly class discussions, students wrestle with competing theories. Are they interested in the psychological reality that Stanislavski was seeking, or are they intrigued by some sort of heightened acting style? Do they want to clearly underline political and sociological messages as Brecht did, or do they want to uncover more human moments in a subtler fashion? Do they believe the most effective way to create a tight acting ensemble is through physical exercises, as Anne Bogart writes, or will intellectual pursuits yield better results?

As a final project, I challenge students to write their own manifestos. I encourage them to interrogate themselves: What will my theatre look like? How will I make it? Why do I direct plays?

In this chapter, I highlight six authors who exemplify different tasks that directors encounter. For each writer I'll give a quick background on their life and times, and then focus on key ideas that we will explore throughout the book. Here's our six:

- Aristotle: Plot Master
- The Duke of Saxe-Meiningen: Deep Reader of Texts
- Konstantin Stanislavski: Acting Coach
- Bertolt Brecht: Crafter of Details
- Peter Brook: Instigator of Improvisation
- Anne Bogart: Physical Ensemble Maker

One could write a detailed history of directors and theatrical essayists, covering hundreds of writers. I picked these six because their formative theories guide us through the rest of the book. As you read about each thinker, ask yourself, is this a technique that I embrace? How can working with this approach change my own process? What practices still resonate hundreds or thousands of years later?

Our first thinker, Aristotle, didn't write or direct plays, but he lectured about theatre during a pioneering moment in the Western world. His descriptions of classic Greek tragedy have influenced theatre makers ever since.

ARISTOTLE: MASTER OF PLOT

Born in 384 BCE, Aristotle lived when Greek thinkers and politicians were developing the core institutions of Western democracy.

Aristotle studied under master philosopher Plato for twenty years, learning and experimenting with his theories of discovery through dialectic. When his mentor died in 348 BCE, Aristotle founded his own school. He taught kings, philosophers, and scientists. He lectured on such far-ranging topics as botany, government, geology, psychology, and dance. He loved to classify the observable world; often his goal was to discover the "best" form of something.

When Aristotle writes about *Politics*, he asserts that the best possible society is his own society, the Greek City State. He goes on to describe what he believes is the best form of government: an aristocracy where the benevolent elite care for the masses. When Aristotle writes about *Ethics*, he seeks the ideal way for people to live. He asserts that ethics teaches us to live well, or in his words choose to do the right thing for the right reasons.

He never wrote about plays. An unknown student compiled Aristotle's notes on dramatic poetry and created *The Poetics*. True to form, the philosopher delineates the ideal form of theatre:

> Tragedy is an imitation of an action that is admirable, complete and possesses magnitude; in language made pleasurable, each of its species separated in different parts; performed by actors, not through narration, effecting through pity and fear the purification of such emotions.[1]

Aristotle was describing a very specific form of theatre, the Greek tragedies written by playwrights such as Euripides, Sophocles, and Aeschylus. These plays often put a great person in the center of a crisis, depicting their eventual downfall. Aristotle believed tragedies were well-suited to both entertain and educate audiences about morality and human behavior. Unlike narrative or epic forms, which only describe human action, tragedy shows people making choices live. Want to learn about how humans behave? Best to see them in action.

Aristotle lays out six elements to any tragedy: plot, character, thought, diction, melody, and spectacle. He crowns plot the most important element. He claims a well-made plot could make you cry if somebody told you the story from beginning to end. By watching a tragedy, we view a representation of that plot, played out by actors.

Aristotle remarks that one of our great pleasures is watching imitations, or representations, of human interactions. Even as children we act out stories, and through creating and watching simulations, we learn about the world. Great tragedies inspire empathy for the main characters. We fear for their safety as their life takes a turn for the worse, and then pity their suffering. Imagine one of your favorite plays; could you tell someone the story plot twist by plot twist and engender empathy for the main character?

Aristotle defines more aspects of successful tragedies:

> The imitation is not just of a complete action, but also of events that evoke fear and pity. These effects occur above all when things come about contrary to expectation but because of one another.[2]

By a complete action, Aristotle means that the plot should have a beginning, middle, and an end. It should start, complicate, and then conclude in a fashion that we can follow. Every plot turn must be logical, necessary, and surprising. This is the essence of narrative continuity, which will ensure the best chance at truly affecting an audience emotionally. We should recognize the hero's steps on their journey and identify with their actions as they seeks his goal.

How does Aristotle guide us as we direct a modern tragedy such as *A Streetcar Named Desire*? Tennessee Williams's classic depicts the faded Southern belle Blanche DuBois searching for refuge from scandal and poverty with her sister, Stella. She battles with her new brother-in-law, Stanley, for dominance of the household and her sister's affections.

In the penultimate scene, Blanche and Stanley face off in a fiery exchange. Blanche is tipsy and delusional, but she launches her most complete attack on Stanley, who she views as a brute. He reacts by exposing Blanche as a fraud, countering her insults, and raping her at the end of the scene.

Aristotle instructs directors to create logical steps to progress from the beginning of the play when the two combatants meet, to this final confrontation. Create a first scene that crackles with a whiff of the coming combat. Lead audiences on Stanley's journey as he persecutes, prosecutes, and eventually exiles Blanche. Shock, but don't surprise viewers with Stanley's brutal attack. The play follows a grim logic.

When I watch complete run-throughs of my productions, I employ Aristotle's criteria of narrative continuity. I task my assistant director and dramaturg with letting me know when the story doesn't make sense. Where do we take a leap of logic that the audience can't follow? If we were watching *Streetcar* and Blanche never seemed duplicitous, or Stanley never erupted in anger, their crucial scene wouldn't make sense.

For Aristotle, creating great theatre depended on stringing together a series of plot twists that unfolded logically. The first theatre director, the Duke of Saxe-Meiningen, believed investigating between the plot points helped create truly human behavior on stage.

THE DUKE OF SAXE-MEININGEN: DEEP READER OF TEXTS

In the latter part of the 19th century, a young art enthusiast named Georg II served as the Duke of Saxe-Meiningen, a small principality in Germany. His first triumph came in the Austro-Prussian War of 1866, leading a regiment from Meiningen successfully into every battle of the conflict. As the German empire reigned over a period a relative calm, the Duke was able to focus on his first love: the arts.

Georg dabbled in archeology and history and was a talented artist and draftsman. Bringing his multiple talents to bear, he founded the Meiningen Players, a court theatre troupe devoted to revolutionizing production practices. At the time, most German theatres threw shows together haphazardly, using whatever sets and costumes were on hand. Rehearsals were formalities, devoted to the star actors, and productions were sloppy.

The Duke had seen a tour of the English actor-manager Charles Kean's company, which impressed him with the rigor of the performances and the historical accuracy of the sets and costumes. He researched what was happening in England and took their ideas to the next level, establishing himself as the first modern stage director.

The Duke standardized many of the experimental practices of English actor-managers: conducting lengthy rehearsals, controlling every actor on stage, coordinating the whole production. He didn't appear in the plays but instead stood on the outside, interpreting the text for his company. He established rules that guide our modern concept of ensemble: if you weren't willing to be in the chorus of one play after playing a lead role in another, you were fired. The Duke and his two collaborators, Ellen Franz and Ludwig Chronegk, rehearsed plays for months, sometimes years, before revealing them to the public.

In his essay *Pictorial Motion*, the Duke outlined revolutionary practices taken for granted today: symmetry should be avoided, actors should not stand in a straight line, no one should lean on painted scenery. The Duke obsessed over narrative as he staged plays. "The stage must always depict movement, the continuous unfolding of a story."[3] He compiled pages of notes on stage images, pictorial groupings of crowd scenes, and character motivations. His notes for Shakespeare's *The Merchant of Venice* are exacting:

> Shylock enters ... to a bench in front of the steps of his house, where he breaks down. Behind him runs a group of street boys. It must be carefully considered whether Shylock should *mumble* the following lines or *cry them out:* "My daughter ... she hath the stones upon her, and the ducats."

During this time the street urchins cry out, "The Stones! The Daughter! The Ducats!"

... Enough time would have elapsed since the elopement ... that this is NOT Shylock's first return home since her departure. He has moved heaven and earth to find his daughter and, as we can see from the text, has even been to the doge. All his steps have been futile. Therefore, the words that he speaks as he goes out are not to be spoken as if he has just learned that his daughter has gone.[4]

The Duke has read and reread the play to discern the most logical sequence of events *between scenes* and how those revelations affect onstage behavior. He creates specific behavior to reveal psychology. He's not just interested in how his actors move and speak, but why.

Ludwig Barnay, a celebrated German actor, came to work for the Duke in 1872. Before working in Meiningen, Barnay was used to two or three rehearsals before performances began. Many actors never bothered to completely memorize their lines but instead relied on an offstage prompter to give them help when they foundered. Imagine Barnay's horror when he realized that the Duke expected all actors to fully commit to a rehearsal period that would last for months. Barney eventually drank the Meiningen Kool-Aid, swayed by the ensemble's devotion to craft.

In his journals, Barney recreates a moment of rehearsal as he was preparing for the title role of *Hamlet*. The Duke assembles his ensemble to stage the first scene with the prince and his uncle King Claudius. Barnay strides on behind the King. The Duke stops the rehearsal to redirect Barnay. The Duke reasons that Hamlet and the King must enter from opposite sides to tell the correct story: Hamlet is arriving home for the first time. Claudius is about to give a speech about marrying Hamlet's mother Gertrude, and he wouldn't bother if Hamlet knew the dirt.

They start the scene again, but Barnay bursts onto the stage and says, "That's nonsense!" After a little pause, the Duke calls out. "What do you mean that it's nonsense, Herr Barnay?" Barnay bravely lays out his reasoning: Hamlet knows his father's been dead for two months; he says it earlier in the play. Claudius isn't giving a speech because Hamlet has just returned home. He's making a public announcement because he knows Hamlet won't embarrass the Queen in front of the court. In other words, the speech is a power move. To tell the story correctly, we must see Hamlet forced to enter with the King as part of his retinue.

Barnay recalls a pit opening up in his stomach, "An unearthly stillness followed my words. Then after a long silence, the Duke said, 'Prepare the scene as Herr Barnay has described it. He is right, and I am wrong.'"[5] The Duke didn't care who came up with the best idea. What does the script say? What did Shakespeare intend? What will help the audience understand what isn't said in the script but is implied by the dialogue?

I remember when I was working on *A Streetcar Named Desire* in a production for DePaul University, and I wished I'd read the script as carefully as the Duke. In the second scene of the play, which takes place in early May, Stanley reveals that his wife is pregnant. In the seventh scene of the play, Stella is rushed to the hospital to deliver her baby on the evening of Blanche's birthday, September fifteenth. We rightly understood that Stella was about four months pregnant in the first few scenes, able to hide her condition from her sister. The last few scenes all take place on the night of Blanche's birthday, with the final scene occurring a few days later.

Our mistake came in analyzing scenes six and seven, which depict a night when Blanche goes out on a date with Stanley's best friend, Mitch. The designers and I assumed the date occurred sometime in the middle of the summer, perhaps a month after the first scene. We designed a small pregnancy pad for Stella, and I prepared to stage with those circumstances in mind.

Imagine our surprise during table work on scene six when an actor remarked on Blanche's line, "Oh, my birthday's next month, the fifteenth of September; that's under Virgo."[6] This put scenes six and seven in the middle of August. This changed everything. Not only did we need to change Stella's costume to present her as eight months pregnant, the given circumstances of the scene altered dramatically. Stanley had been suffering through living with his sister-in-law for three sweltering summer months in their small two-room apartment. Blanche had been dating Mitch all summer but had resisted his romantic advances. With these new given circumstances in play, the scenes started to crackle with newfound tension.

The Duke of Saxe-Meiningen created a series of exacting productions based on his close readings of classic plays. He toured their work and between 1874 to 1890 played in thirty-eight cities in nine countries, including Russia, Sweden, Austria, Denmark, Belgium, Holland, and England for a total of 2,600 performances of forty-one plays. Almost every major theatre artist of the early 20th century saw the work and knew that the Duke had raised the bar.

When the Meiningen Players toured Moscow in 1890, our next writer, Konstantin Stanislavski, was dreaming about a theatre revolution.

KONSTANTIN STANISLAVSKI: ACTING COACH

Born Konstantin Sergeievich Alexeiev, the privileged son of a rich textile manufacturer in Russia, Stanislavski loved theatre but hated his own acting. Luckily for us, he spent a lifetime trying to improve his work. In his idealistic memoir, *My Life in Art*, he chronicles his early efforts to match the talents of famous Russian actors. To achieve great heights, he often grabbed at clichés and stock ideas:

> This is what often befalls an inexperienced actor. They want him to cry when he does not want to, laugh when he feels miserable, be miserable when he feels happy, they want him to express feelings he does not have in his heart ... it all ends in tension, forcing ... and a spurious theatricality by which the actor hopes to deceive both himself and the audience.[7]

Stanislavski dabbled as an actor, director, and producer of amateur theatrical productions. He was constantly dissatisfied with the results. Sometimes he would create what he believed was a compelling performance, only to see the results quickly slip away the next night. As an actor he often succumbed to emoting and histrionics, and as a director he struggled to guide his company.

The 1890 tour of the Meiningen Players knocked Stanislavski for a loop. He talked his way into observing rehearsals and marveled at the director's iron control over the ensemble. He noticed that the entire company worked tirelessly to mine their plays for deeper truths. As he worked with his amateur theatrical groups in the late 1890s, Stanislavski strove to find meaning in his plays and inspire his actors to greater performances. He tried out the iron control that he observed in the Meiningen rehearsals but found that while it was sometimes satisfying, it didn't help his actors create nuanced performances.

Late in the decade, he teamed up with a fellow dreamer, Vladimir Nemirovich-Danchenko, and they collaborated to create one of the most influential theatre companies in history.

The Moscow Art Theatre

Stanislavski had heard of the award-winning playwright and producer Vladimir Nemirovich-Danchenko but didn't know that they shared so many values. When the two upstarts sat down for a conversation about a new way of making art, Stanislavski claims they started talking at 2 P.M. and the conversation lasted until eight the following morning. They had ambitions:

> Our plan for our new enterprise was radical. We rebelled against the old style of acting, "theatricality", spurious emotion, declamation, overacting, against stupid conventions in the staging and in the sets, against stardom, which marred ensemble work, against the whole way performances were put together and the triviality of the repertoire of the time.[8]

They decided to join forces and create the Moscow Art Theatre (MAT) in 1898 with the goal of professionalizing theatre in Russia and raising it to an art form. Danchenko would oversee the literary aspect, and Stanislavski would direct the plays.

Prior to MAT, rehearsals in Russia were slapdash formalities, similar to those in Germany. Often the whole process lasted a few days—to put up an entire play! In a letter to his brother Alexander, the fledgling playwright Anton Chekhov sent an account of the disastrous rehearsal for the first production of his play *Ivanov*. He complained bitterly about the producer, Fiodor Korsh, and some of his actors:

> First of all: Korsh promised me ten rehearsals, but actually allowed me only four, of which only two could properly be described as rehearsals, since the other two were more like tournaments for the actors to hone their skills in verbal disputation and invective. The only two actors who knew their lines were Davydov and Glama; All the others trusted the prompter and their own inner convictions.[9]

The results were disastrous: drunk adlibs, people wandering aimlessly about the stage, and a devastating lack of focus. Stanislavski, on the other hand, orchestrated 100 rehearsals for his production of Anton Chekhov's masterwork *The Seagull*. He started by having the actors sit around a table discussing the ideas of the play, revealing motivations behind the dialogue, and studying the director's analysis. For many years Stanislavski insisted that this initial *table work* helped actors created detailed characters.

MAT's productions of plays by Chekhov and other writers plays drew rave reviews and huge audiences. MAT inspired realism took over as the new style in Russian theatre, and Stanislavski's productions became famous for their detailed moments of staging, pregnant pauses, and complex sound designs. In spite of the commercial success, Stanislavski eventually soured on his own shows. Even though the actors were busy recreating realistic human interactions, the acting rang hollow. They could recreate a moment, but Stanislavski never believed they actually felt it.

Stanislavski devoted the rest of his life writing and rewriting what he called a grammar of acting to help actors discover what he called a *measure of true feeling*.

An Actor's Work

In 2008, Jean Benedetti released a new translation of Stanislavski's classic training manual, *An Actor's Work*. The book takes an unusual format, told from the point of view of an aspiring student working for two years with a master teacher. The imaginary class focuses on "Experiencing" in the first year and "Embodying" in the second.

Early in the book, Stanislavski introduces an idea that will revolutionize actor training: *The Magic If*. Actors must believe in the imaginary circumstances the play gives them and then act accordingly; act as *If* they themselves had lived the character's full life and were confronting the problems within the play.

Using the penultimate scene from *A Streetcar Named Desire* as an example, the actor playing Blanche can arm herself with some juicy given circumstances:

> *If I was raised in a Southern Plantation;*
> *If I was humiliated and had to leave my hometown, penniless;*
> *If I was stuck with my brutish brother-in-law all summer;*
> *If my brother-in-law told me I had to leave his apartment;*
> *If I consoled myself with liquor; and*
> *If he confronted me about my lies;*
> *Then:*
> *What would I do?*

Actors must read the play over and over first to discover the imaginary circumstances the playwright has provided. Then actors work to inhabit and bring those circumstances to bear. But the script doesn't provide all the answers—the director and actor must fill in gaps in the evidence. What happens between scenes? Why does a character make this choice rather than another? What hidden secrets from their past guides current behavior?

After identifying the given circumstances, Stanislavski encourages actors and directors to read the play carefully seeking conflict, action, and desires. For each scene of the play, Stanislavski charges the actor to determine what the character wants most of all. Why do they want it? Why can't they get it? What obstacle blocks the way? Typically, the other character in the scene hinders their desires. Their *Task* is to overcome the *Obstacle* and achieve what they want. How can they overcome the obstacle? By pursuing an appropriate *Action*.

Stanislavski lays out the basics in *An Actor's Work*.

> Life, people, and circumstance, and we ourselves endlessly set up a whole series of obstacles one after the other and we fight our way through them, as through bushes. Each of these obstacles creates a Task and the action to overcome it.[10]

Turning again to the penultimate scene in *A Streetcar Named Desire*, the actor playing Blanche DuBois is facing homelessness and ruin. She wants safety above all. Unfortunately, she is faced with a sneering, leering Stanley Kowalski who taunts and upbraids her. She's alone with him for the first time in months and fears for her safety. What should she do? What is her action? First, she may try to *make Stanley treat her with respect*. Or perhaps she may attempt to *keep Stanley at bay*? Or maybe the best idea is to *put Stanley in his proper place!* (See pages 89–99 for more on applying Stanislavski's methods to rehearsing scenes.)

From the founding of the MAT up until his death, Stanislavski directed plays, taught classes, and continued to revise his grammar of acting. For many years he experimented with the building blocks of coaching actors: given circumstances, tasks, obstacles, and actions. In 1938, at the age of 75, Stanislavski was directing a production of Moliere's play *Tartuffe*. One of the actors confessed she'd kept detailed notes on every rehearsal with the master teacher and didn't know what to do with them. Ever dramatic, Stanislavski told her to "burn them."[11]

He planned to take the cast through an entirely new acting process.

Active Analysis

Vasili Toporkov, leading actor in *Tartuffe*, wrote a thorough account of Stanislavski's process, *Stanislavski in Rehearsal*. The master teacher was interested not in a final product but in developing a new idea of how to rehearse a play.

Stanislavski's final experiment: Active Analysis.

In this new process, Stanislavski throws out the meticulous table work he'd become famous for; instead the collaborators investigate action and conflict on their feet. The director and actors read a scene quickly and try to figure out the relationship between the characters, the basic situation, and the main conflict. Then the actors stand up and improvise the scene, using their own language instead of the author's text. Toporkov recalls the nerve-wracking process:

> He absolutely forbade us to learn the lines. That was an absolute condition of our work and if, suddenly, one of us began to speak Moliere's words he immediately stopped the rehearsal. He considered it a kind of impotence in an actor, if he clung to the script, the words, the author's exact words. He considered it a great achievement if an actor could demonstrate the pattern of physical actions in a scene with the minimum of words. Words were to play only an ancillary role.[12]

After improvising, actors read Moliere's scene, checking to see where they strayed from the plot. Armed with new information they would improvise again, then pore over the script anew. During the improvisations, actors sought to create physical actions that told the story: the conflict, the actions, and the tasks. Eventually when they set a staging they loved; they'd match Moliere's text to the physical actions.

A few years ago, I experimented with Active Analysis at DePaul with the play *Really Really* by Paul Downs Coalaizzo.

We didn't have Stanislavski's luxurious months long rehearsal period, but we tried out the general method. We'd look at a small chunk of the script, investigating the actions and obstacles for each character. Armed with their tasks, the actors put down the script and improvised dialogue and staging.

If the actors found an action that worked for the scene, the actual lines from the script came easily. If they chose a verb that didn't seem appropriate, they wandered all over, not sure what to do. If a scene was really about a roommate *grilling* his friend about what happened at the party last night, but instead he tried to *berate* him senselessly, the actor got lost. Switch to *grilling*, and lines very similar to the script popped out of the actor's mouth. It was like magic.

The process was inspiring but incredibly slow.

After three weeks, we still hadn't run the play. With a week until tech, I called the actors together. "Folks, I think we need to bail on this experiment. We'll never get there." "No," they countered, "we started this way and we're going to end this way."

We were just days from our first preview performance and we still hadn't finished staging. Again, I encouraged us to abandon ship and again the actors said no. The day before our first preview we ran the play for the very first time. I was astonished. The actors knew the script inside and out. They made active choices grounded in character. They *played*.

Stanislavski discovered that actors play when they interact, embracing the actions and conflicts *implied by the words on the page*. Active Analysis returns us to essential questions: How do you rehearse? What is a play? Is it the words on the page? The actions implied by the language? A combination of the two? Throughout his career, Stanislavski sought the essence of how directors can best collaborate with actors; a century later, his methods are taught widely in theatre training programs.

Our next writer, Bertolt Brecht, admired Stanislavski for his attention to detail, but burned with a desire to create a more politically active theatre.

BERTOLT BRECHT: CRAFTER OF DETAILS

Bertolt Brecht made a career of narrowly escaping prison for making political work.

As the Nazis gained power in the 1920s Germany, Brecht wrote and directed plays such as *Man Is Man*, meant to educate the workers on the values of socialism. Clearly in the cross hairs of the oppressive regime, he fled to Switzerland and eventually to the United States. While in America, he unleashed plays that criticized capitalism and nationalistic war machines. For his sins, Brecht was hauled in front of the House Un-American Activities Committee. He fled America for postwar Germany and spent the rest of his life working with the Berliner Ensemble.

Brecht rejected both Stanislavski's realistic acting style and Aristotle's plot-driven model of constructing plays. Traditional plays seduced an audience into empathizing with the characters, lulling them into complacency. In a world where everyone needed to be educated about the evils of capitalism and repressive governments, Brecht believed audiences would be better served by pulling back and scrutinizing what they saw. Don't hypnotize, alienate.

By educating rather than stupefying, Brecht hoped to inspire a political revolution. He popularized Epic Theatre—works that constantly reminded audiences of underlying societal inequities at play. He wanted to alienate the audience from what they were watching, encouraging them to analyze every turn of events.

> The modern theatre mustn't be judged by its success in satisfying the audience's habit but by its success in transforming them. It needs to be questioned not about its degree of conformity with the "eternal laws of the theatre" but about its ability to master the rules governing the great social processes of our age; not about whether it manages to interest the spectator in buying a ticket—i.e. the theatre itself—but about whether it manages to interest him in the world.[13]

To better craft his political message, Brecht outlined a rigorous production process. First, he would analyze a play for its social significance. Next, he'd figure out the important story nodes and imagine ways to highlight the political implications of each plot point. Brecht would design and cast the play and quickly sketch in a rough staging. Finally came the grueling detail work. (See Appendix 1 for Brecht's Phases of Production.)

> Each detail is rehearsed individually, ignoring the final tempo. The actor builds up his character's attitude to the other characters and gets to know what he is like.[14]

Brecht obsessed over making sure that actors investigated all the possible social implications of a gesture or phrase. He could spend hours on a moment where a character picked up a baby or handled a telescope. Not surprisingly, this phase of rehearsals lasted months.

Brecht's assistant Hans Bunge took scrupulous notes and even went so far as to make audio recordings of the 100 rehearsals the Berliner Ensemble conducted for the *Caucasian Chalk Circle*. One day Brecht was working on a scene where a woman discovers a baby on her doorstep, and he found her first instinct sentimental and unrealistic. Brecht walked the actress through her actions step by step. A person wouldn't just go outside if they heard a knock. She should poke her head out slowly and look around. Also, the actress picked up the baby too quickly for Brecht's taste. Bunge reports Brecht's instructions:

> Ok, you see a small bundle lying in front of the door, isn't that so. Now that is a very unhealthy thing, isn't that so, and it's also dangerous, the baby could be sick with anything on earth: plague, cholera. People are mistrustful they don't just take in even a dog. In order that that should be really clear, you could perhaps just let it lie there for a while. Who left something lying there?[15]

Even lead actors weren't safe from Brecht's unstinting gaze. He argued with Angelika Hurwicz, the actress playing Grusha, over the size of a bundle she was carrying. Hurwicz came into a scene with a smaller load, reasoning she had to get rid of things during her journey.

Brecht countered that while that seems logical, it left out the possibility that perhaps Grusha had been stealing things and adding to her bundle. He cautioned her against making assumptions based on character. Bunge reports Brecht's arguments:

> One should never start out on the basis of a figure's character because a person has no character. For Grusha, given the circumstances under which she lives, the times even demand that she steal, at least when it is essential, and this reinforces her "positive character." It is consistent with the main thrust of the play to show what it costs Grusha to take care of the child.[16]

Brecht constantly highlighted inconsistencies in characters. He inspired actors to look for the opposite tactic to the main thrust of their action. People don't act on one desire but out of various contradictory motives. They might love their daughter but betray her to an enemy out of fear. Hunger trumps loyalty.

I obsessed over the details and contradictions of a single moment when working on the Midwest premiere of Anna Ziegler's *Boy* for TimeLine Theatre in 2018. Dramatizing David Reimer's life, the play depicts a historic case of a misguided gender reassignment surgery. It charts a young person's journey from boy to girl and back to being a man.

One simple moment in the play mystified us. The young man, Adam, runs into a woman named Jenny at a party. Jenny knew Adam when he was being raised as a girl long ago, but in the moment she doesn't recognize him. Adam tries to work up the courage to flirt with Jenny but keeps backing away. Jenny has had a couple of beers, so she makes the first move. Ziegler's stage directions propose:

> *She does something flirtatious, putting her hand on Adam's leg or arm. Adam's longing is heartbreakingly clear, but he moves away from her.*[17]

This little moment took the entire rehearsal process to figure out. Adam tried leaping away from Jenny as if he'd been scalded: too abrupt. Jenny subtly put her hand on his arm: not dangerous enough. They tried staring at each other for a moment and then he pulled away: No, we all agreed—untruthful and illogical. We worked the scene with our intimacy coordinator creating draft after draft. Everything seemed close; nothing felt perfect.

During the final hour of rehearsal before the last preview, we broke down the moment detail by detail. Jenny is drunk and relaxed so she should just flop onto the couch, sinking deep into the cushions. Adam, on the other hand, is nervous because he's trying to embody the role of a flirtatious man for the first time. He should sit on the edge of the couch, away from danger. He wants to lean back but can't. When Jenny has to slide forward to look at him and finally puts her hand on his knee, Adam can gently maintain his dignity by sliding away graciously and then changing the topic of conversation.

This version was probably the hundred and first attempt at the moment. By focusing on the societal pressures on the characters, and examining every detail, we unlocked the staging. It was a group effort, one that eventually paid off because we never gave up.

Figure 2.1 *Boy* by Anna Ziegler. Directed by Damon Kiely for TimeLine Theatre Company. L–R: Emily Marso, Theo Germaine. Set: Arnel Sancianco; Lighting: Jared Gooding; Costumes: Samantha C. Jones; Sound: Karli Blalock; Dramaturgy: Josephine Kearns. Photo Credit: Lara Goetsch.

Brecht obsessed over every moment of his productions, looking for the details of staging or intention that would highlight the unseen sociological tensions. There was no moment too small to try three or four ways, no gesture too insignificant that couldn't be mined to help the audience see the bigger picture.

The English firebrand director, Peter Brook, deeply admired Brecht's intentions, but favored a looser, improvisational rehearsal process.

PETER BROOK: INSTIGATOR OF IMPROVISATION

In 1946, at the age of twenty-one, Peter Brook was on the cusp of stardom. His work in smaller venues garnered the attention of the Royal Shakespeare Company. They took a chance and hired him to direct a large-scale production of *Love's Labor's Lost*. In his seminal book, *The Empty Space*, Brook describes fearfully preparing the night before. He knew that actors and stage managers scorned directors who didn't know what they wanted.

He sat in front of a model of the set with scraps of cardboard and tried to figure out the first entry of the court. He had cast forty actors—many of whom had years of experience—and he needed to give them marching orders the next morning. He recalls the fraught moment in *The Empty Space*:

> Again and again, I staged the very first entry of the Court, recognizing that this was when all would be lost or won, numbering the figures, drawing charts, maneuvering the scraps of cardboard to and fro, on and off the set, trying them in big batches, then in small, from the side, from the back, over grass mounds, down steps, knocking them all over with my sleeve, cursing and starting again.[18]

The next morning, he walked in with a fat prompt book and used his most commanding voice to tell the actors how to organize themselves. He divided the cast into groups, assigned them numbers, and gave everyone their orders on how, when, and where to enter.

Immediately, he knew it was no good.

Actors moved differently than cardboard cutouts. Some walked faster than he imagined, others took their time, and a group stopped walking too early. No one was standing in the right place. How could he move forward on his meticulous plan? Should he drill the actors into conforming to his pre-written notes?

> One inner voice prompted me to do so, but another pointed out that my pattern was much less interesting than this new pattern that was unfolding in front of me—rich in energy, full of personal variations, shaped by individual enthusiasms and lazinesses, promising such different rhythms, opening so many unexpected possibilities. It was a moment of panic. I think, looking back, that my whole future work hung in the balance. I stopped, and walked away from my book, in amongst the actors, and I have never looked at a written plan since.[19]

He realized the foolishness of assuming an inanimate model could stand in for a person. He needed to trust his instincts in the moment as well as empower his cast of actors. *Loves Labors Lost* kicked off an unrivaled string of critical hits, establishing Brook as the go-to director for reimaging classics.

At the height of his powers, two decades later, Brook helmed *King Lear* for the RSC.

Charles Marowitz, the critic, playwright, and director, assisted Brook for many years and wrote about his experience working on *Lear*. Traditionally, directors portrayed Lear as a pitiful old man, hoodwinked by his conniving daughters Regan and Goneril. After a deep read of the play, Brook and Marowitz decided to tell a different story. Wasn't Lear capricious and demanding? He gave up his responsibilities but not his rights. His daughters read to them as concerned children rather than stock villains.

After explaining his new take on the play to his cast, in the early stages of rehearsal Brook hung back, allowing actors to wander about without much guidance. When they asked him questions about a scene, he usually responded, "I don't know." He believed that if actors were left to their own devices, they would discover crucial moments on their own. Marowitz reports Brook's insights in his article, *Lear Log*:

> The greatest rehearsal factor is fatigue. When you get so thoroughly exhausted from grappling with a certain problem and you think you can't go on—then—suddenly, something gives and you "find something." You know that marvelous moment in a rehearsal when you suddenly *find something*.[20]

When Marowitz pointed out inconsistencies between the text and what the actors were doing, Brook pushed them aside. He assumed that actors would figure it out for themselves in a week or so. If they didn't, then he would nudge them in a direction.

After the first run-through, Brook championed his actors, telling them they'd discovered the bones of each scene. Now they needed to start thinking of how the entire production will work. Marowitz reports Brook's speech to the actors:

> We've spent all of our time structuring individual scenes and have necessarily lost sight of the whole. Now we must begin looking at one scene in relation to the next...You must keep in mind that when your particular scene is finished, the play still goes on. You must keep the ball in the air being passed from one to the next without a fumble.[21]

Permissive in the early days, now Brook gave strict instructions. He delivered technical notes on falling inflections, cautioning actors to keep up the tone at the end of scenes to launch into the next. Since he'd taught actors about continuity and structure, now he could dispatch specific directives: *break the speech up* or *more pace*. Specificity became the watchword.

When I advise MFA directors on their productions, I'm most effective when I channel Brook's wisdom:

- Read the script as if it's never been done before, challenging typical or received wisdom
- Every play needs a different design
- Every actor brings unique gifts and requires a distinct approach
- Don't focus on details early in the process; inspire creativity and say yes to everything
- Toward the end of rehearsals start to edit with a clear and unsentimental eye
- Just before opening, focus your actors on craft: clarity, pace, language skills, storytelling

Brook's *King Lear* flourished critically and commercially, touring all over the world. Eventually Brook turned the production into a film. Still working almost seventy years later, Brook has directed masterpieces by classic writers, created devised pieces with ensembles, and adapted literature and nonfiction with panache.

My graduate school professor, Anne Bogart, has spoken eloquently about her admiration for Brook's improvisational methods with actors. She taught me the value of creating ensemble primarily through physical exercises.

ANNE BOGART: PHYSICAL ENSEMBLE MAKER

I had the great luck to study under Anne Bogart in her first years teaching at Columbia University. Shortly after she was hired, the MFA directing students went to see her production of *The Medium*. Bogart had devised the play with her SITI Company, and it blew me away. The show didn't present a straightforward narrative, instead illustrating the ideas of prescient media guru Marshall McLuhan through a series of loosely connected episodes. The play took his iconic phrase, "The medium is the message," and made it tangible.

I can still remember images from the show: a group of actors spouting theories about mediated language while acting as if they were in a TV Western; a line of performers revolving backwards as if gliding on an enchanted turntable; Marshall McLuhan stuffed into the underside of a coffee table; magical TV remotes. I didn't know how they'd created the show.

Then, I started studying Viewpoints with Anne and I found out.

Bogart learned about Viewpoints from the educator and director Mary Overlie, who invented the movement technique as an offshoot of her work with the Judson Church Dance project. Overlie desired a new language for movement—one inspired by the freedom of contact improvisation rather than the rules of ballet and modern dance. Overlie noticed artists often employed a *vertical* hierarchy of values. Listed in order of importance from top to bottom, the typical components were:

- Story
- Character
- Emotion
- Space
- Movement

Overlie believed that artists should view the elements of their creations *horizontally*. No one element is more important than another. She focused on a new collection of components—ones she felt were important in creating any live performance.

Space   Shape   Time   Emotion   Movement   Story

Anne Bogart studied the Viewpoints with Overlie at New York University, and went on to adapt them and create her own system of training, collaborating with director Tina Landau. Bogart and Landau introduced theatre makers to their own collection of Viewpoints: Spatial Relationship, Kinesthetic Response, Shape, Gesture, Repetition, Architecture, Tempo, Duration, and Topography through workshops and their publication, *The Viewpoints Book*.

Through Viewpoints training, actors work on each of these principals individually and as a group. Just as actors run verbal drills to improve their diction, they can also heighten their spatial awareness and gestural work. The Viewpoints give ensembles ways to discuss what is happening on stage in terms that don't involve story, character, or emotion. Bogart and Landau extol the virtues of working physically in their training manual:

> Viewpoints awakens all our senses, making it clear how much and how often we live only in our heads and see only through our eyes. Through Viewpoints we learn to listen with our entire bodies and see with a sixth sense.[22]

At Columbia, Bogart led me and my fellow directors through physical exercises that introduced each Viewpoint one by one. First, participants moved back and forth in lanes, only noticing where they were in relation to each other in space. They would move on to interacting with the architecture or working on gestures. I learned not to question when or where to move but to trust my instincts.

Slowly Bogart introduced all the Viewpoints and as a group we started improvising. Standing on the outside, I was astounded by the beautiful images and stage pictures ensemble members created spontaneously. When I participated as an actor, my body often surprised me. *The Viewpoints Book* echoes my discoveries:

> Viewpoints relieves the pressure to have to invent by yourself, to generate all alone, to be interesting and force creativity. Viewpoints allows us to surrender, fall back into empty creative space and trust that there is something there, other than our own ego or imagination, to catch us. Viewpoints helps us trust in *letting something occur* onstage, rather than *making it occur*.[23]

When I trained my own ensembles with Viewpoints, the actors bonded quickly, connecting on a nonverbal level. On some projects, Viewpoints improvisations created arresting and surprising staging. I would guide the actors in creating a repeatable movement piece. Once set, the actors would float the lines on top of the movement. We noted where a line or phrase would pop in unusual ways.

I remember working on *Black Mask,* an original devised theatre piece inspired by film-noir, for the Ontological Theater. Our physical improvisations led to the creation of a crooked plastic surgeon, twisted in body and mind, fleet-footed and combustive police detectives, and slinky femme fatales dripping from the set pieces.

Figure 2.2 Black Mask by Damon Kiely and Frank Bradley. Directed by Damon Kiely for Ontological Theater. L–R: Bryan Webster, Rob Donaldson, Johanna McKeon. Set: Vicki R. Davis; Lighting: Michael Gottlieb Costumes: Carol Bailey; Sound: Jeremy Bernstein. Photo Credit: Gerry Goodstein.

THE LESSONS OF THE PAST

I love teaching a class we call Directing Seminar: all six MFA directors convene once a week to talk about their works in progress. At the end of each production we do a thorough postmortem, pointing out breakthroughs as well as setbacks. Directors also bring problems and challenges from their current rehearsal to the group. *I'm having trouble helping this one actor find the character. I'm running out of time to get to a run-through, what should I do now? I can't seem to unlock the sexuality or danger of this scene.*

As a group we analyze their issues and offer suggestions. Often, we draw from the lessons of the past.

If a director is having a problem with the overall story of the play we encourage them to turn back to their Aristotelian analysis. Have they found a way to link their plot points from beginning to end? Are they following a complete action by the main character? Or perhaps we will encourage them to dig into the play again like the Duke of Saxe-Meiningen, looking for the hidden given circumstances lurking between scenes.

We often turn to the language of Stanislavski when they are having trouble guiding an actor toward a complex characterization. Perhaps the director and actor have slipped into seeking results rather than sticking to the basics of given circumstances, relationships, actions, obstacles, and tasks?

Unsure how to unlock a specific moment in the play? Often it depends on the actors involved and the complexity of the moment to find the right path. Should the directors follow Brook's example and let the actors stumble about in the dark for a bit? Or should they drill down to the specifics like Brecht, working and reworking little moments together?

Sometimes an ensemble hasn't gelled as a group in the early days. In that case we might suggest leading a Viewpoints session or some other movement exercises to bond the actors through nonverbal communication and collaboration.

Sometimes we can't find anything helpful from the examples of history and are better served by listening the ideas of directors working in the field right now. For this book, I spoke to forty directors, digging into each artist's rehearsal process. They revealed their worries, their successes, and their theories on how to unlock scripts with actors.

What did I learn? Let's explore.

NOTES

1. Aristotle, *Poetics*, translated by Malcolm Heath (London: Penguin Books, 1996), 10.
2. Aristotle, 17.
3. George II, Duke of Saxe-Meiningen, Pictorial Motion, in *Directors on Directing*, edited by Toby Cole and Helen Krich-Chinoy (New York: Macmillan Publishing Company, 1953), 81.
4. George II, Duke of Saxe-Meiningen, quoted in *The Theatre Duke: George II of Saxe-Meiningen and the German Stage* by Ann Marie Koller (Stanford: Stanford University Press, 1984), 127.
5. Ludwig Barnay, quoted in *The Theatre Duke: George II of Saxe-Meiningen and the German Stage* by Ann Marie Koller (Stanford: Stanford University Press, 1984), 200.
6. Tennessee Williams, *A Streetcar Named Desire* (1947. Reprint, New York: Book-of-the-Month Club, Inc., 1994), 145.
7. Konstantin Stanislavski, *My Life in Art*, translated by Jean Benedetti (New York: Routledge, 2008), p. 111.
8. Stanislavski, *My Life in Art*, 164.
9. Anton Chekhov, *A Life in Letters*, edited by Rosamund Bartlett, translated by Rosamund Bartlett and Anthony Phillips (London: Penguin Books, 2004), 111–112.
10. Konstantin Stanislavski, *An Actor's Work*, translated and edited by Jean Benedetti (Oxon: Routledge, 2008), 143.
11. Vasili Toporkov, *Stanislavski in Rehearsal*, translated by Jean Benedetti (New York: Routledge, 2004), 108.
12. Toporkov, 111.
13. Bertolt Brecht, *Brecht on Theatre: The Development of an Aesthetic*, edited and translated by John Willet (New York: Hill and Wang, 1964), 161.
14. Brecht, *Brecht on Theatre*, 241.
15. Bertolt Brecht, quoted in John Fuegi, *Bertolt Brecht: Chaos According to Plan* (New York: Cambridge University Press, 1987), 156.
16. Brecht, *Chaos*, 158.
17. Anna Ziegler, *Boy* (New York: Dramatists Play Service, 2016), 9.
18. Peter Brook, *The Empty Space* (New York: Touchstone, 1968), 131.
19. Brook, *Empty*, 132.
20. Peter Brook, quoted by Charles Marowitz in "Lear Log," *The Tulane Drama Review* Vol. 8, No. 2 (Winter 1963), 107.
21. Brook, "Lear Log," 114.
22. Anne Bogart and Tina Landau, *The Viewpoints Book: A Practical Guide to Viewpoints and Composition* (New York: Theatre Communications Group, 2005), 19.
23. Bogart and Landau, 19.

Chapter 3

A Survey of Current Practices

A director launches rehearsal with a script, a cast of actors, a design, and a short amount of time.

In mere weeks they play in front of a live audience. How do directors and actors use those precious days, hours, and minutes readying for opening night? How much time do ensembles want to spend sitting at a table discussing the play? How will you inform your cast about design decisions? Are there tips for creating dynamic and meaningful staging? How can directors and actors collaborate on building performances? Do new plays require a different set of skills?

As I interviewed over forty directors, the sheer variety of methods astonished me. I could easily write forty books—one for each director. Given that most artists suit their process to the production, perhaps I could write 400.

Instead, I pulled together their most inspirational, logical, compelling, and persuasive ideas. Some methods contradict each other, while others dovetail. I chose practices that cut to the heart of the director's job as they work through the entire rehearsal process. This chapter offers approaches to try out, embrace, or resist as you discover your own path.

I've broken this chapter down into the various jobs directors take on as they lead a company of artists from the first read through to opening night.

LAUNCHING THE JOURNEY

- Before the first rehearsal directors read and analyze the play, pull together a cast, and work with designers. The first rehearsal propels a new phase: work with the actors.

- Should you give a rousing speech to your company on the first day? What methods help build a team of explorers? How do you encourage creativity and risk?

EXPLORING THE TEXT

- Why read and discuss the play at the table? Why sit in chairs when eventually actors work on their feet? How much time do you want to spend analyzing the script?
- Do new plays require a different process for text analysis?

CREATING A WORLD

- Plays are more than the dialogue on the page. How can a group create a rich and compelling fictional universe?
- Do you want to incorporate historical research? How can improvisations and games enrich scene work?

SHAPING THE STAGING

- How do you generate staging that helps tell the story and creates flow?
- Are there guidelines for orchestrating movement? Do you want to build a physical structure quickly or craft moment to moment in detail?
- If you want actors to create their own blocking, how can you guide them? What motivates an actor to move?

DETAILING SCENE WORK

- How do you craft a compelling scene? Should you stop and start? Run it over and over? What should you adjust?
- Can you guide actors using simple questions? What can be revealed by focusing on the basics: who, what, where, when, and why?

RUNNING THE PLAY

- When should you run the entire play? Early or late? Often or rarely? Should you build up slowly to a run or jump into it without much preparation?
- How do you best give notes after a run? Should you have a long discussion session or a short check in? How do you incorporate notes from designers, dramaturgs, and artistic staff?

COLLABORATING WITH DESIGNERS IN TECHNICAL REHEARSALS

- How do you integrate what you created in the rehearsal room with the set, lights, costumes, sound, projections, and other technical elements?
- Do you want to move quickly or slowly? How do you navigate conflict? Who is in charge of the technical rehearsal?

LISTENING TO PREVIEW AUDIENCES

- How can you listen to an audience while watching the play? What kind of work happens in between first preview and opening?

OPENING THE SHOW

- Since you won't be at the show every night, how do you walk away from the production? How do you watch a show on opening that you likely can't change?

These tasks often overlap. As you shape the staging, you often continue to explore the script. Collaborating with designers often helps detailing scene work. Listening to preview audiences may encourage you to look back to your pre-rehearsal preparations.

I encourage you to explore all the different ideas in this book and then figure out your own methods of rehearsal. If an idea sparks your curiosity, do some more research, or try it out on your own.

My own process has continued to evolve over decades as I teach directing classes, talk to different directors, and read books by inspiring artists and thinkers.

Let's start at the beginning.

LAUNCHING THE JOURNEY

A first rehearsal can be thrilling.

A director works on a play for months, sometimes years, before finally assembling the entire team. The director reads and rereads the play, works with designers to create a blueprint for the physical world, and gathers a group of actors.

The cast is expectant and excited. Some of them may know each other or even worked together for years. Or it's possible that everyone is meeting each other for the first time. They come to the room with their own ideas about character and story, but what will they learn to inspire their further exploration? The designers have spent months creating a hypothesis about the play, and now comes the time to test the theory.

A first rehearsal can also be terrifying.

In a professional setting, maybe the entire theatre's staff and a few board members have come to nosh on bagels and fruit. In some theatres, up to forty employees ring the edge of the room, waiting with bated breath. At DePaul, first rehearsals are similarly large affairs with cast, designers, assistants, stage managers, and others all gathered for the first time. People nervously make small talk. The stage manager introduces everyone and welcomes them to the process. At a certain point, all eyes turn to the director. What do they say?

Some directors pull out a well-honed first day speech.

Crafting a First Day Address

Early in her career, **Jessica Thebus,** Director of the Northwestern MFA Directing Program, typically improvised her opening day remarks and focused on charming the room. She set a fun tone and got everyone excited. It worked well enough. When Thebus started teaching MFA directors full time she started to rethink her opening day routine. As a way to talk about plays and analysis, she started asking her students to craft thoughtful speeches rooted in a personal point of view.

Now Thebus writes out her own invocations, and like her students, she writes many drafts.

Thebus doesn't prescribe a specific structure for the opening day address, and in fact, her own vary widely. On the first day of Sarah Ruhl's *Orlando* she read a twelve-minute essay. Others are only a page of text. Her students may eventually improvise their speech around some basic talking points, but as an exercise, they must write out their ideas. Clear writing flows from clear thinking.

As she guides her students, she waits to hear an exciting idea that will inspire weeks of work. She told me about her process with students:

> You're listening to someone's draft and you think, *Oh they're really smart.* Which I think is the death nail—the last thing you want to do on the first day of rehearsal is sound really smart because that will make the entire room think, *Oh, he's really smart.* Then they are not engaged, and wonder, *Am I as smart, am I going to be able to execute that really smart thing?* It's like shutting a door.

Thebus looks for an idea that feels personal and true—something that stops you in your tracks and makes you say, *Oh. Oh. I want to see that play.*

I asked her for an example, and she described her ideas for *Richard III*. In her reading, Richard was blessed with charisma and wit, but cursed with a deformed body. The wily warrior seethed with fury at God's injustice. Richard sets out to destroy everyone else's gifts in an act of rage and revenge. When I heard that I sat up and thought, *Oh, that's alive. I want to see that production.*

Now when Thebus gives her first day speech, either reading from a page or improvising off of notes, she isn't trying to rally the actors and designers around her personality. She's firing them up around her point of view on the play and the story they will tell together. If the process goes awry at some point she knows she can return to her original impulses. Her point of view serves as a lamp to guide her through the dark.

Curt Columbus, Artistic Director of Trinity Rep Theatre in Providence Rhode Island, goes a step further with his opening day addresses. He crafts manifestos.

Columbus believes every director serves as a sort of book club moderator. All the members will have read the same book, but the moderator highlights certain themes. They guide the discourse—hopefully to unexpected places. For Columbus, a manifesto lets his cast and crew know where he plans to lead the discussion.

I asked him to read me one of his manifestos and he rattled off his first speech for *Beowulf a Thousand Years of Baggage*, which he directed for Trinity in 2016. The modern adaptation of the 1,000-year-old saga featured the famous adventurer who kills the monster Grendel:

> This is a response to fear. This is a response to safety. This is a political act and an apolitical event. This is rock and roll. This is an American story for this American moment. This is about telling and retelling and modes of telling. This is about inevitability and death. This has a thousand years of baggage. This is utterly new. This is a series of connected yet distinct events. This has no rising dramatic action. This does not exist on the page but only in the room and with an audience.

As he read it I got goosebumps. I responded to the sheer poetry, but also he convinced me that the oldest story in the English language spoke to this moment. By launching his first rehearsal with a manifesto, declaring the purpose of the production loudly, Columbus sets the tone for the next few weeks of work. He signals that their work is political as well as personal. He inspires deep thinking.

Reading a prepared speech is too formal for me, but sometimes I type out an address and read it over many times, eventually improvising a version on the first rehearsal. Sometimes I distill my ideas into to a succinct outline and ad-lib around certain points.

I remember the first rehearsal of *Boy* by Anna Ziegler and facing a room full of people: board members, staff, designers, and actors. It was standing room only. I pulled out my outline and attempted to set the tone for the evening:

- I talked about the first time I read the play: How the true story of a young man suffering from a misguided gender assignment surgery riveted my attention and moved me to tears
- I told the story of bringing the play to TimeLine four years ago, the public reading, the delay in securing the rights, and the belief that we were doing the play at just the right moment
- I saw nodding heads when I discussed the need to tell transgender stories, and the theatre's efforts to create an inclusive team on and off the stage
- I defined success: not only should the audience fall in love with the young man and his family, but they should also question how they treat young people in their own lives

- I talked about what kind of play it was for me: a love story with ghosts (an idea I credited to the dramaturg Josephine Kearns)
- I said what it was about for me: the desire to control your own destiny

My speech oriented everyone in the room toward the same goals. They understood the driving forces behind the production and could focus their work. I left plenty of room for discovery and collaboration, but I provided context. Then I turned it over to my design team to share what we'd been working on for months.

Some directors would say I launched an adventure.

Setting the Course for Discovery

Lisa Portes, head of directing at DePaul University, imagines a rehearsal process as a boat going on a journey. The director sets the course for the cast and creative team: she communicates where they are heading and says we don't know exactly how we will get there, and we may take detours, but we know generally where we hope to end up.

In 2017, when California Shakespeare Theater asked Lisa Portes to work on *The Glass Menagerie* by Tennessee Williams, the artistic director asked her if she could do the play with an all Latinx cast. Portes read the play and didn't think it was possible given the strictness of the Williams estate. She didn't think that a Latina could have existed as a debutante in the world of the deep South in the 1920s as the script demands.

Portes then remembered a colleague's research on African American debutantes. She started digging herself and found a trove of information on African American cotillions—a tradition that stretched back to the late 1800s. She also found a reference in the play to Amanda's husband having sent the family a postcard from Mexico. Portes imagined that Amanda, an African American debutante, could have married a Mexican American. The children, Laura and Tom, would be Afro-Latinx. She pitched the idea to the artistic director and he enthusiastically agreed.

Portes told her team that their production would highlight, "displaced people on the American landscape." The Cal Shakes venue looks out on the hills—so it made sense for the show to start with a blank set with Tom silhouetted by the terrain physicalizing the idea of the production. On the first day of rehearsal, Portes made sure to communicate the organizing idea of the production to the cast.

When the designers made their initial presentations, Portes made sure add context for the team's discoveries. Portes framed each design element—the sparse set manipulated by the actors, the period costumes derived from researching displaced people, the specific music choices—to activate the performers' creative work. Portes explained her reasoning to me:

> So that the actors can begin to knit together where this is all heading. I think it's not only necessary for folks to have a sense of where you're going, it's also important that the team recognize that somebody knows where the boat is aiming. Somebody has created a structure within which they can organize their choices.

Portes uses the first day to assure the cast they have a competent captain leading the journey. She and her designers have made smart, clear, and complimentary choices—all centered on an organizing principle. But she also makes sure they know the expedition is

Figure 3.1 *The Glass Menagerie* by Tennessee Williams. Directed by Lisa Portes for Cal Shakes. L–R: Karen Aldridge, Sean San José. Set: Annie Smart; Lighting: Xavier Pierce; Costumes: Raquel Barreto; Sound: Brendan Aanes; Dramaturgy: Phillipa Kelly. Photo Credit: Jay Yamada.

neither complete nor totally set. The actors will travel the final leg of the journey.

When **Rebecca Frecknall**, West End director, was directing the Williams classic, *Summer and Smoke*, for the Almeida Theatre in London, she created an ambitious first day agenda to galvanize the team.

Frecknall and her designers conceived of a stripped-down production of *Summer and Smoke*, performed within a semi-circle of pianos. Actors played two or three roles, and almost every cast member helped create the live score for the play. The goal: escape inherited clichés around the script and reveal its visceral, human core.

They started off the first day of rehearsal with a read through for the staff of the theatre. The Almeida has a tradition of cooking lunch for the cast at the first meeting. As they shared a meal, the actors told the staff what excited them about the play and the staff of the Almeida talked about the company and its traditions.

After lunch, the cast and director went back to the rehearsal room and talked about the stereotypes associated with Tennessee Williams plays. She had the actors pair up and talk about what leapt to mind when they imagined a Williams play. And they made lists. Frecknall detailed the many ideas the cast came up with during an interview with me:

> Marlon Brando and vests and screaming *Stella!* or heat, claustrophobia, neurotic women. And then we talked about the slightly restrictive stereotypes of seeing a Tennessee Williams play and began to introduce the fact that we wanted to kick against those stereotypes.

Next, they did the same exercise to generate of list of the play's central themes. It wasn't until this point that the designer showed up with the model box, revealing their ideas to the cast. They put images up on the wall illustrating how they moved from original ideas to the final drawings and models. At this point, Frecknall drew connections between reading the play, the cast's explorations of stereotypes and themes, and the design concept.

Lead actor Patsy Ferran shared photos from a trip she took to Clarksdale, the small Mississippi town that inspired Williams's play. Ferran discussed the experience of traveling to the claustrophobic hamlet, far from the bustle of London.

Finally, the composer taught everyone some simple piano variations and encouraged them to improvise musically. They began experimenting with different people playing parts of the overture. Through a varied series of tasks and challenges, Frecknall set the course for discovery: actors' ideas would be welcomed and championed, the ensemble should be encouraged to connect with the theatre company staff, designs had been created through a series of discoveries, and music would be central to the production. It was a stirring end to a very full day.

In sharp contrasts, some directors like to downplay the importance of the first rehearsal.

Easing Actors into the Process

Ron OJ Parson rarely uses all of his hours the first day. He prefers a relaxed initial meeting to break the ice. At a theatre that gathers the whole staff for the first rehearsal, he honors the moment with a speech about his vision, but quickly moves to a more social and convivial atmosphere.

Parson prizes getting to know each cast member as a person, not just an artist in the room. He shares personal stories and encourages others to do the same. He likes to have fun. I asked him what that means to him:

> Opening up your personality to let people see what your sense of humor is, what you laugh at, what's funny to you. Getting people loose. Comedy is always a way to break the ice, so to speak. And a first rehearsal is like a first date because everybody is just getting to know each other.

Parson trained as an actor and always tries to create the warm and inviting rooms he longed for but didn't always experience. The more collaborators bring personal experiences into the room, the better the atmosphere.

Robert Falls has led The Goodman Theatre as artistic director for decades and has attended hundreds of initial rehearsals. Lately he wonders if the ceremony of the first day pressurizes actors. The pomp and circumstance of a design presentation, a long speech by a director, and then the first reading of the play—often in front of the theater's staff—turns him off creatively. Falls explained what he meant when we sat down to talk about his process:

> It puts a fear factor into the actors and various artists who obviously are nervous coming into the situation. I'm always convinced every actor feels they're going be fired on the first day of rehearsal. Clearly they're nervous about reading the play and most of them don't know each other and often they haven't worked at the theatre, so they don't know the culture.

If the production schedule allows, Falls only calls actors the first day. He won't bring in costume or set designs. He doesn't want them thinking about being in production, but instead to focus on character and relationship.

In a relaxed atmosphere, he and the acting company read and discuss the play, building a foundation of understanding. On the second day, he invites the designers and theatre staff for an afternoon meet-and-greet. The team enjoys coffee and pastries, and the designers present the costumes and sets. He eases the actors into the world of the play rather than tossing them into the deep end.

Other directors eliminate the ceremony but immediately plunge their actors into complex work.

Jumping into Physical Work

Robert O'Hara, Obie Award–winning writer and director, provoked his cast even before the first day of rehearsal for *Macbeth* at the Denver Center for the Performing Arts in 2017.

O'Hara issued a warning during the audition process. At the start of each callback session he outlined his vision. O'Hara and his designers had conceived of the show as if it was being performed by a group of warlocks—male witches. O'Hara regaled me with his audition process:

> I gave a twenty-minute speech at every callback in each city that was called the *Get Out Speech*. I told them at the end of this speech you should feel free to leave because there's going to be a bunch of craziness in this play. There's gonna be physicality,

you're gonna be playing warlocks, there may be nudity, there's going to be intimate movement, and if that isn't something you're down for then this is your chance to just as they say *Get Out* because this won't be for everyone.

In a way, O'Hara started his rehearsal process during the auditions. He knew that he didn't want to spend the first part of the rehearsal getting seventeen men on board with the idea of an all-male, highly physical, imaginative show. He wanted everyone to walk in the first day already knowing what the show was going to be about—this was a *Macbeth* being told from the perspective of the Witches in the story.

At the beginning of the first rehearsal he divided the seventeen men into twos and threes and told them to improvise a fight—although one without physical contact for safety's sake. The rules: no weapons, four counts of eight, one person had to die, and it had to involve *Magic*. Then each group taught their fight to the actor playing Macbeth. Using their creations as a base, O'Hara quickly sketched out a prologue where Macbeth defeated an entire army of warriors, instantly giving the cast a sense ownership and connection.

He threw everyone into this exercise to circumvent what O'Hara believes can happen when actors spend an entire first day reading a play sitting down—great ideas can sometimes get short circuited by the intellect. O'Hara told me his thoughts on table work:

> You physicalize something and then the body has to negotiate it before the brain dismisses it. As opposed to sitting at a table and asking, *What is this going to feel like and what is this going look like?* and then deciding, *It won't feel right, I can't possibly do that.*

On the first day of *Macbeth* rehearsals, O'Hara set guiding principles in motion. He put his lead actor at the center of the universe and emboldened his acting company to create before they felt ready. He engaged their bodies before their minds and fashioned a highly physical world. In essence he asked his actors to leap before they crawl. Knowing they have the ability to achieve greatness gave them confidence as they returned to the table.

In the workbook section, I encourage directors to ask themselves a series of questions about how they want to conduct their first day of rehearsal. (See Workbook Chapter: Exercises 6–8.) First check to

A Survey of Current Practices 41

Figure 3.2 Macbeth by William Shakespeare. Directed by Robert O'Hara for Denver Center for the Performing Arts. L–R: Thaddeus Fitzpatrick, Kim Fischer, Joe Goldammer. Set: Jason Sherwood; Lighting: Alex Jainchill; Costumes: Dede M. Ayite; Sound/Original Music: Lindsay Jones; Dramaturgy: Douglas Langworthy; Vocal and Dialect Coach: Kathryn G. Maes. Photo Credit: Sam Adams.

see what the institution you are working for or attending requires or expects. Then you might think about what kind of leader you are. Do you excel at inspirational speeches or do you do better with informal discussions? Next consider your ensemble. What do they need on the first day? Do they all know each other and want to catch up and ease themselves into the work? Are they all strangers and would benefit from some sort of bonding exercises?

Consider the play you are working on as well. What will launch the process on your particular script? Is it a new play? Do you want to start digging into the script with the writer? Are there special skills the actors should start working on as soon as possible such as music, dance, or puppetry? Do you have a particular way of approaching a classic text that might not be obvious? What will help bring the actors together? A speech? A discussion? A game?

Don't assume that what worked for someone else will work for you. Look for your own path.

Prerehearsal Workshops

Sometimes Tony Award–winning director **Rebecca Taichman** is handed a new play and the writer asks for notes. These days she demurs. She'd rather hear the play out loud first. Taichman explained what she meant when we sat down to chat:

> I read a play, I think I get it, then I hear it ... and often realize I missed something. A play doesn't fully live on the page, though the text and story are the genesis of everything for me. I've found that the visceral experience of hearing a piece aloud always teaches me more than I can learn from reading.

Even better than a reading is a new play workshop where Taichman can hear the play out loud, ask the writer questions, hear the play again, and ask more questions. She doesn't have to solve anything, or stage anything. She can just listen and discuss. She finds these low-pressure sessions allow her to fully understand the writer's point of view. Taichman told me her priorities directly:

> I consider the writer my partner. When I'm directing a new play, it's essential for me to understand what the writer wants their piece to be—what they see, hear, experience and what they hope the impact will be. As a director of new work, I think of myself as a kind of midwife—helping birth a writer's creation.

Taichman has found more and more that during a workshop she craves as much downtime as possible. She and the writer learn so much in a day with actors, Taichman finds it helpful to have time to process and implement new ideas on the page.

When I'm running a new play workshop I like to ask the playwright what they hope to accomplish. Are there sections they are confused about? Are there character arcs they want to hear? Do they want to just hear the script over and over?

We read the play followed by a discussion and a longer session just between me and the writer, perhaps including the dramaturg and an assistant director. Then we alternate days of working and days for the writer to crank out new pages. When we read we stop to discuss the intent of scenes, investigate character motivations, and interrogate story logic.

At the end of the week or two of work we'll do a second reading—sometimes for an invited audience or a small group of artists working on the show. Typically, the artistic director of the theatre will attend, and we'll follow up with a note session.

When **Bill Rauch** was Artistic Director of Oregon Shakespeare for many years, he insisted on workshops for all new plays. After a while, he realized that classic plays—especially Shakespeare—got the short end of the stick. Why not give plays from the canon a week in a room before rehearsal to try out some ideas?

When I spoke to him, he was in the midst of a six-day workshop for an upcoming production of *Othello*. Part of their work was comparing the different versions of Shakespeare's play, looking at the 1622 Quarto text next to the 1623 Folio printing. Rauch explained why he felt workshops were important to me over the phone:

> Especially for a play like *Othello* because it's one of the longest plays in the canon and there are like a thousand differences between Quarto One and the First Folio, so we spend tremendous time going through and coming up with the text that works for our particular production. We need to treat our Shakespeare more like new work.

The set design was finished, and the costumes were mostly figured out as well, so their discussions weren't theoretical but rather practical. They weren't discussing *Othello* as an intellectual exercise, but instead the specific production they would realize in a few months.

Spending a week in a room without time pressure, uncovering subtext and learning how the language worked prepared the team for their next step in the process. Cast, crew, and director now had time on their own with what they learned to prepare for the first day of rehearsal.

EXPLORING THE TEXT

In the second year of their MFA program at DePaul, students wrestle with half of an act of a classic Chekhov play. I typically lurk in the corner, observing.

The students often spend their first rehearsal sitting at the table, teasing out their analysis. I tell them to ignore me as I sit in the shadows typing notes on my little red iPad:

> *I wonder if you could have asked a question there instead of telling them the answer?*
> *This conversation seems to have reeled off the tracks, is this serving the play?*
> *Don't forget those two are siblings! How would that affect this squabble?*
> *You said the play was about lost dreams, is this a moment to bring up that theme?*

When I review my notes with students, sometimes I sense they don't really know why they were at the table. They know directors should read the play slowly with their actors, but to what end? Are they meant to be opening up possibilities for staging? Setting the actors on a clear path toward a character? Focusing on the specific rhythm of the language?

While we go over the basics of script analysis in class, students find that it's one thing to understand table work in theory and another to lead it in practice. Also, each director starts to discover that they have a different relationship with discussions around the table. While some directors love to gab with actors about the themes of the play, other get itchy sitting and talking when they'd rather be exploring on their feet.

For many of the directors I interviewed, initial discussions form the bedrock of the rest of their rehearsal work.

Analyzing at the Table

Rebecca Taichman loves to spend time at the table, sometimes even a whole week. She labels herself an iterative director. She likes to repeat passages many times. Taichman let me in on her process:

> The actors read a section, we talk, they read again, we talk, they read again, and on...and on...It's very repetitive. I find ideas or impulses accumulate and fold in on each other, creating layers.

It's forensic—sometimes the greatest truths emerge from the tiniest detail. Occasionally the sheer act of repeating brings impulses to the surface that are outside rational thought.

Taichman tells the company they won't lock things down during table work, but rather enliven possibilities. She's learning as much as they are as she shepherds these long reading sessions:

> We're storytellers, and we have to all share a clear vision of what the story is that we are telling. By the time we're getting up, the point of view of the production and the moment-to-moment story should be clear—and the company should be aching to get on their feet. Usually then staging then is fast and exciting.

Tony Award–winning director **Scott Ellis** learned the value of a long table session the hard way, as a performer in rehearsals. Ellis reminded me of where he began in our interview:

> I was an actor for a while, and the worst thing I remember, the worst was getting the play up on its feet before I knew what the fuck I was talking about. I was just terrified, and that stuck with me.

Ellis believes actors often protect themselves as they start rehearsal; it's his job to help them lower their guard. He earns their trust with a long table session. He won't ask them to perform a scene until they understand the basics:

> I want to be able to sit down and talk. I want for all of us to agree—not agree, but to discuss parts of the history of it, or relationships, or things that are never even touched upon in the play. I like having that base. I try to keep it very slow, very relaxed.

A scene will evolve once they start staging, but he likes to discuss the dramatic possibilities in a safe environment. What's this relationship? What's their shared history? What is this character thinking? What do they want?

Rather than table work, Lisa Portes likes to call her initial work on a play a *slow through*. It's a time to read the play, stop, and interrogate the text. Anyone in the room can stop the slow through and ask a question. Typically, actors won't stop the flow at first, so she will interrupt them or break at a logical shift in the action and probe the text:

> Anything that anybody says, I tend to support, affirm, and then if I need to, reframe and redirect. I try never to shut anything down, clamp an idea, say something's wrong. If somebody says, I think Laura's really interested in balloons, I might say, *Well, that's so interesting, I wonder how come balloons?* And then if the discussion starts to go way off the skids, then I'll find a way to bring us back to the text. But perhaps the idea has something to do with buoyancy that we didn't expect about the character.

She also uses this moment to pepper in information from the dramaturg's actor packet.

Portes often finds that these well-researched dramaturgy reports can arrive on the first day of rehearsal in a glossy bundle, disappear into a backpack, and never to come back into play. During the slow through, she prompts the dramaturg to bring up information as needed. She treats the text as if it had hyperlinks:

> *Didn't you have some information on African American Cotillions you wanted to share?*
> *This might be a time to discuss Williams's sister and her shock treatments.*
> *What did you find out about the African American community in St. Louis at the time?*

All of this discussion, dramaturgy, historical research and questions create a room in which everyone begins to swim in the same waters. They steep in the same information, opening up possibilities, and creating the world as a group.

Some directors read a play several times before getting up on their feet.

The Deep Tissue Massage

Jeff Award–winning director and University of Illinois at Chicago professor **Derrick Sanders** guides his actors through the play three times at the table.

The first day, the cast reads through the entire play without stopping. He leads a general discussion about the script's overarching ideas and what the cast learned hearing it out loud. Next, he leads a scene-by-scene breakdown of the text, uncovering the structure of the script: how did playwright construct the flow of the play? They will compare scenes for tone and content. What happens in the first scene that leads to the next? Why is this scene here? Could it be cut? Why not? What have we learned about the mechanics of the narrative?

After finishing this scene-by-scene read through, Sanders performs what he calls a *deep tissue massage*. Actors read a scene, and Sanders probes them about motivations and choices. He asks them to read it again with renewed understanding. Sanders pretended to be in one of his deep tissue sessions for a moment during our interview:

> *Try it like this, what happens if we did it like this. Come a little harder and faster, let me feel that. I wonder if we back off a bit and there's more love in the scene that we originally envisioned.* Then sometimes I'll say, *why don't we just try it like this and see how it feels.* Let it click for them and then move onto the next scene.

Sanders drives actors toward conflict and moment-to-moment reactions. He encourages specificity in individual choices. Are you trying to lambast them? Are you grilling them? How are you using what you learned in the last scene to defend yourself in this one?

On each of his three passes, Sanders teaches his actors to investigate something new. For the first read they touch on theme; on the second pass they analyze structure; during the final pass he drills down on character.

In contrast, some directors like to speak as little as possible when working the text at the table.

Encouraging Actors to Own the Rehearsal

Nataki Garrett, Artistic Director of Oregon Shakespeare Festival, spends her early rehearsals empowering her actors. She spends a long time at the table, at least a few days and possibly almost a week, and speaks as little as possible. She doesn't answer questions and sits in uncomfortable silence until her actors start talking.

If an actor asks her about a line in the show they don't understand, typically Garrett will say she doesn't know. Instead she asks them to talk about it. Garrett explained her beliefs in a sit-down interview with me:

> If they're doing the talking and if they're communicating ideas with each other and they're willing to unpack those ideas and they're willing to express how it makes them feel: So now they're on their own. You know what you do when you're on your own? You start to come up with ideas.

Garrett has found that actors can sometimes resist offering their own ideas or choices. Perhaps they are used to rehearsal rooms where the director gives them more guidance or tells them how they believe scenes should play. Perhaps they doubt their own agency. By denying actors an easy answer Garrett empowers them to speak out bravely. She encourages actors to bring not just their craft and their ideas, but their whole person.

Since Nataki Garrett values actors opening up personally and bringing their own selves to the work, she starts each day by asking them what happened since she last saw them:

> I begin every rehearsal with, *Talk to me, talk to me, talk to me. Did you see the news last night?* And we'll talk about that. *Did something happen in your personal life? You don't have to share if you don't want me to know.* But I get them to talk to me about it and what I'm really doing is trying to get them to talk to each other about it.

Often Garrett directs world premieres of plays that involve racially sensitive material. Work that she calls transgressive. She knows that to represent the work truthfully, actors need to bring elements of themselves to the work. They need to fully embrace any upsetting or troubling aspects of the work—perhaps they need to speak language that will offend audience members or perform blocking that will make some people uncomfortable. Garrett believes her job is to bear witness to these intimate acts. By asking her actors each day to reveal something personal, she gauges their comfort level—how much they will be willing to risk during that rehearsal period.

In contrast, when I work at the table I tend to stay away from the personal and focus my attention on dramatic structure.

Identifying the Action

My favorite way to work at the table is to identify the turning points, or events within a scene. Katie Mitchell clearly defines what we mean by *event*, in her book *The Director's Craft*:

> An event is the moment in the action when a change occurs, and this change affects everyone present. *Event* is really just a simple word for something that happens regularly in life. We regularly find ourselves trying to achieve one thing when something happens which changes what we want to achieve.[1]

Every time a character enters or exits, by definition the scene changes. These are the easiest events to identify. In between entrances and exits are what we call *French scenes*. As I read along in the script I always encourage the cast to stop at the end of a French scene. This is a great moment to discuss what just happened between those characters. What did they want? How were they trying to achieve their goals? Why did that character enter? From where? Where is that person going? Why?

In between entrances and exits, depending on the length of the French Scene, typically we can identify one or more dramatic events. These are slightly harder to discover, but I encourage the cast to look for moments where the action changes or a decision is made. Look for that moment where a character is pursuing one action or task, and then they stop and shift to something else. Often that shift is bracketed by a physical action or perhaps a pause.

Looking at the first scene in *A Streetcar Named Desire* between Stella and her older sister Blanche, at first glance it could seem like there are dozens of events. The sisters talk about the size of the apartment, Stella's passion for her husband, and the loss of Belle Reve. Don't assume every slight change in conversation indicates an event, look instead for moments where a character makes a decision that affects both parties. Imagine if the sister made a different choice at that moment. Would the story of the play take a different path? If so, you've found an event.

In that first scene, I'd suggest the events are:

- The sisters greet each other
- Blanche stops criticizing the apartment at Stella's insistence
- Stella pours Blanche a drink to calm her down

- Blanche realizes there are only two rooms in the apartment
- Blanche reveals their ancestral home Belle Reve is lost
- Stella runs from the room after being berated

Why does an event happen? Typically, in a scene two characters are at odds; they are in conflict. Each wants something different and drives toward their personal goal. If Blanche gets what she wants, then Stella is denied what she's fighting for. Stella doesn't need to pour Blanche a drink, she could let her sister spin out of control. Or she could finally take charge of the scene. Or she could let Blanche know she isn't welcome in her house. But instead, she pours a drink to ease the tension and calm the situation down. An event resolves or changes the conflict.

As we start our table work, I let the room know that the goal is for us to read the play until we find an event and then stop and talk about what we just heard. At first, actors don't like to shout out "Event!" so I break the ice. But eventually everyone joins the game and starts decisively naming decision points. Sometimes convivial disagreements break out, which always signals a healthy collaboration. By arguing over where an event occurs in the script, we strengthen our understanding of the dynamics of the scene.

As the play shifts at each event, the rhythm and tone changes. As the play takes dramatic turns, the entire group contributes in figuring out the structure of the play. If we learn the action, we can play the play.

Some directors like to drill down even farther in their initial pass—they like to work sentence by sentence.

Discovering the Action Line-by-Line

Head of NYU graduate acting, **Mark Wing-Davey**, loves to *action* his script. In this process, actors assign an action verb to every sentence of dialogue. Rules: the verb must be active, the verb should describe what the character is doing to their scene partner, and the same verb can't be used twice in one scene.

It's a slow process.

When Stanley first meets his sister-in-law and says, "My clothes're stickin' to me. Do you mind if I make myself comfortable?" Does he seduce her? Shock her? Intimidate her? Inform her? If you choose *seduce* now—is that too early in their relationship? In the scene? In this example, Wing-Davey would insist on two consecutive verbs (one per phrase) to follow the thought change: Stanley *disgusts* Blanche, then *amuses* her? *Charms* then *scandalizes*?

Wing-Davey encourages the entire group to get into actioning, which sometimes swells into full-throated arguments about which verb accurately describes what a character is doing. Wing-Davey never insists on a verb that the actors don't understand or agree with, but he might encourage stronger or more revealing choices. He insists that in the end actioning doesn't straitjacket actors. Wing-Davey elaborated on his process to me over the phone:

> It's not totally rigid. Whatever you've written in pencil, it can drift away. It doesn't matter as you get on your feet, you can find things that don't work and somehow impulses takeover. But it does mean having a conversation about what people are doing.

When you break down a script line-by-line, you notice each turn of phrase and each new thought. You observe when the writer uses a long, run-on sentence or a series of short ones.

You start to hear the music of the script.

Listening to the Rhythm

Chay Yew, former Artistic Director of Victory Gardens in Chicago, believes long table work session lead actors to discover the voice of the play. As a champion of new scripts, Yew argues each text contains its own specific DNA, its own language. Only by reading the play out loud over and over can the group find out this particular production's cadence.

Sometimes he finds that actors hunger to get up on their feet. He quickly pulls them back:

> Before you sing the song, or before you play an instrument, you need to know the notes. That's the reason why there's a rest there, that's the reason why there's a slur. Once we have this, you're able to sing it the way that you can because you know the song. To sing it the way that you want to sing it before learning what the song is, then you're not doing a new play.

Yew cautions actors to not learn their lines until they master the rhythms of the language. Paraphrasing taints new plays. He charges them to notice where the playwright has put in periods or commas or beats. Each one is there for a reason. Why is the playwright repeating language? Why are some sentences short and others run on? Assume every line has a purpose.

In this way Yew echoes ideas of some Shakespeare directors.

Many directors of Shakespeare believe his punctuation was less for the eye (reading) than for the ear (speaking). These directors believe Shakespeare employed commas not for grammatical sense, but to indicate a slight shift in thought. Periods are the only place to take a breath, because those are where complete thoughts come to an end. A colon might mean open out to a larger audience, while a semicolon indicates leaning into one listener privately.

Kim Rubinstein, award-winning director, teaches her actors to do what she calls *punctuation walks*. This is a technique that was popularized by the British director and vocal coach, Cicely Berry, but that Rubinstein came to on her own. The actor speaks a speech and lets the punctuation tell them how to move. Begin by moving forward and speaking; change direction when you hit a comma; leap forward to a new idea at a colon; change direction sharply at a dash; only stop at a period, question mark, or exclamation point. Rubinstein explained her process to me over the phone:

> The text tells us through the language more about what is going on in the interior. So, we do punctuations walks—sometimes I do it just in little pieces, you know what I mean? As a part of learning the basic jazz of a character. Yes. Or a way of realizing, oh my God, Blanche Dubois speaks in exclamation points and dashes...and what does that mean for the way in which she interacts, right?

Rubinstein is wary of spending too much time sitting with her cast in the early weeks. She knows that some of them will learn better on their feet.

Discussions in Chairs, Not Tables

Award-winning DC-based playwright and director **Aaron Posner** champions the work that needs to be done at the table, but not *table work*. When he first started directing, Posner used to conduct what he identified as a traditional form of table work in which the entire cast sits around talking about the play scene by scene. Now he does that same dissecting of the material, but he does it scene by scene, only working with the actors involved.

When the actors arrive to work on their scene, Posner pulls up chairs in a circle and they will read and reread the scene and discuss it. These discussions go over what Posner believes are the basics of scene work: Who is in the scene? What is their relationship? What do they want? What does this language mean? If he has three hours set aside to stage a scene, he might spend two hours and forty-five minutes *in the chairs* discussing the work. Posner defined the difference between table work and work *in the chairs* in a sit-down interview with me:

> And then very often, my first staging it is, *Okay, we have fifteen minutes left. Let's say this happens down right. Okay, that's pretty good.* So, it's just that I don't sit around the table with everybody for a long time—where everyone gets bored and it's not in their bodies. Because some people are only working in their bodies. When you're sitting around the table, only the five people who are confident enough to talk ever talk. But, if you go right to the scene, then the people who are in the scene can talk.

Posner found when he led what he calls a traditional table work session, he might talk about a scene intellectually, but then not actually stage it until a week later. He felt that actors often forgot the work at the table. He'd much rather gather his actors, discuss the scene for as long as it takes to get clear, then throw the scene up on its feet quickly.

Posner's work *in the chairs* mixes the practical with the personal. He ask many questions we recognize from Stanislavski's work: What's going on? What's the basic situation? What is the web of relationships? What's the tension? What's the conflict? What tactics are you using to get what you want? How does it affect everyone that this event occurs? How are you hearing this information?

A phrase Posner uses often is "actually actually":

> No, no, you're actually *actually* having to bring the news that somebody's wife and children were just killed. So, what does that mean to you—have you ever had that experience?

He doesn't want his actors to *sort of* tell someone terrible news, he wants them to *actually* experience it. Posner believes his best shot at motivating actors to dig deep is to work on the play in small chunks, pushing his actors to confront the ugly truths.

Some directors think the best method to work the text is to eliminate discussion entirely.

Working the Script on Your Feet

Tony Award–winning international star director **Ivo Van Hove** used to spend weeks with his actors at the table. He trained in the European style of rehearsal, which typically lasts two months. Van Hove would spend the first week or two sitting around the table talking about the play in an intellectual way. Then he had at least six weeks to stage the play in preparation for technical rehearsals and previews.

In 1999, New York Theatre Workshop hired him to direct *A Streetcar Named Desire*, which was his first time working under a shorter, American-style rehearsal period. Van Hove discovered he only had four weeks before the first audiences. He realized there was no time for the reading and talking part of rehearsal, so he skipped it. Instead, he immediately leapt into staging and working the scenes:

> I found it so liberating not to talk about the play but just to act it. To immediately have someone come on stage, say a line, someone responds, I could say, *Stop try it this way*. So, in fact we discovered the whole play while we were just playing it and that came for me like a new guideline. It's much better to make a production based on playing it than talking about it.

Van Hove discovered that he prefers working fast by accident, but now insists on compressed rehearsal periods for every show. Actors must come in with their lines completely memorized and receive their costumes the first day. The theatre will construct a facsimile of the set for the rehearsal space. Technicians install sound systems and, if necessary, video apparatus.

At the beginning of the first rehearsal, Van Hove starts working on the play from the top, moving slowly through the script on his feet. He's able to leap into detail work because he and designers and dramaturg spend at least a year talking about the play in detail:

> So, when we come to the first day we have a pretty good idea about the world that we want to create on stage, and I have

a very good idea about the possibilities of every scene. But I didn't make up my mind about every scene because rehearsal is always a journey, a discovery. I call it my little backpack, you know, I have a backpack full of preparations that I don't bother my actors with if not necessary.

When Van Hove gets to work on the first day, he is working on the text, but not theoretically. He's not trying to understand the scenes or moments intellectually—he puts people in motion. In this way Van Hove collapses many parts of the rehearsal into one process: he digs into the text, while staging the play, and delving into the details of scenes. Van Hove doesn't believe this process works for everyone, but he's found that both he and his actors learn better through experience, rather than through discussion.

Van Hove's elimination table work before staging allows us to look back at the other directors' views on how best to start the rehearsal process. If a director has a three or four-week process in a rehearsal room, some will spend fully one third or one fourth of that time sitting in chairs discussing aspects of the play. These directors believe that actors work best when they are confident intellectually and verbally with the scenes of the play before they stand on their feet to start playing. During that time some directors bring in dramaturgical research, others will go over the structure of the play, others simply lead far ranging discussions. Some directors will drill down to examine each sentence or even every punctuation mark.

Exercises nine through eleven in the workbook section offer a few ideas about how to conduct effective table work. I encourage you to ask yourself questions about the process of analyzing the script with actors. Do you want to develop a process that you use every time? Or do you want to shift your methods depending on the script you are working on or the ensemble you're leading? Will your cast benefit from developing an understanding of the script only by reading the language? Or will your play only truly come to life on its feet?

Reading a play over and over can help a cast find the logic or DNA of their play, but for some directors, exercises, games, improvisations and other techniques offer a more tangible way to learn about the world. They help casts discover the rules of the universe through the back door.

Table Work on New Plays

Rebecca Taichman loves to read the script over and over in the first week or two of rehearsal, especially with new plays. Occasionally after hearing a section of the script, Taichman senses something isn't working. She'll pull the writer aside:

> Usually I know if there's a problem, and the questions to ask. If the issue is in the text, often only the writer has the right answer. I think of questions sometimes as provocations. I'm happy to brainstorm ideas or answers, but just the act of asking can spark the writer's imagination.

Taichman sits the writer next to her during table work and emboldens the cast to ask questions. She encourages everyone to see the work through the writer's point of view.

The playwright typically learns a lot during these sessions as well. If an actor is struggling with a section, this gives the writer information. Taichman's careful though to make sure table work doesn't turn into a note session. Working on a new play is collaborative, but she labors to keep boundaries clear. As always with Taichman, provocative questions help create a fertile room for discovery.

Nataki Garrett also likes to have long sessions at the table on new plays, at least a few days but perhaps up to a week. As noted earlier, she likes to speak as little as possible during this period, allowing the actors to fill the silences. She encourages her writers to take her cue and not speak much either. She's more interested in the actors trying to make sense of the script rather than having the writer explain everything. The last thing she wants is for a writer to prescribe a certain line reading. She wants to give the play time to come into its own first.

Not only does she want to empower the actors, she also wants to give the playwright confidence in their own material. She was recently working with a first-time playwright and felt like her job was to protect the play. The writer was nervous and as soon as they heard something that seemed a bit off, they wanted to rewrite. Garrett cautioned that perhaps it was too early to make changes, that the actors might find a way to make the language work as written:

> Without clarity about why they [the playwright] were in the room the writer tended to want to fix things as they were

> coming up in the process. My job was to protect the play first. We can't fix the play we're just gonna work on this play as it is. Your job is not to fix it—your job is to give the play room to come into itself.

Of course, eventually the writer might make changes to the script, but in this case Garrett suspected that the text didn't need changing just yet. She wanted to let the actors discover the play around the table and own the script before the writer started making alterations.

Broadway director **Leigh Silverman** takes the opposite approach; she tries to get through table work as quickly as possible. After a certain amount of time she believes there's only so much a writer can learn by listening to the words:

> If you're working with a writer who needs to see something in order to understand how to work on it, then the longer you stay around the table, the shorter that process is for the writer. If I can spend three days at the table or four days at the table and then I can stage a whole first act in four days, then that writer's getting a lot of information.

She knows from experience that as soon as she starts staging, the writer will have ideas, and start crafting rewrites. Silverman wants to save as much time on the back end for building performances, so she tries to jump start the writing process.

CREATING A WORLD

I was working on *She Kills Monsters* at DePaul University and looking for ways to help the cast live in the universe of the play.

Qui Nguyen's imaginative script centers on a woman whose younger sister died, leaving behind her Dungeons and Dragons or D&D module—a sort of map for a quest. In an effort to get to know her lost sibling better, the woman engages the help of one of her dead sister's friends and dives deep into the role-playing saga. To play D&D, gamers imagine they are mythical creatures or human adventurers with certain powers and abilities. A Dungeon master creates scenarios, and players make choices about how best to accomplish a task. When they want to attack a monster, or cast a spell, or even lie to an opponent, they role different sided dice to determine how well they did.

We'd read and reread the play and started working on the many epic fight scenes, but we had questions. What feelings do campaigns generate? How do the various competitors connect? How do adventurers relate to the person controlling the story, the dungeon master?

We put down our scripts and picked up our many-sided dice. The cast was pumped:

> *I'm going to throw my battle-axe!*
> *Your weapon glances off your enemy. The Kobald strikes back, you're injured.*
> *Okay! I take aim at two Kobald's at once with my long blow. Release!*
> *The arrow flies through the air, and slices right through the both of them! You've won the battle!*

Figure 3.3 She Kills Monsters by Qui Nguyen. Directed by Damon Kiely for the Theatre School of DePaul. Featured: Ensemble. Set: Ashley Wang; Lighting: Jay Koch; Costumes: Angela Mix; Sound: Lauren Porter; Dramaturgy: Mary Kate O'Gara; Fights: Jaq Seifert. Photo Credit: Joe Mazza.

Everyone roared, high fiving all around. Then we discussed what the campaign taught us. We learned that our imaginations were key in making the game successful. We also found that we all were surprisingly caught up in the danger in a short amount of time. We truly cared if we killed the monsters and accomplished our quest.

By playing a game of Dungeons and Dragons ourselves, we were learning not only about the nerdy universe of our characters, we were diving into the pretend world of *She Kills Monsters*. Every play takes place in a fictional universe. Some universes feel very close to our own world, but still they have their own rules that are particular to how the play works. Other plays take place in completely made up universes, where the language, power structure, space, and time behave with their own internal logic.

Robert Icke, award-winning playwright and director, is known for his sleek contemporary adaptations and productions of classic texts by Schiller, Shakespeare, and Aeschylus. You might expect him to take a lot of time at the table unlocking the complexities of these dense texts. Instead, he might spend a half a day on group analysis but certainly not a week. Icke explained his thinking over Skype:

> Because I've learned over the years that anything agreed around the table is built on sand, and is sort of fundamentally flimsy and weak, when tested against the experience of standing up and actually acting it.

As an example of his methodology, he told me working on Friedrich Schiller's *Mary Stuart* at the Almeida in London. The play follows Queen Elizabeth's struggle to maintain power over her popular cousin Mary Queen of Scots. Icke noticed right away his two leads didn't understand what it took to be a queen. The rest of the cast also didn't quite embody what it meant to be in the presence of royalty.

Icke could have spent time at the table uncovering research about the lineage of Queens or the specific ways in which royals of the 1500s consolidated power and behaved. Instead he invented *the Queens game*. He divided the cast into two teams, each with a Queen in charge. He gave them a map of the surrounding neighborhood that defined the boundaries and a quest: take a picture of the opposing team's Queen and bring it back to the rehearsal room. Anyone on the team could propose a scheme for nabbing the photo—but the Queen had the final say.

The actors raced out into the streets and went to extreme lengths to win. One Queen hid in a bush, another started yelling "help" loudly while running down the street to get passersby to shield her. This was all on day two of rehearsal. Icke told me his next steps:

> What you do is you bring them all back and you say, *Okay, well what did we learn?* And of course, they immediately start to talk about what it feels like for the Queens both to be powerful and to be hunted. And how the anxiety of power and the anxiety that you've got a target on your back is the same sort of feeling.

The cast discussed the group dynamic. They related how they started snapping at each other and jostling for position. In this way, he built the fictional world of the production through action and role-playing, rather than discussion. When I saw the West End transfer of the production, I marveled at how the two queens exuded control over their people, and how the court felt like a dangerous viper's pit.

Other directors combine this sense of play with an injection of hard research.

Activating Dramaturgical Research

Mark Wing-Davey cut his teeth as an actor and as a director with the Joint Stock Company in England, known for their extensive research and workshops in the creation of new plays. Company members conduct interviews, collect information, and run workshops around ideas and themes, all to provide dramatic fodder to playwrights. Famously, Wing-Davey, Caryl Churchill, and a group of actors traveled to Romania just after the 1989 revolution to gather material for the play *Mad Forest*.

I assisted Wing-Davey on the premiere production of *36 Views* by Naomi Iizuka—a tangled romance shaded with deception set in the Japanese art world. Wing-Davey asked the theatre company, Berkeley Rep, to set up interviews between the actors and experts in the Bay area who might shed light on the production. The actors met with professors of antiquities, art dealers, and investigative reporters. Typically, the experts in the field had some connection to the character the actor was playing.

After the interviews the actors returned to the rehearsal hall to sit in the hot seat one by one. They had to answer questions from the cast in the guise of the person they interviewed. They didn't have to mimic the person, but try to embody them, passing along important tidbits. Wing-Davey told me about his practices over the phone:

> And those interviews—the embodiment of those people gives you all sorts of information. Not just behavioral but also factual information and different prisms of how the main subjects of the play are viewed. You aren't saying you've got to play your character like that person, but it gives everyone a richer tapestry from which to get inspiration.

Wing-Davey also assigns research topics for each actor, challenging them to briefly present their findings to the company. For *36 Views*, actors gave talks on printmaking, the art world, academia, the Japanese artist Hokusai, and other topics. The ensemble delighted each other with their presentations, uncovering new insights into the world of the play:

> To feel like the director has to have all the information is a fiction and it means that the company is always looking in one direction. They're always looking to the director and that can be quite wearying both for the director, but certainly for the actors.

When Wing-Davey was working on Sarah Ruhl's *Passion Play* at Epic Theatre Company in New York, he assigned topics to help flesh out the script's scenario. *Passion Play* follows three small communities who perform the story of Jesus's crucifixion. One team of actors ventured into greater New York, studied different religious ceremonies, and recreated them for the rest of the cast. An actor playing a fishmonger learned his trade and brought a fish into rehearsal—which he promptly scaled, gutted, and cleaned. Wing-Davey loved the presentation so much he added the action, and the fish, to the show every night.

Other directors look for influences in the world of art and music.

Finding Inspiration through the Back Door

Kim Rubinstein encourages her actors to access the world of the play through the subconscious and tangential. In the first days of rehearsal she asks her actors to bring in images and objects that relate to the play or to their character. Actors don't have to be worry about being logical, they can trust their impulses. They also bring in music: one piece that speaks to their character and one that speaks to the themes of the play.

While they listen to the music everyone gathers around large pieces of paper. Cast and crew draw and write whatever the songs inspire. Then they debrief. What did they draw? What's that phrase of language? How do these impulses help feed the world?

In a separate exercise, Rubinstein encourages her cast to personalize their relationship to their physical environment. When she was working on a production of Lorraine Hansberry's *A Raisin in the Sun*, she knew the cramped residence needed to feel lived in. In the classic play, five family members must stuff themselves into a small apartment on the South Side of Chicago. The stress everyone feels living on top of each other drives the dramatic tension.

She devised an exercise where the actors inhabited the set, just living in the space rather than playing a scene. She detailed her ideas to me over the phone:

> Maybe they'll bring in a couple of phrases of language from the play. And they're just learning to pattern their habits in this house. What they do together in this little space? Like where do they go to try to hide? Where did they go when they don't want to bother people? How do they deal with everybody else's noise? What are the celebrations in the house? What are the rituals?

Rubinstein had worked on previous productions of different plays where the actors got up on their feet but had no idea where to go or what to do. They had no feeling for the room they were in or the landscape they inhabited. They wandered around aimlessly. By building up habits of behavior and associative connections with place, Rubinstein found that actors started from a more grounded reality. They could truly live in the circumstances.

Many directors believe controlled improvisations create shared experiences and help build the world of the play.

Improvising Past Events

Robert Falls has refined his theories on rehearsal over time. At first, he envisioned a line graph: as time passed the cast and director learned more and the play improved. Now he views plays as paintings that accrue layers. Different exercises and activities add layers to the overall picture. One process reveals the turning points in the script. A focused exercise grounds the cast in the physical rooms of the set. One afternoon of exploration creates rich character biographies.

As Falls delves into character histories, he charges his cast to read the play closely, searching for clues. He might send off a group of family members to pore through the play looking for details about their shared past. Falls then guides his cast in acting out events that happened before the play begins. He'll create an *etude*. An etude is a short presentation by one or more actors where they improvise dialogue inspired by a prescribed set of given circumstances. (See exercise twelve in the Workbook for more on using Etudes.)

In her book *The Director's Craft*, Katie Mitchell talks about the importance of clearly structuring etudes:

> Planning improvisations as if they were scenes from a play, giving the actors immediate circumstances, events, intentions, and a clear sense of place and time. The more concrete the information you can provide for each improvisation, the better—and remember that actors can cope with more information than you might imagine.[2]

I tried this method once while working on Jordan Harrison's play *Maple and Vine* for Next Theatre in Evanston, Illinois. Harrison's biting satire imagines a burned-out New York couple who seek rejuvenation in a gated community where everyone pretends it's 1955. An earlier miscarriage formed the foundation for the couple's despair.

We improvised the moment the husband regrouped with his wife after the miscarriage. We created a makeshift gurney and the recovery room. We decided that he would try to comfort her, and she would resist until he reached a breaking point. I remember the improvisation vividly, almost more clearly than moments from the production. The actors' pain was so raw and upsetting. It imprinted the event on their memories, and whenever the miscarriage was referenced in the play, they had a shared experience to draw on.

Scripts tell us what people say. But they hide just as much as they reveal. It sometimes takes group exploration to find the hidden spaces.

Mapping the World

Early in rehearsal I run a game to map out our production's atlas. I divide the entire room—actors, assistant directors, and dramaturgs—into teams. I remember working on *A Streetcar Named Desire* and making three teams. One focused on the apartment, the second created a diagram of the New Orleans of the play, and the third worked on a map of the entire globe.

The apartment team dug through the script and listed every fact they could discover about Stanley and Stella's home. For example:

- There are only two rooms
- One room has a bed
- There is a hanging light in each room
- The is a bathroom off the bedroom

The New Orleans team looked out further, seeing the Big Easy as filtered through the script. Some of their findings included:

- The apartment is on a street with other row houses
- The L&N Railroad runs through the city near the apartment
- There is a bowling alley around the corner
- There is a bar that plays blues music around another corner
- There is a factory where Mitch and Stanley work

The world team thought globally but only the planet that Tennessee Williams describes. Some of the facts they found:

- There is a bus that travels from Laurel Mississippi to New Orleans
- Shep Huntley lives in Texas
- Blanche DuBois teaches French—and knows about France
- Mitch and Stanley fought in World War II, which took place in Europe and Asia
- Stanley has a sales route that takes him to parts of Mississippi

I gave each team twenty minutes to get their facts together and then make diagrams, maps, or drawings of their findings. One team presented an architectural plan for the apartment; another a large map of the world. The third created a pictograph of New Orleans. Each group made a brief presentation, helping us expand and deepen our knowledge of the universe. We continued to build ensemble and set the groundwork for putting the play up on its feet.

Workbook exercises twelve through fourteen barely scratch the surface of what directors try in rehearsal to help actors capture

Figure 3.4 A Streetcar Named Desire by Tennessee Williams. Directed by Damon Kiely for the Theatre School of DePaul. L–R: Joshua Torres, Jonathan Kitt, Rashaad Hall, Edward Karch. Set: Lauren Angelopoulos; Lighting: Casey Diers; Costumes: Richie Fine; Sound: Toy Delorio; Dramaturgy: Kelly Hires. Photo Credit: Ross Hoppe.

the specific world of their play. I've watched movies with my cast, had people play scenes as if they were different genres of television shows, and challenged the actors to tell the entire story of the play in a series of short tableaus. On pages 24–26 I outlined the basics of how directors such as Anne Bogart use Viewpoints training to create physical ensembles as well as generate ideas for plays.

For those who spend a week or two analyzing the script and utilizing different methods to help flesh out the world and the characters, at some point they start to put the show on its feet. They start to stage the play in space, crafting entrances, exits, and everything in between.

SHAPING THE STAGING

I was about to head into previews for *Luck of the Irish* by Kirsten Greenidge at Next Theatre in Evanston, Illinois, and I felt pretty good about my work.

The play chronicled an upwardly mobile African American couple in 1950s Boston shunned by realtors in an upscale neighborhood. To get around the racist system they pay a struggling Irish American family to "ghost buy" it for them, with the hopes they will one day pass it along to their children. The action took place in the present day and the 1950s, in the backyard of the disputed home, at a diner, and in different apartment buildings.

I asked my colleague Kimberly Senior to watch a run. Her first comment: "You're using the same part of the stage over and over—there's no variety and so my eye got bored." Immediately, I realized she was right. I overused center stage—ignoring the corners both upstage and down. I was about to tell my audience that everything was equally important, and therefore, nothing was important.

I spent the next day quickly restaging the play, just before audiences walked in the door.

Reading the Playing Space

Alexander Dean and Lawrence Carra offer clear advice on avoiding staging mistakes in their seminal textbook *Fundamentals of Play Directing*. When Senior noted my monotonous production, she channeled their advice on Picturization:

> Picturization is the visual interpretation of each moment in the play. It is the placing of characters in a locale that suggests their mental and emotional attitudes toward one another so that the dramatic nature of the situation will be conveyed to an audience without the use of dialogue or movement.[3]

Step one of Picturization: create stage pictures that help capture the basic situation of the scene. Do you have a king in your scene? Is he in a place of power? Does the love scene generate heat? Does the fight create a sense danger? When I watch run-throughs of plays directed by my students, I ask: if a non-English speaking audience saw the play would they understand the narrative?

Step two of Picturization: place your scenes in the correct part of the stage. Assuming you're working in a proscenium house—with the stage on one side and the audience facing it on the other—you can read the stage emotionally. Each part of the stage, according to Dean and Carra, will generate a different kind of sentiment or feeling.

I like to teach the emotional map of the stage by using beanie babies—little stuffed animals—with my MFA directors. I give the directors a short amount of time, a bag of beanie babies, and the directions to stage iconic scenes by creating still pictures:

- a ghost scene
- a royalty scene
- a romantic scene
- a scene of intrigue
- a fight
- a gossip scene

I then have them imagine an end stage proscenium stage and divide it up into the six traditional areas:

- up right
- up center
- up left
- down right
- down center
- down left

Next, they need to put each scene in the zone of the stage they think will best serve the image. Should the ghost be down center or up right? Finally, determine which area of the stage has the most impact and which the least—and show the scenes off from weakest to strongest.

According to Dean and Carra, the scenes should go in the following order:

- The weakest place on stage is up left and is best for ghost scenes.
- The second weakest is up right and can be used for romantic images.
- Next strongest is down left and should be used for intrigue scenes.
- Next is down right and should be used for intimate scenes.
- The second strongest place is up center and is best for scenes of royalty.
- The strongest place on stage is down center and is best for fights.

Areas of the Proscenium Stage

Upstage Right:	Upstage Center:	Upstage Left:
Romance Illusion Distant	Royalty Status Stability	Ghost Unsettling Infinity
Downstage Right:	Downstage Center:	Downstage Left:
Intimacy Monologues Warmth	Fights Heat Intense	Intrigue Gossip Business

Audience

Figure 3.5 Areas of the Stage, Proscenium.

Why this order? We read from left to right and so images that are to our left are warmer and more familiar—those to the right feel colder and more distant. Similarly, it's easier to connect with things that are closer to us. Up left feels far away, so it's best for scenes that fill us with dread. Scenes that need to pack an emotional punch should be close to us. Hamlet's ghost should enter up left but Hamlet should die down center.

I follow these guidelines when examining a ground plan. Are we staging a romantic scene in an upstage corner? Should we move it? Do I want to subvert any of these guidelines to dramatic effect? Should we frustrate the audience by hiding the lovers away? Marrying topography to emotional impact prepares me to stage effectively.

If you're working on a three quarter or thrust stage, some of these rules still apply. Use down center, or more accurately plain center stage to punch up your fights, it will still feel the closest to most audience members. Placing people up center automatically grants them status because for most audiences they are in a position of power with some distance from the spectators. The downstage corners remain intimate spaces and the upstage corners distant—but there's no advantage to right or left given the audience sees the show from so many angles.

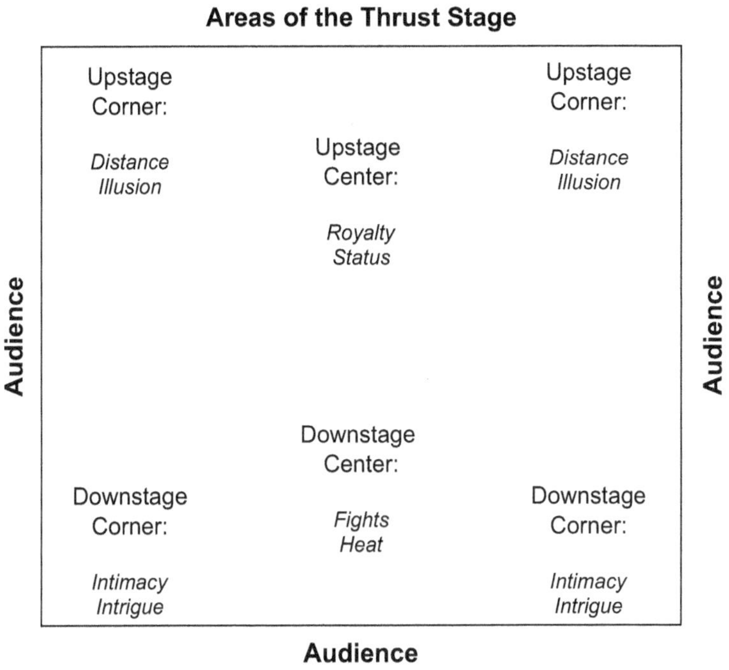

Areas of the Thrust Stage

Upstage Corner: *Distance Illusion*	Upstage Center: *Royalty Status*	Upstage Corner: *Distance Illusion*
Audience	Downstage Center: *Fights Heat*	*Audience*
Downstage Corner: *Intimacy Intrigue*		Downstage Corner: *Intimacy Intrigue*

Audience

Figure 3.6 Areas of the Stage, Thrust.

If you're staging completely in the round, all these rules go out the window. Someone close to one audience member is far away from another. While one person is reading the stage from left to right, someone across the way will be reading the mirror image. Holding any picture for long will block audience sight lines, so it becomes challenging to create images that read to an audience emotionally. The only constant is that center stage bestows more power than the edges, but even then, if an actor faces one direction for too long, somebody is stuck looking at their back.

Working in these configurations requires careful consideration of how the actors are moving: or in other words the blocking.

Blocking the Actors

In his pithy book, *Tips: Ideas for Directors*, Jon Jory suggests effective blocking can make or break a show. Directors with a talent for nothing but moving actors around a stage, have often forged successful careers. Jory extols the craft of blocking in one of his tips:

> It provides focus by directing our eye and ear to the necessary place. It provides physical punctuation for the text. It reveals character through its details and story through its juxtapositions. It makes metaphors that enhance meaning. It creates rhythm that deepens attention and gives pleasure. It clarifies what happens between people and is a sort of visible emotion.[4]

One method to develop blocking: identify logical behavior for the situation. If a scene is in a kitchen, there are countless reasons for a character to fetch a cup, grab some food, or stow a knickknack. Are they fiddling with silverware to avoid direct eye contact? Are they busy rushing around the room, barely engaging in the conversation?

Blocking emphasizes beat shifts or conversational turns. When the stage is still we assume the characters are in stasis. When the actors relocate, they draw our eye and we sense something has changed emotionally.

In their book *Notes on Directing,* Frank Hauser and Russel Reich encourage directors to think of each scene as a chase scene. One character wants something; the other doesn't want to give in and probably wants just the opposite. A chase begins when the first character advances and the other retreats. Hauser and Reich suggest that to maintain drama, the characters should always maintain some distance from each other as they engage in the chase (see page 90 and Exercise 18 for more on the chase scene theory of staging):

> When blocking, imagine an elastic band connects the characters. When they come together, the tension is gone, the chase is over. Look for ways and reasons to separate them, to reestablish the tension, the chase, the very reason for watching.[5]

The term blocking comes from the tradition of 19th century theatre makers using different colored blocks to represent the actors, which they would move around a miniature set model to figure out their staging ahead of time. (See pages 21–22 for Peter Brook's experience with cardboard stand ins for actors.) This practice of preblocking shows at home and transferring the movement to actors in rehearsals is almost never used any more. Directors typically collaborate with their actors in the room to create staging. That said, while directors rarely arrive with a fat prompt book, some do like to stage in detail from day one.

Staging Moments Specifically

Since Anne Bogart's SITI company is best known for popularizing the physically improvisatory Viewpoints training technique (see pages 24–26 for more on Viewpoints), many people assume Bogart's rehearsals are improvised. Not so: Bogart stages each play quite precisely from the moment the actors get on their feet. She mentioned her fear for staging when we sat down to chat:

> Terrifying. But I live by what Pablo Picasso said, which is the first stroke on the canvas is always a mistake, and the rest of the work is to fix that mistake. So, the courage on the first day is to make big fat mistakes knowing that everything else is trying to work on that mistake.

Bogart stages slowly and meticulously. She might say, "You start upstage. Now come downstage left five steps." Sometimes actors will propose changes or try something different. They all know the task: create a specific repeatable set of movements to go with their dialogue, something they can repeat. Bogart defines the job as creating a *physical container*. The container will change during rehearsal, but company members must set something concrete from the first day of staging.

When Bogart starts staging, she stops talking about emotions or psychology. She only speaks in physical terms. *Move here, walk over there, grab her like this.* She manipulates proximity, speed, distance, and touch as a way to provoke her actors. Bogart believes a precise physical track frees up the space for emotions; actors rule their own psychology and feelings, not directors.

As she stages, Bogart is looking for ways to distort pedestrian human behavior. Sure, two people will shake hands but how? Slowly? Too slowly for comfort? Quickly and abruptly?

> You try to make music out of the behavior that exists. It's behavior that's recognizable but is reified through one's musicalizing of it and making it strange, really. It's about awakening what's asleep. A lot of human behavior is sleepy. In addition, you have to raise the bar so that it actually costs you more to walk across the stage. Or it costs you more to shake hands with somebody.

Bogart fashions a theatrical language by manipulating common human interactions. She stages actors in unison, instructs them to repeat a gesture over and over, or slows down their cross from stage left to right. She's crafting stage poetry—working with actions rather than words.

Obie Award–winning director **Anne Kauffman** also stages quite precisely, controlling the visual picture. She believes audiences understand a play through the movement. Of course, they hear the language, but actors' movements and location on stage affect theatregoers viscerally. Kauffman expanded on her thoughts when I interviewed her:

> We're animals. The hair raises on the back of our neck if spatial relationships are violated. And we've taught audiences how people are supposed to move onstage. We are taught that if somebody is performing a speech, nothing else can take focus, nothing else can be happening. So, if someone is sitting in a chair talking, and someone else crosses in the background during the chair sitter's speech, I think that the audience goes, *What?* There's a tiny little refocusing because of how we've educated audiences about the rules of movement. So, when we break those rules, it's unsettling and provocative in a subtle way.

Regardless of the play she's working on, Kauffman always tries to disquiet an audience by awakening their senses. In the same way that Shakespeare uses rhythm or alliteration to arrest the ear, Kauffman attempts to reengage the audience with motion and action. For these reasons, precision is her watchword from day one.

In contrast to this method, some directors like to encourage complete freedom in the beginning of the staging process.

Running without Staging

When I was working on a new play called *McMeekin Finds Out* for Route 66 Theatre in Chicago in 2010, we'd spent a solid week at the table discussing the play. After we finished reading through the final scene I announced, "Okay let's run the entire play on its feet." This two-act comedy featured changes in location, complicated physical action, and punchy dialogue. The lead actress yelped, "Great, let's go!" and readied herself to leap into action. The lead actor sputtered, "We're gonna what?!" I quickly explained the rules of the run-through:

- *There are no wrong choices*
- *Mime violence, no actual contact*
- *Here's a table and some chairs*
- *Make entrances and exits at will*
- *Let's go!*

I looked over at the lead actress—she was raring to start. I looked over to the lead actor. He said, "We're actually going to do this?" I nodded and off they went.

The transition from the table to staging can be awkward. Ideas that made sense when just sitting seem foreign when trying to speak, move, and connect with a partner. The unpracticed run-through rips the bandage off this process.

The surprise run-through gives actors confidence—even those who start out terrified. I learn about each actor's first instincts: where they are comfortable, where they don't know what they are doing, and where we need to work most. We always have a quick discussion afterwards to see what they learned.

> *Wow it moves fast!*
> *I didn't realize how much time I sit in one place.*
> *I'm racing all over.*
> *You're all so funny!*
> *I can't wait to get this script out of my hand.*

A few years ago, Robert Falls got bored staging plays meticulously. He has built a successful career on the basis of his inventive and precise blocking, but he craved more spontaneity. He traveled to Russia to see master directors work on etudes (See Exercise 12 for more on etudes). He obsessed over veteran director and author

Mike Alfreds and took his book *Different Every Night* to heart. Alfreds prizes life on stage:

> If actors know in advance how their partners are going to deliver a line or play a moment or, indeed, how they themselves are going to respond to that line or moment, there can be no spontaneity, no surprise, no risk and therefore no true creativity—the actor is safe, playing a facsimile of what once was.[6]

When he can, Falls follows Alfred's method for rehearsing plays. He spends the first few weeks analyzing the script and world-building. He and the actors break down scenes beat by beat, identify intentions and actions, and sometimes improvise dialogue. He encourages actors to create detailed biographies and relationship webs. (See pages 62–63 for Fall's work on world-building.)

Falls was able to follow this method when he worked on *Uncle Vanya* at the Goodman Theatre in 2016. After weeks of world-building and text analysis with his cast, Falls thought they were ready. He said, "Okay let's run the first act." Falls told me what happened next when we sat down to discuss his process:

> They would play all of Act One on their feet from beginning to end, knowing all their lines, all their intentions, knowing their characters, knowing where they were coming from, when they came onstage or left, and I loved the work they did. It was triumphant. Everyone said, *Wow, I can't believe I did that.*

Falls didn't discuss the run-through much with his actors—he wanted the work to stand for itself. He videotaped their work to capture their first instincts. When the actors ran the act a second and third and fourth time they made completely different choices, which he expected. Eventually he started guiding actors toward choices that he liked best: curating their choices to craft a production.

Nataki Garrett will tend to let the actors lead the way when she starts staging. Just like her table work sessions where she leave silences for actors to fill, when staging she'll leave empty spaces. She's giving license to her actors and making sure the staging both feels and looks organic:

> I don't like to move people around spaces...I like to collaborate with people. I need them to feel empowered. I need them to

be empowered. I create blocking based on what they're doing anyway because of course you want it to be as organic as possible. It's their movement and they have power over what their bodies are doing in space.

Garrett allows actors to just stumble around the stage for periods of time. She feels if she jumps in too quickly she will cut off their instincts. She may ask provoking questions, but she won't tell them what to do or how to do it.

Other directors look for a middle ground between complete freedom and precise blocking: they create a loose sketch.

Sketching a Physical Structure

Rachel Chavkin, Tony Award–winning Broadway director believes directors must make staging choices in the rehearsal room early and often. Chavkin believe actors crave structure. Staging doesn't happen by accident; directors craft physical choices. A director who takes charge of a process doesn't stifle creativity—she sets it free.

When teaching at NYU Chavkin noticed her students avoided blocking. They seemed afraid to craft a structure, believing staging would appear by magic. Chavkin doesn't believe there are rules for good or bad staging, but she likes to quickly zip through a few truisms for her students. She outlined her guidelines to me in an interview over the phone:

> The first rule is the text doesn't mean anything until you decide what it means. The second is every decision leads to at least five more decisions. The third is that you can't make a better choice until you've made a choice. And the last, which is just a formula, is the amount of time in the process equals the number of choices you can make over that process.

She encourages her students to stage their plays early and fast. At least they should make choices about where people enter and the big turning points of the scene. They might decide on a style of movement—is it a play with a lot of action? Is it a play where people sit around a lot? Some combination of the two?

Once they create a sketch, directors can go back and change the outline, or add in detail. A sketch will be rough at first, but it provides structure.

Daniel Kramer, former artistic director of the English National Opera, enters plays primarily through the body. He trained in Viewpoints and started his career devising plays. When Kramer starts putting shows on their feet, he sketches in the big ideas, and worries about details later:

> What's the floor pattern, what's the basic movement of the piece? I think that a director should go in knowing all of that as a metaphor. Of course, it changes with the actors, but you've designed a set—you should know the topography, the flow patterns, the shapes. And in those first two weeks I'm doing all the floor patterns, basic shape work, the basic intentions.

Kramer believes that story, metaphor, and physicality go hand in hand. Are you working on a play where people move in circles or at right angles? Does this scene move fast or slow? Is this scene still and the next one frenetic? Kramer believes that if you can set a basic pattern for the actors in the first few weeks you give them a structure to play within.

Broadway director **Kimberly Senior** continues to change how she stages plays. When she started directing, Senior meticulously blocked her plays, crafting her actors' instinctual choices. Staging illustrates the psychological story of the characters—why move toward or away from someone? Why stand up on this line but sit on this one? Do you want to be closer to the kitchen or farther away? Early in her career she dug into carving out the specifics of her storytelling by controlling the picture.

Eventually, her interest shifted to provoking action. She stopped staging scenes, acts, and sometimes, entire plays. Instead of blocking, she led actors toward conflict, character, and objective. After actors ran large sections, they discussed their takeaways from the run. Actors had complete freedom night to night as to where they stood or how they physically attacked a scene.

Now she's found a middle ground in her work:

> And I used to say things like, I don't believe in blocking, but the truth of the matter is, is I don't believe in me blocking the show. I believe in letting the actors figure it out. And it might

take three weeks and I can give them feedback on that. But truthfully, they end up finding the right way to do it. There usually is only one way to get from A to B.

Senior and her actors discuss which sections of the play should be different every night and which need to be the same. Combat and dance must play precisely every performance to ensure actor safety. But a small character interaction? That might change:

> I give them a map, right? There's a map of this town that is this play, there are specific landmarks, there are certain things that have to happen...and you can go a lot of different ways from the library to the grocery, but you have to go to the library and have to go to the grocery. Are you taking the most direct route? How is that working? Are you noticing the things you pass by?

Senior isn't giving up control of the play—she makes sure that every scene, every moment, every joke has been examined and turned over. In essence though, she works on scenes rather than staging them, and by working them, the staging materializes.

Exercises fifteen through seventeen in the workbook offer suggestions on tuning up your staging. As with other parts of the process, ask yourself how you like to stage. Are you interested in crafting details from the first day? Do you feel like you speak the most clearly in physical terms? Does your play demand finely tuned staging throughout? Or do you want to be looser? Are you interesting in creating a playroom where actors create their own movements? Perhaps you want to combine the two methods? Do you want to allow actors to find their own pathways in early rehearsals and then finely shape scenes toward the end of the process? Or perhaps different parts of the play ask for different methods? Maybe intimate two person scenes can be left looser while crowd scenes require a conductor's hand.

In order to provide more detail, I have separated out two intimately linked tasks: shaping the staging and crafting the details of scene work. In this last chapter I focused on how different directors tackle the challenge of either directly blocking stage movement or editing physical choices made by actors. The next chapter drills down to the heart of coaching actors on creating rich detailed performances.

If staging is form, then acting is the content.

Staging a New Play

When Chay Yew first came to Chicago he was surprised so many actors came to auditions with their lines memorized. Their dedication impressed him, but he noticed some actors added in beats or words. They didn't hear the writer's rhythm. These actors rarely made the cut.

When actors memorize their lines before rehearsal, often they learn the cadence incorrectly, and will have to unlearn those mistakes. When Yew starts staging, he encourages his actors to hold their scripts so they can hew to the prose precisely:

> Also, there may be a sense of possession for actors who get off book too early. They may want to hold onto a moment they found early in the process. And the playwright has cut it because the moment now doesn't make sense dramaturgically. And guess what? There's now a more interesting moment to play.

If an actor builds their performance slowly over the course of rehearsal, they can learn how their character thinks and speaks, even as rewrites appear. By previews, actors should know their character so well they could handle a fresh speech easily. They've learned the DNA of the person and can easily rattle off any new language.

As **Will Davis**, new play director, stages world premieres he encourages actors to embrace change. He tries to stage a play quickly to stimulate the writer. A first pass inspires a writer to toss out old ideas for dialogue or scenes. He let me know how he champions his intrepid actors:

> What success looks like in this room is new pages. So, if new pages come into this room it is because you are doing something that is creating ideas. The actor animal will think new pages must mean I did a bad job. They have to re-write because I am so bad.

Davis asserts the opposite: revisions aren't fixes. Writers deepen and expand themes based on what they saw in the room. Davis cautions actors that new work takes bravery: you can work in minute detail on a moment one day, only to have it thrown out the next.

> Leigh Silverman attempts to activate every part of a new play as swiftly as possible. She'll stage a first draft rapidly. As soon as one draft is finished: she starts working on any script changes. Perhaps a scene changed locales, or the writer is trying out new dialogue:
>
>> If you spent an entire day staging a scene and then the next day the writer brings in a whole new version, it can be a real waste of time. Unless of course there's a specific thing that a writer is really looking for and then you want to stage it as accurately as you can. You should spend a lot of time on scenes that need a lot of work and you should spend a lot of time on scenes when they're in process so the writer can get what they need.
>
> Silverman attempts to home in on the writer's needs. If the writer wants to hear a scene over and over, she works on the scene in detail with the actors. If the playwright knows they need to do a rewrite on a scene on their own, Silverman will let it lay fallow for a few days.
>
> Silverman says she often ends up staging a play four times. Her first pass gives the writer something to react to and helps Silverman get a sense of the whole. She'll start staging again if she gets new scenes or wants to refine performances. Once in technical rehearsals, Silverman often finds herself staging the play again based on what the set, lights, and costumes are telling her. Finally, after seeing it during previews, she might restage the play one last time based on what she learns from an audience.

DETAILING SCENE WORK

In order to apply for the MFA directing program at DePaul, candidates direct a short scene in front of myself and Lisa Portes. We tell the candidates we know it's an artificial exercise: nobody knows each other, time is short, and people are watching. Regardless, we learn what directors think scene work entails. It's fascinating.

Some candidates run exercises throwing balls of energy or invent chasing games. Others stage precisely from the first moment. Some conduct a short table session then slowly work. Afterward, Lisa and I feedback to the director. Usually I lead with, "Don't interrupt the actors so much."

Often, candidates stop the actors every couple of lines or even mid-line to offer an idea or adjustment. I encourage directors to let actors flow longer. Interrupting an actor jolts them out of the scene. They learn to play for your benefit rather than working with their scene partner. I encourage directors to set boundaries, "Let's start here and end here. Then we'll chat." Actors play for a bit, hopefully with a specific goal in mind, and then the director feeds back. I believe it give actors agency, while letting them discover moments themselves.

Some directors couldn't agree less.

Crafting Every Detail

I visited Chicago Shakespeare Theatre in 2018 to watch Aaron Posner work on his magic-laden production of *Macbeth*. He interrupted his actors constantly. He stopped them every other line—sometimes mid-line—to give a small note about the pitch of a word, the stress in a phrase, or an opportunity for comedy. *Turn out there so the audience can see you. Don't drop the end of your sentence.*

Posner said he might allow his lead actors to occasionally run a scene once without being bothered, but typically he will stop and start constantly. He interrupts actors to focus their attention and hone their language. As an example, Posner broke down the moment Macduff discovers that Macbeth has murdered all his children at once.

> This isn't just a general metaphor this is a specific metaphor. *My pretty chickens in one fell swoop*. He's talking about a bird coming down and swooping up chickens. It's one fell swoop. It's not just general; it's specifically that. So, getting the language to a specific and hard edge, as discovered, as coined as possible.

Posner worked that muscle a lot when I was watching. He stopped actors when it seemed like they were reciting precious language. He encouraged them to speak the lines as if they've never used those words before. As they work he inspired actors to react as truthfully as possible to their scene partners. Posner told me his theory on what helps create truth moment to moment:

> I never talk about listening. I always talk about processing. Because we don't listen—we process. Everything we hear we're putting through our own processing device. We're hearing it,

we're cataloging it, we're remembering it, and we're going, *Oh, that's interesting.* So, I'm trying to get people to process with as much specificity as possible.

In a slightly meta moment of the interview, Posner analyzed the interaction the two of us were having. He noted that we know each other casually, like each other a bit, and we're doing an interview. But that's not everything that's happening. I caught him at the end of a long day:

> I'm tired, I'm like, *interesting, I wonder how he's hearing me because he's a director*? I'm curious, am I trying to impress you a little bit, is that my intention?

If a casual encounter between two colleagues contains that many layers of subtext, what's underneath a scene of two spouses planning to murder a king?

Figure 3.7 Macbeth by William Shakespeare. Adapted and directed by Aaron Posner and Teller, in the Yard at Chicago Shakespeare Theater, 2018. L–R: McKinley Carter, Theo Germaine, Ian Merrill Peakes. Set: Dan Conway; Lighting: Thom Weaver; Costumes: Mara Blumenfeld; Sound: Andre Pluess; Magic Designer: Johnny Thompson. Photo Credit: Liz Lauren.

Making Small Adjustments

Anne Kauffman says the only way she knows how to understand and direct a scene is by noting the details. She perceives that a detail seems off, has an instinct it should change, and passes a note along to an actor:

> And I can get weirdly granular. I'll look at my notes, and I'll be like, *Well, that's a dumb note because that seems, like, we don't even know what we're doing and I'm giving them this note.* But somehow it strikes me as important, you know what I mean? *Well, can you pick up the pot at that point?* But it somehow feels structural to me.

Kauffman works through the play twice in this fashion, looking at small sections and giving minor adjustments to behavior, blocking, or intention. This might take three weeks—most of her rehearsal process. Only then will she pull back, look at the larger picture, and see what she's made.

Kauffman likened her process to building a car but starting with the smallest parts rather than say the outer body. She starts putting together the combustion and exhaust system before she knows what kind of engine she's fashioning. Once she figures out the engine, she constructs the frame or builds the suspension. At this point, she doesn't know if she's building a Ferrari or a Prius.

Late in her process, just before technical rehearsals, Kauffman often has a moment of reckoning with her cast. They've built up many details in their performances, carved out minute moments of staging, but do they know what's happening in the play? They might spend a whole afternoon talking through the script scene by scene, asking what is happening, looking for the dramatic arc. Kauffman has learned over time that her best work come from starting with the smallest detail and working her way up to the overall structure of the play.

In direct opposition to that idea, some directors move in the other direction, from the general to the specific.

Sketching before Detail Work

After a long period at the table reading the script over and over, Rebecca Taichman likes to create a rough draft of the play, without too many details. She tries to move as quickly as possible the first time through, so she can slow down for her second and third passes.

Taichman encourages flexibility and variety. On her first pass through the play, she alters the staging often:

> It can get scary for actors if they fear blocking isn't going to get set. I always say to them: *Fear not. Ultimately, you might get frustrated by how set it is, depending on what kind of actor you are.* By then end I'm compulsive visually. I believe a story should be told on stage visually with purpose and it can get pretty compulsive. How to guide the eye, what the moment-to-moment images say and how they move an audience ... I love that part of the process. I think of directing as very much a visual art form.

Once she's into her second pass, Taichman gets iterative. She likes to run scenes again and again, but with small changes each time. What will she alter? She'll modify anything from a bit of blocking to a character idea to an intention:

> Do it again with this tiny little modification. This tiny little modification again. Over and over and over. Layers and layers accumulate.

Sometimes actors want a clarification for the change and sometimes she will explain her instincts, but more often she'll ask her actors to just do the scene again. *Don't talk about it, just repeat it.* She'll run a scene three, four, five times with very slight adjustments. It's almost like a chiropractic adjustment, one more little crack and the spine of the scene clicks into place.

How does she know what to change? Intuition. Something doesn't feel right or specific enough or honest enough:

> I want to be *moved*. I hope to move an audience—so if I'm not moved how can I imagine they will be? I hope that we can open an audience's hearts and minds to the mythic questions... Theater is usually good at that—asking questions that are so profound they really don't have an answer. Those are among the questions I think we need to keep looking at over and over and over as a community, as a culture.

If something isn't gripping her she asks—what's wrong? Why isn't it affecting me? She's not trying to figure out what's cool or interesting. She doesn't want to show off her actors' talents. She's focused on the narrative. What's the most powerful version of this story?

Chay Yew similarly crafts a sketch and then goes back to work on each individual unit. He won't run the play until he has worked on each scene in detail. After his sketch, he'll ignore scenes that he feel work perfectly on a first go, ones that seem to land as the playwright intended. Others need more attention.

When a scene isn't working, Yew is blunt:

> Oh my God. I'm bored. Can we run that again? And I explain: I say, *I'm bored*, means that I know what's happening in the scene and it's no longer exciting. So that problem is actually not yours, it's mine. I need to know why I'm bored.

Yew knows you can watch a great scene over and over because it's full of suspense, tension, and surprises. So why is this scene dead? Are the actors not taking care of the specificity of the text? Is Yew's staging off? Does Yew believe the actor in the moment, or does the acting seem forced? The scene made sense yesterday, but not today. Why?

It could be they've misdiagnosed the basic circumstances of the scene.

Understanding the Situation

I was lucky enough to visit the Moscow Art Theatre School in 2016 and watch master acting teachers work with students from Wayne State University as a part of their Month in Moscow program. In one session the teacher instructed each student to choose an animal, place that animal in a situation, and fashion a little drama.

A young woman shares her exploration: she's a frog. The actor gets down on all fours and starts her scene. Ribbit. Hop. Ribbit. Sees a fly, watches it buzz around, hops over, and gulp. Dinner. The end.

The Russian teacher praises her first for her movement techniques saying he could really see the gyrations of the frog. He was impressed by her body work. Then he launches into a series of questions:

- How old is this frog? Young or old?
- I can't tell—is it hungry or not hungry?
- Is it hot out? Cold out?
- Why does it eat the fly? Is there a reason?
- Is it morning? Afternoon? Evening?

He rattles off a few more questions and something starts to click for me. When a director watches a scene, they need to understand the basic situation. What is happening? In this case, the actor hadn't created a specific time, place, or set of circumstances that could feed her work.

I remember working on the final scene of *A Streetcar Named Desire*. Blanche DuBois has been sexually assaulted by Stanley: everyone knows it, but silently denies the situation. Stanley and his friends are callously playing poker, while Stella waits for someone from a mental institution to fetch Blanche. Stella confesses to her friend Eunice that she has misgivings, but her friend is firm: If Blanche made up an insane story about Stella's husband, she must be crazy. She has to choose who is telling the truth, her husband or her sister.

As we were working on the scene, I remember the cast members whooping it up while they were playing poker, having a grand time. They were playing the situation casually. I reminded them—everyone has heard the rumor that Stanley raped Blanche. What will happen to him if that rumor gets out? Could he go to jail? Will the rumors tear their community apart?

Immediately the tone changed. Everyone knew the secret but was trying to pretend they didn't. The poker game was a cover for their guilt and shame. It seemed people were suddenly walking on eggshells, and every line seemed to be about the hidden subtext. I didn't ask for tension or tell everyone to take the scene more seriously; I only commented on the basic circumstances of the scene.

In her book *The Director's Craft*, Katie Mitchell encourages directors to limit their notes and observations to a short list of criteria: time, place, given circumstances, events, intentions, relationships, and character histories.

She believes a director can spot these principles in action through keen observation. While the below may seem obvious, I've often found that directors can lose sight of what they should be viewing. Mitchell lays out the basics in an early chapter on craft:

> When you are watching the actors' work, look closely at what they are doing. This means you have to look at their whole body and not just their face. Pay attention to every tiny physical detail such as a flick of an eye, a twitch of a foot or the way they sit down heavily on a chair. Observing physical detail precisely is a skill that you can train yourself in.[7]

Mitchell isn't suggesting directors tell actors how to behave in scenes, rather she's encouraging them to tune up their observation skills so they can recognize if actors are truly embodying the given circumstances. If someone is hot they may adjust their clothing. If someone receives shocking news, they might sit stock still for a long moment. People who haven't seen each other for a long time might approach each other warily.

Mitchell encourages directors to stay away from giving notes on emotions, tone, or staging—stick to what's clearly observable. Is the relationship clear or unclear? Is the actor's use of their backstory fuzzy or on point? Did the physical behavior exhibited give evidence that the actor was pursuing a clear objective?

I often see student directors struggle to give notes. Something feels off—but what? I encourage them to put on a pair of *glasses* through which to view the scene. If you worry about staging while you watch the scene, you will notice where the actors are standing. If you focus on the relationships, you will see how people treat each other. If you concentrate on action, you'll be able to track it.

I encourage students to try my Post-it note theory of directing. Write the words "Who, what, when, where, and why" on a Post-it note. Then write the word, "How" and cross it out.

Who is in the scene with you? What is the state of your relationship? What do you want from them? What are the facts of this scene? Where does the scene take place? Are you clear about where everything is in your imagined surroundings? Are there any time pressures? Why do you say that line? Take that action?

Let's drill down on each of these questions and see how they relate to scene work.

Who's in the Scene?

Derrick Sanders was directing a family drama and the main couple wasn't clicking. He couldn't pinpoint the problem, but he didn't buy the relationship. One afternoon he was working on a scene in the couple's kitchen. The actor playing the wife brought out her husband's coffee with cream and sugar. Sanders stopped the scene and gently probed the actor:

Sanders: Why'd you bring cream and sugar to him?
Wife: I put cream and sugar out when people have coffee.

Sanders: How long have ya'll been married?
Wife: Thirty-five years.
Sanders: How does he take his coffee?
Wife: Black.
Sanders: So, why'd you bring out the cream and sugar?

Sanders didn't really care about the cream and sugar, he questioned whether the actor had deeply imagined her marriage. Had she dreamed on the relationship, envisioned the many breakfasts she'd cooked up? How could he help the actor more fully connect to her scene partner as someone she'd lived with for decades?

While it doesn't happen often, occasionally, an actor will ask Sanders how he wants a scene played. "Do you want it slower, faster, angrier?" Sanders guides the actor away from results and toward more active choices. He spurs actors to delve into relationships and motivations. He sparks them to dream on their shared histories—the pace and tone should take care of itself.

When I coach auditions in acting class, I focus on relationship first. After an actor makes a go at an audition scene, I ask, "Who are you talking to?" My students quickly figure out that the right answer isn't merely, "My sister." They need to expand their answer. "My sister Blanche who I love dearly, but who needs to live in the real world." Now we have something to work with.

What factors shape relationships? I offer students categories to investigate as they break down a scene. Let's think of Stella's views on Blanche:

- Shared history, language, inside jokes
  - *We grew up together and we think lemon Cokes are the best.*
- Differing views on past events
  - *Belle Reve was stifling. I had to get out, but she loved it.*
- Historical status between the two
  - *She always treated me like a bit of a servant.*
- Current status between the two
  - *Now she needs my help, which I'll gladly give on my terms.*
- Past events that only affected one person—but they bring to this relationship
  - *She can't possibly understand my deep love for Stanley.*
- Competition—often for a third person's attention
  - *Sometimes she seems to be flirting with my husband—she should focus on Mitch!*

- Love—familial, erotic, friendship
  - *She's family, nothing is stronger, but I do have a new family now...*

I encourage actors to home in on the problem they want to solve with their scene partner. This problem stays constant throughout the play, and each scene presents a slight variation on the theme. Conflict defines relationships.

What do Blanche and Stanley think about each other?

Stanley: Blanche is a sexy woman and my wife's sister, but I don't trust her influence on Stella, and she keeps calling me coarse. She needs to understand that I am the king of this castle.

Blanche: Stanley is offering me refuge for the moment and is certainly handsome, but he is a vulgar thug who treats my sister like dirt. He needs to treat me better, clean up this apartment, or let Stella and I leave in peace.

When Stanley and Blanche first meet, he dominates the household in subtle ways—he examines his liquor bottle, takes off his shirt, and grants her permission to stay. He's the ruler of the roost. In their final scene together, Stanley destroys Blanche to prove his sovereignty. He kicks her out, exposes her lies, and eventually rapes her.

Once an actor unravels their complex relationship with one character, they must crack the secret formula for every character in the play! Blanche has one problem with Stanley, a quite different one with Stella, and yet another with her young suitor Mitch. How does she treat Pablo? The tamale seller? Eunice? Also known as *channel work*, defining a relationship with each different character in a play helps actors create detailed, human performances. (See Exercise 13: Character Webs.)

Once I feel an actor understands the relationship, I follow up: "So what are you fighting for?"

What Do They Want?

I was rehearsing *The Seagull* by Anton Chekhov for a student production at DePaul University. We wrestled with the long final scene between Nina and Constantine, childhood friends and ex-lovers.

Nina ran off with Constantine's mother's lover, lost a baby, got rejected, and struggled to make ends meet as an actor. She blows into the room upset, bordering on lunacy, but Constantine begs her to take him back.

I asked them each what they wanted. Constantine wanted Nina to return his love, telegraphing his passion in every line and every action. Nina suggested she desired forgiveness. We got to work but the scene lay flat. Constantine forgave Nina immediately and the scene had nowhere to go. I had an impulse.

What if Nina wants to be punished for her sins by the one person who knows her best?

Immediately, the scene leapt to life. When Constantine praised Nina, she furiously delineated more of her wrongdoings. When he approached her, she ran away. She was only happy when he lashed out.

In his seminal guide, *An Actors Work*, Konstantin Stanislavski trained actors to access their creativity every night, rather than relying on the whims of inspiration. The actor's most potent question to unlock truthful work: what does the character want? (See pages 13–14 for more on Stanislavski's grammar of acting.)

Stanislavski encourages actors to divide the script into logical bits, or units, and search for what the character wants most of all in that section. Next, what stands in their way? What is the obstacle? The obstacle is almost always found in the other character, but occasionally it will be internal. Now, how will they overcome their obstacle and achieve their goal? They may need to try several approaches.

Stanislavski offered clear terms for actors: The problem to overcome in a scene is the actor's *Task*. A character embodies an *Action* to achieve their task, and *Tactics* are the subtle different methods for going after what they want:

> Learn not to play the result onstage but to fulfill the Task genuinely, productively, and aptly through action all the time you are performing. You must love the Tasks you have, find dynamic action for them.[8]

If actors jump straight to outcomes, they will tend toward emoting, forcing product, and clichés. In his inspirational book *A Sense of Direction*, William Ball translates Stanislavski's actor training into a guide for directors. Ball substitutes the word *objective* for task:

> The only real reason a director is needed in rehearsal is to perform the following function: persistently to draw the actor to a more meaningful and appropriate choice of objectives, and then to persuade the actor to lend his full commitment to those objectives.[9]

At this point, Ball helpfully points out that in the world of theatre there are many names for essentially the same thing:

- What is your task?
- What do you want?
- What are you doing?
- What are you playing?
- What are you fighting for?
- What's your objective? Goal? Intention?
- What do you need?
- What is your action? What is the verb you are playing?[10]

Looking back at the example from *The Seagull*, the scene finally leapt to life not just because we found strong actions, but because we found actions that conflicted. Nina wanted Constantine to punish her and Constantine wanted to rekindle their love affair. Each time Constantine tried a new tactic to restart their romance, Nina needed to find a new way to inspire him to hate her.

Conflict: the key to generating heat in scenes.

What's the Conflict?

In *Notes on Directing*, Terry Hauser and Russell Reich drop a simple potent idea for working on scenes. Every scene is a chase scene:

> Character A wants something from Character B who doesn't want to give it. If he did the scene would be over. Why does A want it? In order to...what? Why does B refuse? Usually when someone chases someone else they move toward their object, and the object feeling the pressure, moves away.[11]

Figure out who is chasing whom and scenes unfold in a series of attacks and parries, cat and mouse moves, thrusts and evasions. (See page 70 and Exercise 18 for more on this concept.)

Look at the first exchange between Stanley and Blanche in *A Streetcar Named Desire*. At first glance they might seem to be exchanging pleasantries:

Stanley: In Laurel, huh? Oh, yeah. Yeah, in Laurel, that's right. Not in my territory. Liquor goes fast in hot weather. *(He holds the bottle to the light to observe its depletion.)* Have a shot?
Blanche: No, I—rarely touch it.
Stanley: Some people rarely touch it, but it touches them often.
Blanche: Ha-ha.
Stanley: My clothes're stickin' to me. Do you mind if I make myself comfortable? *(He starts to remove his shirt.)*
Blanche: Please, please do.
Stanley: Be comfortable is my motto.
Blanche: It's mine, too. It's hard to stay looking fresh. I haven't washed or even powdered my face and—here you are![12]

Are they putting each other at ease? Greeting each other? Is Stanley making Blanche feel at home? Not if we believe conflict is the soul of drama. If Stanley doesn't have an obstacle, why does he need an action or a task?

I remember working this scene in the rehearsal hall and it was just lying flat—playing as a mild first meeting between strangers. I asked Stanley what he thought about Blanche. The actor believed he'd already heard about Blanche from his wife and assumes she'll be snooty and judgmental. I reminded him of some of the given circumstances: he's come in sweaty and stinky from bowling. Some of his liquor is gone—who drank it? I encouraged Stanley to really take over the apartment. He took off his shirt entirely and moved toward Blanche. I remember the actress shrieking a bit in surprise. We upped the stakes and created more life.

Stanley's text says, "Have a shot?" but his subtext says, *I'm in charge here.*

What's the Subtext?

Scott Ellis trained as an actor at the Theatre School of DePaul back when it was the Goodman School of Drama. His teachers drilled him on action, intention, and subtext. He takes that training into his rehearsal halls when he directs plays. He encourages his actors to question every line they speak, looking beneath the surface. He related some of the questions he uses to spur action:

> Why am I saying this? What am I trying to get when I say this? What am I hearing? Which will change how I now attack. Through that process you find the character. You find the physical action of that character, which will help define what's happening in that scene.

Ellis encourages actors to constantly reassess what their partner is communicating under the surface. He distinguishes between *listening* and *hearing*. If you *listen*, you understand the words your partner says. If you *hear*—maybe you sense hidden intentions:

> How am I taking that? How am I hearing that? You can say a statement, and three different people can hear it three different ways. Or that character can hear it in three different ways, which can affect how that character reacts the next time.

Perhaps you understood what the other person said, or instead you completely misheard them. Maybe they are lying, or hiding part of the truth? I could be you're only hearing what you want to hear. Are you sure? Should you reevaluate the relationship? The situation? The underlying facts of the scene?

What Are the Given Circumstances?

Nataki Garrett sometimes sees actors trying to *get it right* or *say the line correctly*. She encourages them to not worry about how the line sounds, and instead focus on what is happening in the scene:

> Young actors tend to do this more often than anyone else. They ask, *When I say this line should it sound like this?* No, it should sound like you're in that circumstance and you don't want to be in it and that's why you use that language.

The best plays concern people making questionable choices. Garrett probes her actors: *How did you make that decision? Why? What do you want to do about it now? How will you get out of this pickle?*

The playwright has given you language: How can you use it to solve your problem?

Stanislavski taught us that the best way to discover the correct action or tactics in a scene is to have a firm grasp on the given circumstances. Actors need to embrace *the Magic If*: if these facts are true, then how would I act? (See pages 13–15 for more on Stanislavski's thoughts on given circumstances.)

Actors and directors should read the play thoroughly to compile evidence about character biography or events that happened earlier that day. They can build up their given circumstance pile by conducting research into the historical period:

- Blanche grew up on a plantation, Stanley clearly in shabbier quarters
- Stanley has a good job, Blanche is out of work
- Blanche and Stanley have never met
- Blanche just revealed to Stella that their ancestral home was lost
- Stanley's been bowling

Directors and actors glean some facts on a first read, but great plays often raise more questions than answers. Some questions can be answered through research or a close read of the play, but many can only be solved by working on the scenes in rehearsal:

- Are Blanche and Stanley attracted to each other?
- What has Stanley heard about Blanche? Vice versa?
- Did Stanley grow up poor? Was he taunted as a kid?
- How lavish was Belle Reve before Stella left?

Directors can train themselves to spot given circumstances at work. Does Blanche look like she's hiding a secret of some sort? Is Stanley noticing what Blanche is wearing? Are they both sweaty and tired? How do they react to seeing each other for the first time? Again, you don't need to ask for results in a scene, but rather you can just remind actors of information that fuels the action.

To delve into the details of scene work, directors and actors try to flesh out who is in the scene. They pore over character histories and deepen relationships. To activate conflict in scenes, collaborator look for the most vibrant desires, actions, obstacles, and tactics.

To ground this action, directors and actors discuss the facts of the scene. A key part of the given circumstances: location.

Where Are They?

Blanche and Stella grew up on a plantation, in a huge white house with imposing columns. As children they probably played on grounds that spread out as far as the eye could see.

Compare that to the small rented flat Blanche will be crashing at for the foreseeable future: it's a two-room apartment with a bedroom, a kitchen, and a bath. Blanche will sleep on a rollout bed, which we assume needs to be put out every night and away in the morning. Blanche has some choice words for Stella after being in her home for mere minutes:

Blanche: Oh, I'm not going to be hypocritical, I'm going to be honestly critical about it! Never, never, never in my worst dreams could I picture—Only Poe! Only Mr. Edgar Allan Poe!—could do it justice! Out there I suppose is the ghoul-haunted woodland of Weir! *(She laughs.)*
Stella: No, honey, those are the L & N tracks.
Blanche: No, now seriously, putting joking aside. Why didn't you tell me, why didn't you write me, honey, why didn't you let me know?
Stella: Tell you what, Blanche?
Blanche: Why, that you had to live in these conditions![13]

By scene six, when Stanley storms in to gather Stella for a date, a director can provoke dramatic tension by restating the givens:

- Three people have been living for months in a few hundred square feet of space
- The married couple have either not had sex out of respect for Blanche, or they have, and Blanche has been listening
- The normal routines of bathing, dressing, and eating have become incredibly complicated
- It has been hot, it is hot, and it will be hot for the foreseeable future

Stanley bursts in, intimidates Blanche with hints about her seedy past, and blows out:

Stanley: I'll wait for you at the Four Deuces!
Stella: Hey! Don't I rate one kiss?
Stanley: Not in front of your sister.[14]

Just a few months ago, Stanley ruled as the king of his castle. Now, he passes through like a guest.
He's a victim of time and place.

When Does the Scene Take Place?

You can spur actors with simple questions around time: What is the time of day? What is the season? What is the year? When in the play does this scene happen? What happened before or after? What's coming up next?

During another moment of rehearsal for Chekhov's *The Seagull* I found that Act Three was playing sluggishly. At the top of the act, famed actress Arkadina and her younger writer boyfriend Trigorin decide to cut their vacation short. Her son Constantine and brother Sorin beg her to stay, but to no avail. Juicy circumstances, but we couldn't seem to find the stakes.

I employed a short exercise. I helped actors ground themselves in the dining room of the estate. "What do you see? What do you hear? What's out that door?" Then, I encouraged them to walk around the room with purpose. When they encountered someone else, they could only say "you're leaving" or "I'm leaving." I was trying to get them invested in the event of the act—the parting of celebrated guests.

Immediately, I diagnosed the problem. Actors wandered around slowly and lugubriously, melancholy at their friends' departure. No wonder we couldn't generate any drama. I changed the exercise. Now they had to say, "You're leaving soon" or "I'm leaving soon". Immediately the actors took on the stakes of the circumstances, they zipped from person to person, trying to make connections before time ran out. They fully embodied the dramatic event at stake.

All of a sudden Chekhov's clues about how to play the act jumped to the foreground. Characters make declarations left and right about their need for speed and alacrity during Act Three.

- *We're going to be saying goodbye and probably...we'll never see each other again.*
- *You're leaving, and it's depressing for me here, alone.*
- *They're bringing the horses around...I hope you're all packed.*

- *It's already time, dear lady, to leave for the station.*
- *One more minute.*[15]

The Seagull takes place in the late 1800s in Russia when relatives typically visited once a year. Travel in winter was often treacherous or even impossible. There's a saying in Russia—in winter there are no roads, only directions. Everyone expects Arkadina to stay all summer but she's cutting out after a few weeks. Her loved ones are desperate to either convince her to stay or communicate their love to her before she takes off.

For Bill Rauch, a small throwaway line in *Othello* unlocked a key design element. Late in the play, Desdemona's cousin Lodovico arrives to order her husband Othello back to Venice. With this mandate to leave Cyprus for home, Shakespeare generates time pressure.

On the fateful last evening of the play, when Iago provokes Othello into a jealous rage, it's suggested a formal dinner for Lodovico would be apropos. Rauch and his designers pounced on the idea. He told me about his decision-making process over the phone:

> So, that little detail which I think would be easy to blow that off, *Yeah they can have dinner it's not a big deal.* We actually hinged a big part of our design on that. We don't see all of our characters in formal dress with naval uniforms until that dinner. And the night that Desdemona is gonna die and Emilia is gonna die and Iago is gonna die and Othello is gonna die, that night when everything is going to hell in a hand basket, they're having to sit together at their most dressed up and their most put-together.

The final night of Othello's life, as his world unravels, he's straightjacketed in a formal dinner coat. Did the formality of the evening provoke Othello's tip into delirium? Dressing every officer in Navy whites serves as a metaphor: the crust of civility holding back raging fury.

As directors excavate who, where, what, and when, they arrive at the juiciest question: Why?

Why Are You Doing That?

When he first started directing, **Brian Kulick,** former artistic director of Classic Stage Company, primarily coached actors through his staging. He relied on his blocking to animate his theories about a scene. By moving the actors, he illustrated the action. These days he peppers his cast with questions. He told me a few during a sit down interview:

> Why, why you do you do this at this point? Why did you do that? What do you mean by that? What do you want? What are you doing? Are you getting it? Did you really get what you wanted? You didn't. So, in life, what would you do with this? Now what? Now what? Now what?

Kulick asks these questions in the early phases of rehearsal, as he's doing a first pass on the play. He doesn't expect answers. Or if his actors do respond, he assumes they will change their answer over time. Questions should provoke the actors' imaginations to give a different answer in the rehearsal hall, during previews, and even into the run of the play.

Asking questions propels actors to specify their behavior and create the staging themselves. Sometimes he observes an actor on autopilot, not paying attention to their partner, and not tracking their tasks or objective. He'll launch into more questions. *Why do you want this? Why are you talking to them? Why do you say that next?*

Just asking why over and over can inspire the action of an entire scene:

- *Why do you enter?*
- *Why do you speak to this person?*
- *Why do you bring up that topic of conversation?*
- *Why are you fighting?*
- *Why do you give in?*
- *Why do you say those specific words? In that specific way?*
- *Why do you leave?*
- *Why do you stay?*

Asking why keeps a director curious. Questions can backfire on directors if they already know the answer to their query—when they just want to have their preconceptions validated. Sometimes directors ask questions when they really want to give a command. True questions spur learning. Kulick exhorts his students to enter a scene with an open mind. Ask *why* to be surprised:

> The thing that I find with young directors, is they don't ask questions. They just take the text at face value, as opposed to: *Why didn't the scene turn out this way?* Which is one of the Stanislavski's greatest questions. Play what it could have been as opposed to what it is. What was the character's expectations coming in?

If you ask an actor why they do something, they start to dig into their character. Actors don't just perform an action; they question their own motivations. Without this rigor, often directors can only deliver the bare plot of a scene. Through questions we uncover the reason we perform plays—to understand the strange choices human beings make.

Examine the first scene between Stanley and Blanche. They face off in a cramped hot apartment. Blanche has traveled hundreds of miles in desperation. Why does Stanley pick up the liquor bottle? Why not just leave it? Why does he make a joke rather than confront Blanche? Why does Blanche lie rather than admit the drink? Why does Stanley ask if he can take his shirt off? Would he keep it on if Blanche said no? Why does Blanche say yes? Why? Why? Why?

Guarding the Secret of Why

Charles Newell, Artistic Director of the Court Theatre labors to keep his actors in the dark about their partners' motivations. The last thing he wants is for actors to agree. During scene work, he will often pull an actor aside and discuss ideas on psychology or relationship—but he'll be sure to keep the conversation private. Newell related the theory behind his practice to me in a sit-down interview:

> I call them secrets, character secrets, because then the actor feels kind of ownership of something that is uniquely theirs. And then the fun thing, of course, is to create secrets that are contradictory. So, then they are operating out of conflict with each other. Even though they're only playing their own truths.

An actor will start playing a scene and become completely frustrated with their partner, *Why is he doing that? That's not what I want at all!* Newell loves when actors are baffled by their scene partners, because he believes it mimics life. Human beings enter into situations with different intentions, then improvise. We never agree on terms in the middle of an argument.

He finds his actors constantly try to confer on parts of the scene, either how they will approach a moment or a certain given circumstance. Newell doesn't allow any consensus—he'll throw a flag or a towel if actors lurch toward a shared understanding:

> *No! Stop! We're not gonna agree that we all last saw him twelve years ago. We're not all going to make the same assumption because that doesn't happen in life.* Right? So, even what seems like the most obvious, biographical, or historical fact...my tolerance for agreement is incredibly, incredibly, sharp.

In Newell's opinion, when actors fight for what they want in the dark, they do their best work. They try to achieve their goals, never succeeding, thwarted by their scene partner. When they can't get what they want, they shift tactics moment to moment. Newell finds this method gives his scenes life.

Most of the ideas in this chapter come straight out of Stanislavski's playbook, and are based on his grammar of acting that he laid out in *An Actor's Work* (see page 13–16 for more on Stanislavski's journey). Exercises eighteen through twenty in the workbook offer more insights on scene work. I would argue than any scene can be viewed by a director through the lens of basic questions: who, where, what, when, and why. When I first started directing all I could ever see was where people were standing or how they were moving. As I developed my craft I began to discern that actor's movements are influenced by what they want, or how they view their relationship, or even the time of day.

As I mentioned at the end of the last chapter, separating staging and scene work is slightly artificial. The two tasks intertwine intimately. Where actors stand or sit on stage affects how they relate to their scene partners. As directors delve deeper into scenes, looking for more detail, inevitably the staging alters.

When directors work on scenes and guide the physical details of scenes, typically they work through the play scene by scene, building toward the best test of their work: a full run-through.

RUNNING THE PLAY

I visited Moscow in 2016 and was lucky enough to speak with legendary theatre maker Dmitry Krymov about his process.

Krymov started his career as a designer, creating fabulous sets for many years before turning to directing. He and his students experimented, creating devised masterpieces. They tinkered in a theatrical lab with themes, ideas, and simple materials. The results dazzle and delight.

Opus No. 7 meditates on a generation of lost Russian Jews, reincarnated by hurricanes of paper, black paint, and empty shoes. *Eugene Onegin* imagines four clowns impishly relating the story of Alexander Pushkin's life and illustrating his famous novel.

I asked him about running his productions in rehearsal. He said you must run the play ten or fifteen times to really hear the music. Then he said something that surprised me:

Krymov: I'm with them on stage.
Kiely: You're with them on stage?
Krymov: Yes, I interrupt them. They cannot feel their roles yet…I don't wait to the end of the whole run.
Kiely: You give notes in the middle?
Krymov: Yes, of course, many days, many days. *I'm so sorry*, I tell them, *I'm sorry but I will interrupt you*. It's unusual?

I let him know that yes, typically directors don't interrupt in the middle of a run-through. That's why it's called a *run-through*. Krymov defended his process. When he no longer wanted to interrupt, the play was ready:

> At last there is a moment. I am interrupting less and less and less and one day I tell them, *Now, I don't want to interrupt you*. I stop my job when I see that I cannot do anything else, and if I interrupt them it doesn't matter. It's a moment you can feel it. Maybe they will understand some things by themselves more clearly than I will explain to them.

Krymov often rehearses plays for a year. He complained recently he had to economize: he only worked six months. It's not surprising that he might have fifteen full runs with him interrupting as the actors worked.

Most rehearsal periods in the United States last three or four weeks. This time crunch demands a tight structure.

Seeing the Whole Picture

Derrick Sanders slowly but deliberately builds his productions on the road toward technical rehearsals, or *tech*. He layers character, situation, beat work, and rhythm through several passes on the play. I asked him how he structures his few weeks from the first rehearsal until tech. He rattled off a quick sketch of his schedule:

> A first pass, stumble through, a deeper pass, a run, a more detailed pass and then run, run, run, run, notes. Run act one, run act two, run together, notes, notes, notes, run act one, run act two, run it together.

Let's break down Sanders's quick outline:

- Table work
    - Clarify basics of relationships
    - First pass at scene structure
    - Deep inquiry into motivations
- Sketch of the play
    - Actors still holding their scripts
    - Decisions about entrances and exits
    - General take on a scene—what is it about?
- 1st run
    - Notes and discussion
- Deeper pass on scenes
    - Actors off book
    - Add layers to character work
    - Deepen relationships
    - More detail work on staging
- 2nd run
    - Notes and discussion
    - Check the status of the show
- Final detailed pass
    - Work specific moments
    - Set minute details of staging
- 3rd run and notes
- 4th run and notes
- 5th run and notes
- Technical rehearsals begin

If Sanders only has two weeks of rehearsal instead of three or four, he will compress his timeline. Also, he changes his process production by production as he assesses what the actors need. Regardless of how the process moves, as Sanders watches runs and goes back to do more detailed work he checks each scene for variety. He introduced me to some key phrases he often uses after seeing the entire play:

> We've already used this. Didn't we use this before? We can't use it again. We already played this card.

If actors come in playing hard actions two scenes in a row, Sanders knows this doesn't depict the relationship developing over time. It's not logical. Audiences glaze over without variety to help them differentiate one scene from another. Looking at the two scenes, Sanders and his actors will make a choice—perhaps this one starts off cooler and this one hotter. Then, they check it all again with another run.

The goal of a run-through is to see the entire play in one go; to understand the music of the piece.

Surveying the Landscape of the Play

Robert O'Hara employs a unique method for looking at the whole and fixing problems—he calls it *landscape* and *triage*. O'Hara will stage a sketch of the play after very little table work. Then he's able to see the entire play as if he's looking out over a *landscape*. He doesn't get bogged down in every bump and twist; he's looking out at the horizon.

After creating this first landscape, he stumbles through the play, and then asks the actors to write down the moments they want to work on. He tells them they will be able to run their scenes without interruption many times. Actors should write down the little beats they want to work through slowly, dig into the details, and figure out something confusing. *Triage* is inherently collaborative. Sometimes actors feel like asking for rehearsal time is selfish, O'Hara told me he encouraged his actors to ask for what they need:

> It doesn't matter if the entire cast has to be there, this is a selfish time for you. Where does it hurt? Where do you need me as a director to concentrate for you? I don't want to spend three

hours on something that already works for everyone. I want to deal with something that doesn't work, that is where I want to spend my time.

Every actor in the room is free to write down any and all of their *hurt* moments on a piece of paper, without discussion, and hand it to the stage manager. O'Hara will begin to work through the list and typically several people will want to triage the same part of a scene. If everyone is confused by a particular moment, O'Hara knows where to put his focus.

After working through his list, O'Hara stumbles through the show again. Each landscape run is a chance to try new ideas, then triage again. If he doesn't finish his triage list, he'll add those moments to the next day's work. He's always trying to put the work in the actors' bodies, working on problems, and then running what they have:

> And then as you run the show something else starts to hurt. Because once you run you realize, *Oh, it wasn't that part, it's this part that I need to work on.* Then we'll triage that.

O'Hara focuses in on the small moments, then pulls back to see the whole.

Kimberly Senior pulls back to see the whole often. When I spoke to her, she was in previews for *Support Group for Men* at the Goodman Theatre in summer 2018. She ran the play ten times before she got to tech. In a three-and-a-half-week process, she spent almost two weeks running the show every day.

Senior says she developed this idea when she started working on her Broadway debut, *Disgraced* by Ayad Ahktar—a tense ninety-minute drama about a Muslim American lawyer's marriage dissolving in one night. She felt certain that the play was best experienced as a wild ride; once you get on you can't get off. She wanted the small acting ensemble to experience that journey many times, like building up to run a race. She had a hunch the actors needed to work like athletes.

She proposed that once they had a rough staging of the play, they run the show daily. Upon hearing this, the lead actor resisted. Senior insisted, feeling she needed to take charge of the rehearsal process. The actor said, "Well, it has to have a purpose." In that moment Senior came up with an inspired idea "Of course. We'll have a target for every run-through."

It used to be that I did a run-through and then three days of scene work and then another run-through. The expectation was that the next run-through was going to be better than the one before. Better is not the goal anymore. I don't feel like Wednesday's is better than Tuesday's and Thursday's is better than Wednesday's. They are all different. They're all drafts.

Senior sets a different group objective for each run. Today actors *clarify their through line of thought*. Tomorrow actors *focus on loving their scene partners*. The next day she asks actors to *hone their precision with language*. After each run, she speaks with the actors about what they learned. Ideally, she will run in the morning, give and discuss notes, and then work smaller sections of the play in the afternoon. (See Appendix 2 for Senior's list of run-through targets.)

I try to run my productions at least once a week. After each run-through we circle up and I ask everyone how it went. For one person this run was great, but for another it didn't go well. The next run could be the exact opposite. I ask stage managers and assistant directors to share their thoughts. Actors self-diagnose each time we go through the entire play. They learn where they need to work harder and where they've figured out a scene. With student productions I've noticed that the earlier we run, the earlier the actors get off book.

In contrast, some directors almost never run the play in the rehearsal room.

Delaying Run-Throughs

Scott Ellis delays run-throughs until his actors are ready. As a performer, he hated being forced to run a play when he didn't know what he was doing. He wants his actors to be confident the first time through without stopping:

> I tend to want to go through the whole play rough, so we have some sort of idea of the journey. And then you go back, and you do it again, and then you start doing some detailed work.

His first sketch helped him understand the play, and now he's ready for detail work. During his first quick pass he not only diagnoses the play, but his actors. He figures out who is confused and needs more guidance.

Ivo Van Hove famously pushes this theory to the logical extreme. He will often not finish staging a play until moments before the audience arrives for previews. As noted earlier, Van Hove requires his actors to come to the first rehearsal with their lines memorized. He starts at the first scene and works through the play slowly, focusing on performance details. He doesn't move on to the next scene until he finishes with the first—until he feels the scene is ready for an audience.

Van Hove works with his designers in the room from the first day of rehearsal. He will have sound and music from the beginning, some semblance of the set, and even costumes. He allows his designers to speak to the actors and at first it might seem like a bit of a free for all:

> For some that's surprising the first two days. *Oh, wow the director's not talking to me.* But also, everyone feels it is liberating because there's a lot more people to talk to. At the end of the day I make the ultimate decision.

With this amount of collaboration and this deliberate approach to the work, the play gets built quite slowly. This is by design. Van Hove doesn't want to create a show that "isn't finished." But he often will not complete the play before technical rehearsals.

Van Hove trusts his process. He doesn't need to see the whole until almost opening night. Others want to see parts of their play almost every day.

Building up the Muscles of the Play

Artistic director of Cornerstone Theater, **Michael John Garcés** will see the beginning of his play almost twenty times.

When Garcés starts working the play on his feet he'll work methodically starting from the beginning of the script. The next day, he'll run what he worked the first day, then move on to the next section. The following day, he'll run from the beginning to where he left off. Then he'll keep going. Each day starts the same: run from the beginning of the play to where they left off, then continue forward. Each day more and more of the rehearsal is spent running and less time is spent working on new material.

By going back to the beginning, Garcés solidifies the journey of the play while continuing to explore and deepen the discoveries. Like Van Hove, he might not work on the end until he's in technical rehearsals with his entire team. If the theatre company or the designers need to see a run-through, he'll show them what he's got so far.

I asked him if this method didn't preference the beginning of the play. You'd run the first part of the play say fifteen or twenty times and the last scenes once or twice. I wondered if his beginnings were better than his ends of plays:

> The beginning of the play leads to the ending, experientially for the audience and for the performer, regardless of the linearity of the text, so if you don't have a solid beginning, your ending is going to suck, it will have a weak foundation. In the end, it's actually preferencing the end of the play, right? It makes the ending stronger. Because you have to get there in the best possible way.

Lisa Portes heard about Garcés's method and adopted it for herself. Like Garcés, she will start staging at the top and the next day she'll review what they staged the day before. Then she'll push forward and the following day she'll review from the top. If she's working a two-act play then she'll do this until she's finished Act One and then move on to the second act. But if she's working a ninety-minute one-act she'll keep reviewing from the top. She acknowledges there's a danger that things will get set:

> So, I always say, *This is a review, it's not to set it, it just to walk through the map that we made yesterday, and if there's stuff you don't like or if there's stuff that you're feeling differently: feel free. It's open, we're not setting, we're reviewing to get a sense of where we are before we go on.*

Even when the actors get to the point where they are doing the entire play, Portes won't call it a run, she'll call it a review. She cautions them to not set anything completely. They should continue to explore the route and try new ideas:

> They're driving the roads, and they're saying, *Oh, there's a tree here, I didn't know there was a tree here. Or oh, there's an alley I didn't notice before, I'm going down that alley.* They're

not just walking through it, it's not a mark through, but it's a review with curiosity.

The last time the cast plays from beginning to end, right before tech, Portes declares the cast ready for a run. They've built up their knowledge of the map; they want to drive their Ferrari along the course.

When should you run your play? It depends on your learning style, the play you're working on, and the cast of actors. If you know that you can't personally learn anything from a run that is somewhat messy, you might want to hold off on running the play until you've created more detail with your ensemble. If on the other hand you like looking at successive drafts of a play you might consider trying to run at least once a week. Just as vital is discovering what your cast needs to build a repeatable performance. Too much lag time between work sessions on a scene make it hard for actors to hold onto details.

Exercise twenty-one in the workbook section talks about creating a rehearsal schedule; a crucial part of making an effective schedule is figuring out how and when you will run the play. Regardless, after you run the play, actors crave feedback.

Giving Notes after a Run

As I watch a run-through I either dictate ideas to an assistant or write down my own notes as they occur to me. I tend to capture my stream of consciousness musings on how the play is proceeding. If at all possible, I like to have a note session with the cast the next day. I like to take my reactions home and look them over. Are there three or four notes that could be combined into one idea? Do I suspect that the actor is still experimenting with a part of their performance and giving feedback now will upset their creative process?

What kind of note I give depends on where we are in the process. If it's our first run-through in the room, I'm more likely to engage in a conversation. Notes in the beginning serve as springboards for deeper dialogue about the production. If I'm watching the play later in our process I might give many technical notes about diction, energy to the end of a line, or operatives.

Lisa Portes says timing notes correctly is an art form, one she's still pursuing after a lifetime of directing:

> I take a bunch of notes in a run or a review and I won't give about half of them. Because it's not time yet, or it's not useful right now. One of the lessons that I think takes the longest to learn is gauging when the note is useful. I'm still learning that.

Whether she gives many notes or just a few, Portes makes sure to give every actor some feedback on every one of their scenes. She wants them to know that she sees them. Portes believes the actor's job is to try new ideas, be in the moment, and build toward performance. The director's job is to feedback on what she sees.

In a note session, Jessica Thebus typically will let the cast know when she senses a moment isn't working. Maybe she noticed that the power dynamic was off in the scene, or that the tension peaked too early. Sometimes she has a suggestion for a solution, but other times she only can identify the problem:

> But sometimes I don't know why it's not working. *Guys this is not working, and I don't know why.* When I was younger I was more likely to think that I needed to solve the problem and tell them what to do.

These days, Thebus knows that by the time she's running the play, the actors know their characters better than she does. An actor might diagnose their own problems: maybe I'm fighting for the wrong thing, or entering from the wrong door, or my physical action is off.

When Leigh Silverman gives notes, she tries to keep them quick and simple, and she prefers giving them individually. Unless it's a tightly woven ensemble piece Silverman has found that a group note session is a waste of time:

> I usually give some like, big broad notes, like I'll say, *This section really worked, this section we killed ourselves on and it's still not working.* Then I send people home. I feel like after a run in the room people are drained and exposed and everyone just sort of wants to get the headlines and then go home and think about it.

Silverman gives individual notes to actors the next day, sometimes handing out typewritten missives. If a note involves more than one person, she takes time to work it in rehearsal.

When I'm advising student directors I encourage them to give notes the same way they've directed the rest of the play. If they've spent their time focusing on creating complex relationships, then after run-throughs offer notes about how characters connected. If they've been highlighting given circumstances, then note when actors seemed to embody the facts of the play and when they seemed to slip. Often the most helpful note is to just remind actors of the actions they were playing in rehearsal.

As directors prepare for final run-throughs in the rehearsal room, typically other members of the production team or the producing organization will attend. These run-throughs can feel nerve-wracking at times because the director and actors have been working diligently for weeks, but they may not be totally sure if their play is working or not. Production team members and producers, or in the case of student directed shows, faculty advisors, serve as the first audiences.

What will these newcomers think of the show?

Incorporating the Rest of the Production Team

When Jessica Thebus is doing her third run of the play she truly loves receiving a few choice notes from the artistic director. The first two run-throughs she likes to just keep for herself and the actors. By the third time she's ready for feedback. Sometimes she needs confirmation that a scene she's lost faith in is actually still working. Is this still funny? Do we believe in that?

> I love an artistic director that gives me three big notes. That's my favorite thing in the world. If they give me twenty then fuck them. But if they give me three like, *I don't have a sense of danger, she is holding back her comedy, and that sight line is screwed up.* I say, *Oh my God the sense of danger! Totally! I took my eye off that ball because I was in the details.*

After seeing a student's work, she tries to practice what she preaches by only giving a few clarifying notes. Her notes fall into two varieties: taste and craft. Taste: *I wouldn't make that choice, but it's up to you.* Craft: *All of my experience says that you must make a change, or your play won't work.*

When I directed Anna Ziegler's *Boy*, for TimeLine Theatre, we struggled to crack the character of the boy's father, Doug. Set in rural Iowa in the 1980s, Doug is a working-class dad who doesn't possess great communication skills. He doesn't feel confident speaking to his child.

In one scene, the father has a long talk with his son and finally opens up about how much he loves him. The artistic director kept giving me the same note—*the scene is too easy for Doug*. I agreed but the actor and I couldn't figure out how to execute the note. How do you play, *not easy to say*?

The actor and I went to work. I asked him what he wanted in the scene—he said to connect to his son, but that led us right back to the same issue as before. We took a shot in the dark and tried to play the scene *awkwardly*. It didn't lead to much beside a general sense of anxiety. He tried leaning into the given circumstance that he was resentful at his son for being put in the position of trying to teach him, but the text didn't support the resulting hard actions. We knew Doug desperately wanted to connect with his son but didn't know how.

I don't remember if the actor, or my assistant, or the artistic director finally said, "why doesn't he try not giving his son any eye contact." Finally, the scene made sense. Doug had a lot to say but wasn't sure how to say it. He was worried about how it would land on his son, so he judiciously avoided looking at him. It was a clear physicalizing of Doug's obstacle in the scene. At the very last moment, Doug gathers his courage, looks his son in the eyes and says, "I think you came out of your mom just the way you are, this kind, gentle boy."[16]

The artistic director had clearly identified the problem—but it took the entire creative team to figure out the solution. Luckily it came to us as we were heading into technical rehearsals. For the *Boy* process I followed my typical rehearsal schedule: I tried to run the show about once a week, followed by note sessions where we discussed larger thematic trends. Then we dug into detailed scene work to refine our work. Each week of work was bracketed by a run-through. In this way we tried to learn as much as possible about the play before we added in all of the technical elements.

COLLABORATING WITH DESIGNERS IN TECH

At the end of a long day of technical rehearsals, the creative team wrestled with an impossible question: how do you recreate a baseball World Series victory on stage?

We were teching *Miracle*, a world premiere musical in a commercial production at the Royal George Theatre in Chicago, that celebrated the 2016 Cubs finally breaking their 108-year losing streak. The story focuses on the denizens of a mom and pop sports bar near the Cubs home field. The show climaxes when the Cubs dramatically beat the curse and the fans erupt in paroxysms of joy.

For those who aren't long-suffering Cubs fans: in 2016, the team battled their way to a climactic winner-take-all game seven. On the brink of victory, disaster struck: a late inning home run by the opposing team tied the game, sending it into extra innings. If you knew Cubs' history, they were destined to blow it again. But to the shock of fans everywhere, after a tense seventeen-minute rain delay, the Cubs pulled off a dramatic comeback in the tenth inning.

Our challenge: represent the fateful scoring rally on stage.

Major League Baseball approved use of video from the game, but which clips should we play? How should the characters on stage react? We tried a dance sequence synched to the key moments, but it played awkwardly. We needed the audience to focus on video highlights so they could experience the win. The composer rightly argued that the show seemed to stop for a minute while we watched television—it was a musical!

In a fit of frustrated inspiration, the composer said, "It should sound something like this!" I whipped out my iPhone and started recording. He mimicked a piano, humming a dramatic riff. Then he started reading the text in rhythm: we'd boiled down the rally to a handful of key plays. Every time something climactic happened in the game, he slammed his hands down as if he was playing a dramatic chord. He hit the climax, and we all cheered.

Now we knew what we had to do. We had to translate those forty-three seconds of audio into theatrical magic.

The composer scored a version of what he'd improvised for his musical director. My assistant director and the playwright huddled with the sound designer, recording and re-recording the announcer sound bites that would tell the story. The video designer pulled clips to correspond with the audio. The choreographer devised a simple physical vocabulary to represent cheering fans. We spent hours working through the timing moment by moment, syncing up the video and the audio, getting the actors to take their cue from the musical director, and finessing the lights to highlight the moment.

Figure 3.8 Miracle: Music and Lyrics by Michael Mahler, Book by Jason Brett. Directed by Damon Kiely. Featured L–R: Elise Wolf, Allison Sill, Brandon Dalquist, Jonathan Butler-Duplessis, Veronica Garza, Michael Kingston. Set: Collette Pollard; Lighting: Christine Binder; Costumes: Izumi Inaba; Sound: Ray Nardelli; Projections: Cat Wilson & Michael Tutaj. Photo Credit: Michael Brosilow.

Eventually watching those forty-three seconds with an audience was thrilling. People would cheer, clap, and get swept up in the climax of the play and the World Series. If only they knew how many hundreds of person hours went into making it work.

Teaching Directors to Run Technical Rehearsals

When I advise MFA directors during technical rehearsal, I settle in next to them for hours. Many of them have never worked on a fully supported play before. Well over a hundred people bustle around the theatre doing their jobs. Actors warm up, faculty advisors nudge their designers, and stage managers drill their crew members. Directors know they need to strike a delicate balance between giving the artistic team clear direction without shutting down their creative instincts. If departments don't agree on an approach, directors will need to make the final decision.

It can be a bit overwhelming.

Sometimes I see student directors shrink into their seats as the theatre buzzes around them, unsure of how to best embody their role. While we've spoken at length about the technical process, and they've worked as an assistant director on a school production, now they are directing the technical rehearsal in real time. They are learning by doing in these rehearsals, sometimes by making a choice that helps the collaboration, but sometimes by gumming up the works inadvertently.

When the team tries to tech their first transition, some directors wonder how to lead. Should they hang back and wait to see how the team tackles the problem or dictate the transition step by step? During inevitable lulls, should they be encouraging the stage manager to move forward? Talking to the actors? Biding their time?

I encourage my students to focus on three aspects of the technical rehearsal:

- Story
- Collaboration
- Time

Let's take a look at each of these angles in turn.

Championing the Story

For Thebus, tech is the moment where all of her preparatory work pays off. Long before rehearsals begin, Thebus gathers her designers and talks to them about why she's doing the play. Her discussions with designers mirror her first day addresses where she tells the story of the play from her point of view. (See pages 32–33 and Exercise 1 for more on first day addresses.) Thebus explained how her point of view helps guide the design process:

> If you hold the lamp up by the dark forest path, that is your point of view, and everybody can see the way you're going to take. Of course, there are going to be things that surprise you. You want to give your designers their freedom while having them with you on your story.

Every lighting moment, every costume, each sound cue, should dovetail, creating a coherent outlook. The combined storytelling elements should align with Thebus's point of view, which deepens and complexifies through the design process. Eventually, the point of view becomes shared by the entire team. During tech, she only needs to remind the team of their perspective on the story to guide the rehearsal.

During tech, Jessica Thebus believes her job is to let her competent designers and stage managers take care of the details, while she tries to see the whole stage. When she was a younger director, she often leaned into moments, trying to figure out exactly when a light cue was called or how a sound cue worked. But now she tries to lean back and focus on the overall story. She tries to watch like an audience member, not a technician. Thebus used a film reference to explain her technique during tech:

> Pull your camera back. The more I can do that, the more I am able to see the dynamics. That's what directors are for. Seeing the big problem, not a forest for the trees. The story has to be delivered.

Thebus knows that lights and sound can either help or hinder the delivery system of the story. Her job is to look out for the overall dynamics of a scene or a transition. If the scene is meant to be funny and buoyant, but the lights are dour and cloudy: something is off. If the story is accelerating, but the transitions are lagging, she'll encourage her designer to adjust.

For some directors, images tell the story.

Creating Cinematic Images

Barbara Gaines, Artistic Director of Chicago Shakespeare Theatre has been directing Shakespeare's plays for decades. As she plans her seasons years in advance, she's always reading one play or another from the canon, hoping something will spark her interest. If images pop into her head as she's reading, she knows a play is ripe for a remount. She told me in an interview how she relies on these vivid, clear visions:

> Thank God they come. I suppose I'll know I have to leave if they stop. I've always felt like a conduit. I have never felt responsible for the images that have been sent to me. When I'm reading Shakespeare, it is most often when I'm sitting at my desk at home. I see the play as if it were a movie.

Gaines says that about 80% of the images she visualizes will make it into the final play. She brings her ideas and images to the set designer and they work together to make her dreams a reality.

One summer, Gaines was reading *Hamlet*, but nothing sparked her interest. She was about to put the script down when an old Enya song popped up from the depths of her shuffled audio files. The song spoke directly to her feelings about the play. Gaines recreated the moment for me:

> When I heard this it all came together—*Time moves on in the pouring rain / I still think of you and whisper your name / Will I see you once again / I could never say goodbye / To the sadness in my heart you know.*

In a flash, she remembered her father's sudden death many years ago. He passed while Gaines was in technical rehearsals for a huge production of *Troilus and Cressida*, so she never had the time to truly grieve. She just moved on. She drew a parallel to Hamlet's grief, compounded by his mother's hasty marriage to his uncle:

> The grief process for a parent who dies suddenly is a very long process, but you have to go through it. Then I realized why the play was calling me. It was the time for me to face my father's death, and help others, especially Hamlet, to face his father's death.

Her production opened with an image directly inspired by the Enya song: Hamlet stands upstage center at his father's grave in the pouring rain, singing the lyrics of the song "I could never say goodbye." He's weeping openly, grieving. As the grave recedes, Claudio and Gertrude enter downstage in silk pajamas and lingerie, passionately making love.

Gaines quickly establishes the major themes of grief and infidelity through striking images, and then plunges into the story.

Framing each Scene

Lisa Portes trained under master showman Des McAnuff, working as his associate director for the Tony Award–winning, high-tech musical *The Who's Tommy*. On the world tour, Portes would travel ahead of McAnuff, working with the designers to get the show to the director's high standards. Lighting lanes had to be crisp, set changes precise, and everything synched to the music.

Portes still loves clean, clear, bold lighting, and hates mud. I asked her what she meant:

> When it's muddy, I can't tell where to look. I have a very keen sense of when I'm distracted at all from where I need to look or if the tone is off lighting wise.

Does the look of the scene support the story moment? Is the scene meant to be sexy, dangerous, romantic? Audiences need clues as to what they are watching. Are the actors specifically carved out of the space or are they being washed into the background? Is there a way to highlight their faces without blasting light all over the stage? Is each scene specific to itself?

Once Portes and her designers find a look for a scene they turn to crafting a transition to the next moment. As a new play director, she often works on plays with many scenes. When she worked on Ike Holter's *Rightlynd*, a high-octane graphic novel of a play about local Chicago politics, every time the scene changed, she needed the lights to pop. Portes explained what she tries to fashion when creating a sharp transition:

> Framing. What I'm looking for usually in a sequence is framing. In a show like *Rightlynd*, every time you have a transition you're shifting the focus, tone, and punctuation.

What is the situation at the top of the scene? How can you articulate that for the audience? Now how does the scene complicate and develop? And finally—how does it land? Can you highlight that moment visually? Sometimes this means holding on an image for a moment to make sure it resonates, then cutting away to the next scene.

Directing the Story, Not the Tech

As students are working through the play with their designers, I encourage them to speak in terms of story, not technical aspects. I tell them, *You're in the storytelling business, not the cue calling business.*

If they see a dress on an actor and it feels too short, they might say, *Hey, I think that character is a bit more guarded in this scene, she probably wants to wear something less revealing.* If a moment looks too dark, they might sidle up to the lighting designer: *the key to this scene is connecting the lead actor to the audience. Could we see him a bit better?*

When teching a transition from one scene to the next, I encourage them to stay out of pinpointing exactly when the stage manager will call the cue to move the scenery, change the lights, and bring up the sound. Rather than get into the weeds with them, I encourage them to talk story. *Let's take a moment for that last line to ring out, it should feel like he's stuck in one place as the next scene starts to build across the stage, luring him to cross over.*

If you just say *lengthen the dress, brighten the scene, call the cue three beats after the last line*, you're missing the opportunity to have a discussion about the impact of the moment. It's a moment to build true partnerships.

Fostering Collaboration

Ron OJ Parson likes to work with designers who can take the ball and run with it. He hopes to have some conversations early on about the show and then let them do their own work without much guidance. As the design develops, he expects designers will wow him with new ideas.

Once he gets to tech he feels his job is to pilot the wheel. I asked him what he meant by that:

> Keep everybody on track, move it along. Basically, just to steer the ship, that's how I look at it. You're the captain, but you can't do everything. There's no way I can try to control everything. I want people to create, to collaborate.

He's comfortable enough with his designers that while they are building cues, he pops down on stage to work with the actors. He used to call this, "killing two birds with one stone" until a stage manager said, "Why don't we feed two birds with one seed?" Now, that's one of his catch phrases and it speaks to his collaborative style.

Lisa Portes is quite active during tech, always moving around the theatre, checking in with each designer personally. Some directors take notes throughout the day and deliver them at the end, but Portes would rather quickly talk to a costumer about a character's shoes, or the lighting designer about her need for clarity. If she knows the designers are working for a bit, she zips down to the stage to talk to the actors:

> I think it's very important to stay in contact with the actors. Usually there would have been a run-through just before you go into tech and you don't have time to give notes. So often I'm giving notes while the designers are working. Even if we have nothing to work on I'll make sure to get on stage and joke around with the company just to stay in contact. And I always tell the stage managers don't wait for me—when the designers are ready let's move—but in the meantime I try to stay in contact with the actors.

As soon as the break is up, she's back with her designers, looking for ways to solve the storytelling together.

Learning about the Play with All the Elements

Rachel Chavkin loves tech. It's her favorite part of the process because everything begins to look the way it always appeared in her head. Now the designers, actors, and technicians start to see what she's been dreaming about.

Chavkin believes that when all the elements come together—set, lights, costumes, movement, and eventually audiences—the team can finally figure things out. Before this moment, actors and designers make educated guesses about how set pieces or costumes will work. Once tech and previews begin, the collaborators no longer need to imagine, they are finally working with the actual materials.

Chavkin's never met an actor who didn't want more time in rehearsal to make discoveries. They crave time to refine their movements and develop their performances. One could imagine expanding the time in the rehearsal room, during tech, or during previews to help actors build complex performances. Chavkin told me her theory about rehearsal over the phone:

> The time would not necessarily be best spent unlimited in a rehearsal room. It would either be in tech, like you would have a month of tech to really figure shit out, or you would have endless previews.

Often in the rehearsal room there are elements you can't possibly duplicate or even approximate. Chavkin's Broadway musical *The Great Comet* had many staircases: she didn't really worry about how actors moved on the taped-out version in the rehearsal room. She ignored the issue until actors could step up and down the intricate pathways. She knew the most important decisions would be made during tech.

Jessica Thebus remembers a dire moment in tech when she asked all of her designers if a major scene needed to be cut. She was working on the world premiere of *Welcome Home, Jenny Sutter* by Julie Marie Myatt at Oregon Shakespeare Festival in 2008. The play focuses on a female Marine re-entering society after a tough stint in Iraq where she lost part of her leg:

> There's an opening monologue and then a woman with a prosthetic leg gets dressed in silence. She moves from fatigues to civilian clothes and then gets on a bus. The point of the scene is what it takes for her to get dressed. We loved it. Seeing it in runs, I got scared. The artistic director got scared and Julie got scared. It's ten minutes, I think we got it down to six.

She called together her designers to talk about the moment, *Are we putting the audience in silence for too long too early in the play?* Thebus wasn't asking about the sets, or the lights, or the costumes. She wanted their opinion on the structure of the play. Two of the younger designers had cold feet and advised her to cut the scene. The two more experienced designers had more faith, "Let it ride." Thebus talked with the writer one more time: they decided to keep it.

It became one of the most beloved and talked about moments in the play:

> I just loved that everyone was willing to disagree, and everyone was willing to go with it. It's a perfect example of me having to pick. I can ask for everyone's opinion and then I choose. That's leadership. Leadership isn't not letting anybody else talk; it's being willing to make the call.

For Thebus, this is an example of her collaborative style at work. She always tries to inspire her designers to leave their individual silos and focus on the entire story. When she pulls them together at the back of the room she can poll them as a group: Why isn't this scene working? It's falling flat:

> *Is it my blocking? Should we underscore? Thoughts?* I love it when one person says, *give it another run* or another person says, *the actor isn't confident.* There might be too much going on visually. I want to free all of them to feel safe enough to say something.

Thebus loves it when her lighting designer gives her notes on blocking or character. Even better, when a costumer graciously accepts a sound designer's idea, she knows the collaboration is singing. Thebus tries to foster a collaboration where every person on the team feels empowered to be a part of the conversation.

Speaking to the Whole Room

If a student director has an idea to change a moment in tech, I encourage them to speak to their entire team at once. If you think a cue needs to happen sooner, don't just tell your lighting designer, discuss it as a group with your stage manager and sound designer. Pull in the technical director, props artisan, and set designer if seems appropriate. Perhaps the music director or violence choreographer need to be involved. Arouse conversation and communication.

I encourage students to literally speak up, to speak louder. It forces them to own their voice in the room and say what they think, or boldly lead a conversation between collaborators. I'll prod them: *Stop whispering to me. Stand up, go over there, get in the middle of all the designers and explain what you mean.*

If they are running an especially complicated sequence with many moving parts, I encourage them to ask for a microphone and speak to everyone in the room. Make sure the stage managers, actors, backstage crew, and the design team are on the same page. No one ever suffered from too much communication.

I encourage them to only use this technique sparingly. If you stop every five minutes for a group chat, you might never get to opening night.

Managing Tech Time

Jessica Thebus used to luxuriate in her tech time, going over every moment deliberately. A colleague said she was "like a goat in grass." But she learned to speed up:

> I feel like my preference now is to move fast. Sketch it in, then see it. I now know that lighting and sound do most of their work after seeing a first run. Which I didn't know earlier. I thought we had to get every moment correctly. My whole learning curve is: stay out of their way.

Now Thebus resists the urge to finesse each lighting cue and sound cue. She stops if a scene looks completely wrong or if a transition isn't heading in the right direction, but she prefers to keep rolling.

If they can drive to a run, they can diagnose the whole as a team. Have they used too many bright cues in a row? Is that color overused? Does that sound cue seem to pull us out of the show? After a quick run, they have time to go back and bring all the elements into alignment.

Other directors take the opposite approach: they tech inch by inch.

Crawling Your Way through Cues

I asked Barbara Gaines about how she runs tech. She said her techs were legendary for moving at a glacial pace. She suggested I call up one of her frequent collaborators:

> You have permission to go to him and ask, *What are Barbara Gaines' tech like? HELL.* Because I'm very specific. Very specific, indeed.

Gaines says that part of the reason she moves slowly is that often she has moving scenery, which can be dangerous. Safety is her number one concern with anything automated, so she'll crawl through any transition where large pieces move on stage.

She's also crafting the look of each scene:

> You have to establish the palette from the very beginning. Tech always takes longer the first few days because you're establishing the color palette and what kind of lighting it is. Is it Eastern European? Very sharp light, very cold. It pours down like steel and cold. But phenomenal and thrilling. Or is it Vermeer? Soft, beautiful sunlight.

Working slowly means Gaines typically doesn't have time to run the play mid-tech and then go back to the beginning. She counts on her slow and grueling process to sculpt the specific images she desires. She usually has time for one dress rehearsal before audiences arrive. Gaines trusts that the actors will rise to the occasion and deliver.

Ivo Van Hove builds his tech the same way, which can often drive his actors crazy. As noted earlier, Van Hove starts his first day of rehearsal with the actors off book, slowly working through the play beat by beat. He often won't finish staging the play before leaving the rehearsal hall and heading to the theatre.

When tech starts, he goes back to the beginning and works through slowly again. He may not finish the play until right before the first preview. He told a story about working with Bryan Cranston on *Network*; Cranston was a bit worried because he hadn't worked the last scene and audiences were coming soon. Van Hove kept telling Cranston it would be fine, they would rehearse the scene when the moment was there. Finally, a few days before the audiences were coming they rehearsed the last scene:

> We rehearsed it once and it was done forever. So that's what I call working towards the ending. Not knowing the ending before you start, working towards it. After the first time we did it, he said it was wonderful. If we had done it earlier it could have caused a huge discussion and now it was totally organic for him, it came out of everything he had rehearsed before.

Van Hove believes you can't finalize your staging until you understand how the play works from beginning to end. His actors sometimes get nervous, but Van Hove always keeps calm because he knows it will all work. He doesn't say it's for everyone, but he knows that it works for him.

When I'm working with student directors in tech, I preach patience. Student designers must learn their craft in the theatre. Learning is slow work.

I let directors know that they have a bit of control over the pace. They can often decide to either move forward because they trust that everybody has a clear sense of the scene, or to hold back because there seems to be uncertainty. They can talk to their stage manager often, encouraging them to check with designers and keep things on track. Their most effective tool in moving a rehearsal forward is clear communication.

As you head into tech ask yourself a series of questions to prepare. How much time do you have and what do you hope to accomplish? Make a plan with your stage manager and your designers, knowing that plans typically change. It might be helpful to communicate with the team about how you like to tech a show. Do you like to put something up quick and dirty, then run the show and go back to refine? Or are you more inclined to carve out each moment meticulously? Also ask your designers—what do they prefer? What plays into their strengths?

Hopefully by now you've all agreed on the point of view of the show and what story you are telling as a group of artists. While you may learn about new facets of the diamond you are carving during tech, hopefully you have agreed on the general shape of the show. Collaborate as a team to craft a methodology for tech. How will you know when to move on from a scene? Will you just feel it? Is there a benchmark you are looking for? How will you manage time as a group?

Finally, make sure you all know that while you'll solve many problems during tech, you can't figure everything out. You need the real test: the audience.

Giving Notes during Previews

Kimberly Senior let me sit in on a note session for the world premiere comedy, *Support Group for Men* by Ellen Fairey at the Goodman Theatre in 2018. A few previews in, the show was landing well with the audience. The room felt loose. The discussion centered on technical aspects of holding for laughs.

Senior started off casually, "How'd everybody feel last night?"

People in general felt good, they'd gotten some laughs, the audience seemed into it. Senior agreed, but worried the actors were stepping on some laughs at the beginning, squelching the audience response. In the early parts of the play they needed to teach the audience how to listen. Actors should err on the side of holding a bit where they typically get a response.

On the other hand, once the show started rolling, she encouraged them not to sit too long in laughter. Holding for laughs shouldn't feel like an empty pause. In those moments, the actors should react to what just happened or plan their next point of attack—anything to keep the show alive.

She gave different kinds of notes to different actors. One actor forgot to take off a hood the previous night, so she crafted a physical cue that would motivate him every time. She gave another set of blocking notes—turn out here, turn in here, plant and deliver here. One actor anticipated every note, cutting Senior off with a friendly, "Yep, yep."

The cast had two hours to rehearse before the next preview, so Senior went actor by actor and asked, "Is there anything you want to work? Anything not quite clear?" One actor had an issue with a moment where a policeman came to the door—could the cop see the other actor holding a small rhino statuette? Should he notice it or not? Senior added it to the work list.

Then, she quickly outlined the plan for the afternoon: adjust the level on a too-quiet sound cue, finesse a few transitions for timing and storytelling, and rehearse the curtain call.

Finally, she gave the target for their next preview. (See pages 103–104 and Appendix 3 for more on run-through targets.) The previous night actors had been instructed to *love their own character* and *defend their actions*. Tonight, they should *focus on loving everyone else on stage*. They should *chase love, share love, make love the choice*. She left them with a quote from Japanese novelist Haruki Murakami:

What happens when people open their hearts? They get better.

Then they headed into the theatre.

LISTENING TO PREVIEW AUDIENCES

When Anne Kauffman rehearses, she makes it clear to the actors that the show won't be finished until it's in front of an audience. She purposely leaves some parts of the play unpolished or unexplored:

> The rehearsal in the room is just an outline because being on stage and being in front of an audience is a completely different experience. I've learned to keep the actors a little unsettled because they get attached, they think what we've made is the thing, and then if I have to do a one-eighty...I mean...some actors can get pretty upset by massive changes. So, I say, *Ok so now next week we're going to move into the theater for tech and previews...and then the rehearsals will **really** begin.*

Kauffman is only half joking—of course time in the rehearsal room is crucial. Actors learn their lines, set staging, and clarify relationships. They attempt to discover how the play works. But sometimes, what seemed to work in a vacuum doesn't make as much sense when viewed with an audience.

Anne Kauffman remembers working on the world premiere of Amy Herzog's *Belleville* and realizing the opening moments of the play were completely off once she got into previews. The script follows a young woman living in Paris who slowly realizes her husband has been manipulating her for years. Because Kauffman was seeing the show with new eyes, she realized that she'd tipped her hand about the duplicity of the husband too early. The audience wasn't laughing, and they seemed checked out or confused:

> Oh, this beginning is totally wrong. We need to change this beginning. A total shift, which means that the mood, the whole intention of those first five beats just had to change. The play is very funny at first, and we need it to be funny, and the audience was not set up for that.

First, she talked to the playwright. They agreed that a silent prologue they'd built in rehearsal distanced the audience. It needed to go. Next, Kauffman met with her actors and told them she'd made a mistake. She'd had a hunch about the beginning of the play: plant the seeds of the abusive relationship in the first moments. But her instinct didn't yield anything useful. The audience needed to see the couple's love before they could watch it curdle. They set to work adjusting the tone of the opening.

Kauffman believes the first moments of a play teach an audience how to watch the rest of the show. Every play is different, and each production has an infinite number of potentially right ways to kick off the proceedings. Should the inciting incident creep up on an audience? Should we provoke a strong response right at the top? Do we need comedy to prepare us for the later darker moments? In this case, she needed to lead her audience away from the end of the play in order to surprise them later. Lead with comedy and let the plays disquiet creep up on them.

The Moment of Truth

Award-winning British director **Christopher Luscombe** is often hired to direct comedies, from Shakespearian classics to world premieres. Previews clarify everything. Luscombe works rigorously in the rehearsal room, looking for the correct tone for a scene, or the right physical attack, or the development of relationships. But sometimes he finds that what is hilarious in the hall, doesn't evoke the same response in performance. He let me know his theories on audiences when we met to chat about process:

> Audiences, I think, tend to laugh at plot. They laugh when a plot point happens, that they didn't expect. They're not actually that interested in the hilarious character. Or the wonderful funny voice. I think you don't know quite what you're dealing with until you get it in front of the audience. You're working in the dark.

Luscombe doesn't watch the audience watching the show, but he sees the play through new eyes sitting with other people. He senses when scenes are landing or missing. He can hear the laughs. But he can also hear the coughing and rustling. He encourages everyone to be ruthless in figuring out what works and doesn't work:

> I always say to the actors, *Brace yourselves, because when we are in previews, we are going to work really hard*. Because that's the time you've got all the knowledge. The audience don't lie. And we know when they are bored, we know when they are amused. We know when they want to get their train home.

If a scene is dragging, he tries several attacks, but then perhaps he'll remove it entirely. If a joke doesn't land, and they can't make it work, then he'll cut it. Luscombe says you can't really know what an audience will go for until you play it in front of them. During the evening he'll furiously take notes, observing what works and what needs improving. In the afternoon the next day he meets with his cast to offer guidance and make adjustments. It's thrilling work.

Luscombe has worked with varying lengths of previews, although typically he thinks a week is enough time to make changes. One time he was working on a comedy that was heading to London's West End, and for various reasons he ended up staying with the company for a month:

> And I saw the show every single night for a month and we never stopped working. And we loved it! We loved the play, we all loved each other. And it was very creative. I didn't regret the time at all.

On the flip side, he remembers times when he was an actor and the company had months in the rehearsal room with a short time in previews. Sometimes in those cases the final result was disappointing:

> After all that, we weren't really ready. Because the important bit was truncated. You're sometimes needing to make some massive adjustments in that week. You might cut costumes or swap scenes around and every night can be quite scary. Because the actors are dealing with huge notes they have to play. And then suddenly, you've got all the critics in. Sometimes a couple more days would have made a huge difference.

Luscombe says that the longer he works, the more he learns about the craft of creating comedy. He's fascinated watching audiences and seeing what lands. The more he learns, the more he realizes he doesn't know, and the more turned on he is to get back in rehearsal again. For him it's a never-ending process of trying to improve.

He does know that comedies provide a clear litmus test: are audiences laughing or not?

Looking for Closure

During previews, Robert O'Hara continues his process of landscaping and triage that he set up in rehearsals but now he includes his designers. (See page 102–103 for more on Landscape and Triage.)

After each preview, he'll check in with the team to see what *hurts* and needs attention. They can't say the whole play. They need to limit themselves to three things that demand the attention of the entire company:

> Most of the time, just like with the actors, the designers all want the same thing. We all agree that a moment needs help whether it's set, lights, costumes. Once the designers are comfortable we go back to the actors and ask them if there's anything they want to triage. And of course, in both the rehearsal and the technical triage, my triage is done first. Because I'm constantly watching and fine-tuning and looking for moments to dig deeper into, so most times my own triage covers most of the needs of the room.

The margin of error should get smaller and smaller. His goal is to get to the place where he asks his designers and actors what else do we need to work, and there's nothing.

That's as good as it's going to get.

OPENING THE PLAY

I often get depressed after opening night.

The week before follows a typical pattern. On Wednesday the first preview audience and the adrenaline rush lift everyone's spirits. On Thursday the show sags and I consider giving up directing forever. Friday and Saturday shows play unevenly—some people are tired, others full of energy, a new bit of blocking throws someone, another person has a breakout moment. Finally, Sunday arrives. Theatre lovers fill the audience, the cast relaxes, and I finally enjoy the performances. I don't take many notes; just sit back and observe.

The critics and VIPs descend on the theatre for opening night, creating a frenetic buzz. The party afterward thrills, everyone pats each other on the back, congratulating each other for our hard work. I don a special pair of red pants for the occasion.

The next day, I inevitably collapse in despair.

After years of repeating this routine, I figured that my problem was biological. Putting up a show requires every ounce of willpower, stamina, expertise, and judgment for weeks. Once the show opens I lack purpose. My adrenaline pumped as if I'd been sprinting a marathon. Normal life pales in comparison. Also, it feels like I am no longer needed at a great party I threw.

Brian Kulick often feels the same way. He likens it to the moment he dropped his young son off at camp for the first time. The excited ten-year-old gave Kulick a quick hug and joyfully ran off to his cabin:

> No tearful goodbyes, no *I'm gonna miss you, dad*, just the sound of my son's accelerating footfalls as he got further and further away from me. A fellow parent laughed and said, *You did a good job.* I said, *What do you mean? You raised your son to be confident, so he doesn't need you for every little thing, that's the job—raise them so they don't need you anymore.*

Without knowing it, Kulick secretly hoped his son would cling to him, need him for a little longer. He wanted to be the Sun, shining his brilliance, but instead he might as well be Pluto, a cold distant planet no longer needed.

Some directors like to make sure their presence is felt long after they've left.

Setting the Boundaries

Mark Wing-Davey doesn't feel depressed after he opens a show, he's typically on to the next challenge. On the way out the door, he leaves his cast with some gentle warnings.

Wing-Davey was born and raised in England and worked for many decades as an actor and director before coming to the United States. In England it's very common for a director to stick around after opening night. He told me British director Mike Alfreds was known for attending every performance and giving notes after. While he never went that far, Wing-Davey maintained a presence at his shows.

When he came to work in the United States, theatre companies typically handed him his plane ticket on opening night and said, *Here you go. Goodbye!* They clearly wanted him to do his job and get out. When working on *Angels in America* many years ago, he came back to see the show months later. Wing-Davey was jarred by how far the show had slipped:

> I went to the actors and said you need to go back to your scripts and your actions and all that stuff. Because what had happened was, they were great for the first month or so, but then they began

to play the end of the scene in the middle. The show had become very smug. I think that's a danger of a hit. You have a hit show, and that must show how marvelous you are, and that vague kind of smugness takes away from the immediacy of the performance.

Now Wing-Davey warns his cast during the final week as he prepares to leave. During previews he quotes notoriously acidic British director John Dexter who would say, "I don't want your grandmother's notes." Meaning that he doesn't want the cast to be influenced by their friends and relatives during that final week of preparation. *Couldn't you be more sympathetic?* He also cautions them against reading reviews, good or bad, until the show is over. If a review praises a moment in the play, the actor will always approach that point in the performance and think, *Oh, here's that brilliant moment I've got to do*:

> When you're working as a team to make this piece, whatever it is, you want to say, *look, this is the piece that we made, there's flexibility within it to shift and change but not much.* Actors have to be able to find a liveness in it without feeling that to be alive in the moment requires them to destroy things.

Wing-Davey guards against destruction by forming a strong bond with his stage manager. They cultivate an aesthetic connection. Wing-Davey learned that in the United States it's typically the stage manager who holds the artistic flame for the show, monitoring run times and giving notes to keep the show in shape. On larger commercial productions with long runs or on tours, associate or resident directors are charged with maintaining the quality of the show, but in regional theatres, typically the stage manager holds down the fort.

Kimberly Senior makes a big moment of deputizing her stage manager before she leaves. Senior reminds the cast that the stage manager witnessed every note, watched every directing choice, and knows how to sustain the performance. Even if the stage manager hasn't spoken much until now, she calls them a silent partner. She instills trust.

Sometimes, Senior's casts maintain the show themselves. As noted earlier, Senior likes to run her plays many times before tech rehearsals. For each run she creates a target: love yourself, use language precisely, spend it all. After Senior leaves, some casts miss the nightly ritual. Without her asking, actors started assigning themselves nightly goals as a group. A different person each night was charged with figuring out the target for the next performance. (See pages 103–104 for Senior's discussion of targets and Appendix 2 for a partial list.)

> They would connect at the end of the performance; they would ask how tonight went. *Oh, it felt sloppy.* The next night the person who assigned the targets would bring in something about precision. They were in a sense directing themselves. What do we need more of? How do we boost more from here? Where do we go?

Senior nourishes a culture of precision and artistry. She's no longer needed to invigorate and challenge her actors; they are pushing themselves. Her entire rehearsal process focuses on finding action, conflict, and moment-to-moment life. She feels she's succeeded if long after she's left the building, the actors are still building their performances, finding new nuances.

The director Robert Icke has invented techniques for keeping his shows alive night to night that is somewhat extreme: he calls them grenades.

Keeping the Show Fresh Night to Night

Robert Icke was working on his own adaptation of *Oresteia* at the Almeida in London in 2015. He was rehearsing with Agamemnon on a section where the Greek general was supposed to comment on his own tears. The actor asked what would happen if he didn't feel like crying. Icke told him then he should just skip that section and move past it:

> And I suddenly thought, *Oh God, that's so obvious when you're making your own text. To try and support the actor in what they're feeling live in that moment.*

Now he throws in what he calls grenades. He might write two different versions of a speech and once the actor feels comfortable, they can use either one on any given night of the show. It keeps the entire company on their toes because they don't know what's coming next:

> Rehearsal is all about trying to separate the twenty million wrong ways of playing a certain bit or saying a line or a speech or whatever, separating the twenty million wrong ways from

the two million right ways. I realized a few years back that when I was watching the action, I'd think, *Oh I really liked that version and I also liked the version they did yesterday.*

Icke has encouraged his actors to employ grenades even when working on an extant play, such as *Hamlet*. In Icke's production of Shakespeare's tragedy, late in the play Laertes came in with a gun and held it to Claudius' head, demanding to know where his father was. Icke had seen it a few times and then he said to the actor playing Laertes—*look you've done that too many times, we need to find you a new option*. The actor said *I have an idea can I try it tonight*—and Icke told him to go ahead:

> That night he held Gertrude hostage, and so it was great, because of course you saw Claudius have to struggle more than he did when he struggled for his own life, and Gertrude burst into tears. And everyone, everyone really got a lot out of it. And so, from then on, there were two possibilities.

This is an extreme example and of course by that point Icke had set up the idea of grenades and people knew that change was possible night to night. These were a group of professionals who had worked with each other many times and had built up a level of trust that Icke knew he could rely upon.

Letting the Actors Fly

Brian Kulick didn't always know when to leave a show. He was doing his first show at the Public Theater, which at the time previewed shows for weeks on end. He'd keep working and changing for almost a month and then finally open the production:

> I think I must have been in my third week of previews and an actor who I loved saw me after the show. He grabbed me by my shoulders, pulled me close into him, and snarled: *You have to go now.* At first, I was devastated by this response. How dare this actor tell me to leave my own show; but, he was right. There comes a point where, even if the company is still not proficient in executing the show, they cannot continue to grow under the continual judgmental eye of the director.

Kulick says this is where directing rhymes with parenting. The actors need to own their performances now, free from the tyranny of endless notes. Whether you like it or not, a director needs to go away.

Kimberly Senior also finds leaving a show emotional, but she sees it as a natural progression of her role. In the rehearsal room she sits close to the actors, practically on stage with them. When she moves to the theatre, naturally she moves farther away from her cast. During previews she sits even farther back in the room and finally, after opening, she's no longer in the building:

> If you think about perspective in drawing the play becomes bigger and you become smaller. You move to the edge of the frame, the director. A little sad. There's no place for me there anymore. It's about understanding that. We raise our children to leave us, and then we will have done a wonderful job.

Sometimes on opening night, Senior takes out her first rehearsal notes and reads them over. What interested her initially? Has that changed? How did they reach the goals she set out on the first day? Aside from being an ambassador for the institution, Senior knows the director has no job on opening night. She'll find out what the theatre needs from her and try to be a good party guest.

Then typically she does what she calls an *Irish Goodbye*: she just leaves.

Leaving the Building

Curt Columbus hasn't watched an opening night performance since his very first show in Chicago many decades ago. He imagines himself watching the critics and squirming every time the show didn't land perfectly.

On opening night, Columbus acts as an ambassador for his theatre company. He talks to long time audience members and chats up the press. He gathers his production team for one last moment:

> I make some kind of speech to the cast, thanking them for their collaboration, and I always try to remind them of why we wanted to stage the play in the first place and why we want an audience to see it. Then, I leave.

Columbus goes out to dinner with his husband Nate and returns either for intermission or for the final curtain. Once he's back in the building he congratulates the actors and hosts the opening night party, mingling with his guests, safe in the knowledge that he spared himself the agony of watching the actual performance.

When I was artistic director of American Theatre Company, I went through a process to figure out how to watch opening night. At first I sat in the back, positioned to watch the critics, trying to read the tea leaves of every single laugh or sigh or scribble. A good review from the lead critic could mean the difference between paying the next rent check on time or begging for an extension.

Watching critics drove me crazy. I started going out during the show, heading for dinner like Columbus. But I couldn't enjoy myself. How was it going? Were there any disasters? I couldn't do anything about mistakes, but maybe I should be there?

Finally, I discovered an alcove where I listened to the show without watching it. I heard all the lines, monitored the pace, relished all the laughs, and quietly drank a glass of scotch. I could resist the temptation to guess how the critics or audience were enjoying the show, and appreciate the work.

ANIMATING THE SCRIPT

I once had two shows running in Chicago at the same time.

One theatre company gave me a political satire to read. I liked it well enough and loved the theatre, so I dutifully did my job. I put together a great cast, constructed the scenes, and delivered the laughs and the irony. We opened to generally favorable reviews and I went on my way.

I brought another theatre an experimental play about a woman's complicated relationship with her sickly mother. The cast and I struggled to figure out the tone, how certain scenes landed, and the multifaceted relationships. The script strummed personal chords. My own father was ill, and it felt like a story that needed to be told. The opening was rocky; reviews were mixed.

I went back to visit the first one and the show had taken a rough turn. Actors were pushing for laughs, and when they didn't get them, they pushed harder. Scenes that played at a seven in terms of intensity on opening night were up to eleven.

The second show had bloomed. Relationships had deepened and complicated. Audiences laughed deep laughs of recognition, then caught their breath with emotion the next moment. Scenes we couldn't crack in rehearsal now shone like little diamonds in the theatre.

What happened?

The deep personal connection to the second show allowed me to light a fire under the script. My collaborators felt that burning desire and worked until the closing performance to perfect the story. I used many of the techniques outlined in this chapter. I found my own hook into the show; my passion burned brightly. I shared that hunger with my designers and then with the entire team on the first day of rehearsal. We spent time at the table, unpacking the different types of scenes. Some felt very small and personal, and others felt more comedic and broader. I was often confused and constantly asked questions of my actors as we tried to move toward a coherent vision. We staged that play slowly and meticulously, leading to run-throughs where still we weren't sure what we were making. Technical rehearsals allowed me to hear the thoughts of designers again, and as we moved from the personal scenes to satire, we started to find a rhythm. Finally, the audiences told us what we were missing. They loved the family story and wanted to connect with the lead character. Throughout it all, I had a hunch of why I loved the play and found ways to draw all the other artists on the show into helping to create a coherent vision. By the end of the process, everyone loved the production.

The political comedy was a job.

In both cases, I read the script, figured out a vision, and hired a team of artists. I was able to activate one script and merely deliver the other.

But what about directors who don't start with a script? What about ensembles that co-create the text in the room or devise movement-based projects? How do they generate material, revise their work, and open it up for audiences?

How do you rehearse when you don't have a play?

NOTES

1 Katie Mitchell, *The Director's Craft* (New York: Routledge, 2009), 55.
2 Mitchell, 73.
3 Alexander Dean and Lawrence Carra, *Fundamentals of Play Directing* (New York: Holt, Rinhart and Winston, Inc., 1941), 172.

4 Jon Jory, *Tips: Ideas for Directors* (Hanover: Smith and Kraus, 2002), 78.
5 Frank Hauser and Russell Reich, *Notes on Directing* (New York: RCR Press, 2003), 22.
6 Mike Alfreds, *Different Every Night* (London: Nick Hern Books Ltd, 2007), 25.
7 Mitchell, 128.
8 Konstantin Stanislavski, *An Actor's Work*, translated and edited by Jean Benedetti (Oxon: Routledge, 2008), 144.
9 William Ball, *A Sense of Direction* (Hollywood: Quite Specific Media Group Ltd., 1984), 81.
10 Ball, 80.
11 Hauser and Russell, 33.
12 Tennessee Williams, *A Streetcar Named Desire* (1947. Reprint, New York: Book-of-the-Month Club, Inc., 1994), 117.
13 Williams, 110.
14 Williams, 188.
15 Anton Chekhov, *Seagull*, translated by Curt Columbus, *Chekhov: The Four Major Plays: Seagull, Uncle Vanya, Three Sisters, Cherry Orchard* (Chicago: Ivan R. Dee, 2005), 53, 55, 59, 61, 63.
16 Anna Ziegler, *Boy* (New York: Dramatists Play Service, 2016), 47.

Chapter 4

Rehearsing a Play Without a Script
Notes on Devising

I remember the moment the idea for my play *The Revel* popped into my head.

I was riding my bike along Lake Michigan, listening to Hank Williams belt out his country gospel scorcher, "I Saw the Light." Singing along, feeling exultant; it hit me: the only time I really feel spiritual is when I listen to blue grass hymns. I don't know why, but my next thought was about the choruses in ancient Greek tragedies and their exultant cries to the gods.

Seven years later, after many readings and workshops, The House Theatre of Chicago produced *The Revel* in the fall of 2015. My passing thought on the lakefront turned into a loose adaptation of Euripides's tragedy *The Bacchae*, set in 1930s Appalachia, filled out with old-time country gospel music. Much of the original story line was similar—a group of women convert to a new religion and leave town to revel in the mountains. The leader of the town follows his mother up the mountain to confront the group. In a fit of ecstasy, the women rip off the son's head and parade back into town, where the fever finally breaks.

The seven-year journey from idea to opening night was torturous.

I started with a simple reading of the original play, substituting Hank Williams music for the choruses. The group loved the music, hated the play, and suggested I lean into the Appalachian feel of the songs. I went back to my computer and knocked out another draft, followed by a reading. The play sagged this time. Was it the actors? The music choices? I pored over my script trying to figure it out.

Eventually, the artistic director felt there was enough promise to schedule the play, but he wanted original music. I connected with folk composer Jessi McIntosh and in five weeks we banged out five country gospel songs. Our director, Leslie Buxbaum Danzig, led a group of actors in a workshop to explore musical styles and try out physical ideas. I furiously rewrote scenes. Finally, we went into rehearsal.

As I think back on the production, I remember images, moments, and staging: a woman holding up her son's bloody head in a sack; the chorus of women dancing in ecstasy; a young girl jumping off a high platform to her death.

I can imagine that Moisés Kaufman of the Tectonic Theater Project would ask me—if what I loved in the end were the moments of music, dance, and ecstasy—why didn't I start there? Why did I labor alone for years before collaborating with composers, actors, directors, and designers?

Kaufman's Tectonic Theater Project identifies as a group of artists who devise their work as a company. They don't start with a written text, but with an idea, a historical moment, or with interviews. They begin without scripts and develop their theatrical pieces over time. Every leader of devised or company-created theatre that I

Figure 4.1 The Revel by Damon Kiely. Directed by Leslie Buxbaum Danzig for The House Theatre of Chicago. Foreground: Sarah Charipar, Background: Ensemble. Set: Grant Sabin; Lighting: Lee Keenan; Costumes: Izumi Inaba; Sound: Kevin O'Donnell; Composer/Co-Lyricist: Jess McIntosh; Music Director: Matthew Muniz; Fight Choreography: Matt Hawkins; Clogging Instructor: Barbara Silverman; Dialect Coach: Christine Adaire. Photo Credit: Michael Brosilow.

talked to created material in their own way. One begins with puppetry and song writing, while another writes a dance in real time. Others have no set method but trust the creativity of their ensemble members. Tectonic has their own process called *Moment Work*, where artists start with theatrical improvisations and eventually write a script.

So, what if I started working on *The Revel* with a composer, director, designers, and actors right after that fateful bike ride? Would I have saved a few years? Would I have come to compelling theatrical moments sooner? What shape would the piece have taken?

For devised theatre makers, once they discover the spark—that's the moment to start rehearsal.

THE SPARK

What launches a devised play process?

In their book, *Moment Work: Tectonic Theater Project's Process of Devising Theater*, Moisés Kaufman, Barbara Pitts McAdams, and other founding members detail their devising process. They start with a hunch—a character, or historical event, or a theme that captures their imaginations.

The company's most famous work, *The Laramie Project*, was inspired by the 1998 murder of a young gay teen named Matthew Shepherd in Laramie, Wyoming. Targeted for being gay, attackers beat Shepherd severely and tied him to a barbed wire fence to die. The company asked: Why? Why this person? Why not others? Why now? The writers of *Moment Work* depict the company's inspiration:

> These questions led Moisés to suggest that we should travel to Laramie to find out. His hunch at this point was that something had happened in Laramie that might shed light on the state of the nation as a whole...He was interested in hearing from the people of Laramie: How had they been affected by the crime? What conversations was the murder generating in town?[1]

The company took the bold step of traveling to the site of the murder to interview citizens. They weren't journalists, and they didn't even know if they would end up writing a play. As a group, they had a gut instinct that theatre artists should be a part of the national dialogue.

I interviewed several theatre directors who drew inspiration from either current events or the news of the day. Upon reading a troubling item, these directors were compelled to action.

Starting from a Historical Event

Jorge Vargas, the artistic director of the Mexican multidisciplinary theatre project, Teatro Línea de Sombra, works with film, multimedia, movement, text, and song. He's committed to company creation. His actors, designers, and dramaturgs help generate whatever script they eventually perform.

But first, they need a spark.

Vargas was struck one day by a shocking statistic he found in the newspaper: between 2002 and 2012, ten thousand Mexican immigrants died trying to cross the desert into the United States. Why so many senseless deaths? In their research, they discovered that President George W. Bush increased the length of the border wall by 500 percent. The lengthened barrier forced migrants to cross to the United States in more dangerous places. Thousands never made it.

Vargas decided to open up what he calls *a space for research*. His company worked with non-government-based organizations, digging into a pool of information on migration. They combed through images, films, and articles. During an in-person interview, Vargas told me the company was looking for a theatrical spark:

> First what we do is leave the space for that detonator agent. We don't know when that's going to happen, but it's going to happen. That detonator will untie a series of questions that we call a *system* of questions. Questions that encourage you to investigate the context to find out the possible answer.

Vargas asked: when a man leaves a town in Mexico to go to a city in the United States but never arrives—what happens to the body? Where is that person? Undocumented migrants are trained to be invisible and hide in the shadows. *How can we reconstruct an absent body?* This question sparked the play they would call *Amarillo*.

Personal Histories

In early 2019, **Madani Younis** was named as the Creative Director for London's Southbank Centre, a multidisciplinary arts complex. He came to the position after seven years leading the Bush Theatre in the Shepherd's Bush district of West London, where he oversaw capital projects, tripled the audience, and created internationally renowned theatre projects.

Before working at the Bush, he created plays and theatrical events for Freedom Studios in Bradford, culminating in a 2011 site-specific piece called *The Mill: City of Dreams*. Bradford is one of the many industrial cities in the north of England that were ravaged when the factories that provided most of the jobs shut down in the 1980s. Hulking industrial sites sat empty for decades.

When Younis lived in Bradford in the late 2010s, some mills had been converted into lofts, other into pool halls and trendy bars. During one hazy night in a factory-turned-snooker hall, Younis was struck by the irony that his South Asian ancestors had traveled across the world to work where he now stood enjoying a drink. They'd lived here, raised families, and worked long hours creating industrial products. Their ghosts were just at the edges of the room.

The spark for the promenade theatre piece, *The Mill: City of Dreams* was lit.

Younis and his main collaborator, Omar Elerian, were lucky enough to get permission to use Drummond Mill. The factory opened in 1896 and thrived as a textile plant for over a century, working at a time when Bradford was responsible for over a third of the world's wool production. Younis and Elerian interviewed members of the community, gathering information about Drummond, and even worked with the mill's ancient custodian. Younis told me about his interactions with the steward when we sat down for an interview:

> The caretaker had been there in its glory days, so he'd seen it as a kid and he's now in his seventies. So, he's got objects he's bringing to us, like manuals he kept, and what he's given to workers on their first day.

Eventually they would create a fictional version of the custodian as the guide for their promenade piece. The caretaker took audience members through the vast expanse of the factory—as large as seven football fields. The ghosts of workers populated the massive factory floors, as the caretaker journeyed into the past.

Younis obsessed over honoring his ancestors' narratives. Immigrant communities helped forge industrial cities like Bradford, but no one told those stories. Younis hoped that his theatre piece would expose the truth hiding beneath the myth.

Starting with a Myth

Leslie Buxbaum Danzig and **Julia Rhoads** have worked together for over a decade, co-creating dance-theatre pieces for Lucky Plush Productions, a touring company with a home base in Chicago. Rhoads founded her multidisciplinary company in 2000, sometimes creating pieces herself, and other times working with a co-director. Buxbaum and Rhoads have collaborated on meditations on marriage inspired by the classic melodrama *Gaslight* and investigated the weird waiting limbo of airport lounges.

In 2017, seeking inspiration for a new piece, Buxbaum suggested exploring remorse and regret. Perhaps the myth of Orpheus and Eurydice could be told through the lens of personal disappointment. Rhoads wasn't particularly invested in the ancient story but trusted her collaborator's instincts. She gathered her ensemble for an exploratory workshop period. As they usually do at the beginning of a process, the Lucky Plush company asked Rhoads: *What is this thing we're doing?* Rhoads explained her company's patience to me during an interview:

> Our ensemble knows that it is a long form process. If I tell them it's about *this* it's gonna change. Usually the people involved in our process are really game for the *not knowing* and they understand that you gotta go through a lot of muck...One of the very first days we came in with 3 or 4 different synopses, I believe, of the myth. Then everybody wrote notes on three or four things that they cared about from the story or just something that came up for them or a question that they had.

The ensemble and their co-creators realized that regret was only one part of the story of Orpheus and Eurydice. Some members were interested in the underworld, others in the journey of love, some weren't really interested in the tale at all. The legend became a jumping off place for a piece called *Rooming House*. The company started to picture a story as a home with many rooms. Buxbaum told me about the metaphor when we sat down to discuss the *Rooming House* devising process:

> People want to hang out in different rooms of the house. Some people really like this threshold, and some people are just really in the kitchen. A story is a space that you go in and you hang out in, and what people are drawn to is different. Especially a myth or an old story that gets told and retold and repurposed.

Because there were so many versions of the Eurydice myth, the ensemble felt liberated to create their own take. They weren't bound to telling the narrative in one fashion. Hanging out in the "rooms" of the myth of Orpheus allowed many voices to enter the story.

I can imagine starting work on *The Revel* as a devised theatre piece: I bring my spark to the ensemble: *I think there's a connection between bluegrass hymns and Greek tragedy. I believe we could explore religious ecstasy through music.* They seem game and we dive in.

We read different Greek plays looking for what fits our actors and fires up the group. If we decide we want to focus on *The Bacchae*, we read all the extant translations we can find for inspiration. Ensemble members bring in news articles about religious cults and the power of charismatic leaders. If we get ambitious perhaps we interview members of different churches, especially those who use ecstatic music. We sing some Hank Williams songs, Carter Family ditties, and other old-time country gospel tunes. Perhaps we recreate euphoric dances and religious rituals. This research period would allow us to start to explore the spark of the piece.

At some point we need to start creating theatrical moments. We need to get in a room and play.

GENERATING MATERIAL

When Jorge Vargas starts work on a project with his ensemble, he forms a theatrical laboratory. Any idea can be tried out, refined, sculpted, and eventually accepted or rejected. Each project requires a different amount of time, and each experiment in the laboratory works by its own rules. One idea may take weeks to develop, while another comes together in hours. Trial and error stimulate the heart of Teatro Línea de Sombra's work.

When they started working on *Amarillo*, the company didn't own any rehearsal space, so they rented a squash court. The sports facility was conveniently located, and the physical structure of the room seemed apropos. You enter through a small door on one side to a self-contained chamber dominated by an imposing eighteen-foot wall. It's intimidating.

Vargas sat in the squash court every day and waited for his ensemble. Vargas told me that the company ethos asserts, "Each actor is the author of their own independent artistic piece." Some days no one would show up and eventually Vargas would leave—but he had time to think about the production. Other days, actors showed him what they were thinking about. Vargas related the story of one of his company member's experiments:

> One day Raul [Mendoza] started running towards the wall and jumping and he was there for like twenty minutes. At the end when he couldn't jump any more we talked about his idea. Raul said that the only thing he wanted to demonstrate was that the desire was stronger than the impossibility of the task. Even though he couldn't cross, the impulse of doing it obligated him to jump....*On the other side is what I want.*

Vargas and his company held onto the high wall of the squash court in their final design. The back of the set looked like a concrete border reaching to the heavens. It served as a projection screen, but also an impenetrable barrier. Watching *Amarillo*, I found Mendoza's simple, repetitive, and ultimately futile jumping haunting. It was wordless, but clearly summed up the impossible task desperate Mexican migrants face.

Kristin Marting founded the HERE Arts Center in New York City twenty-five years ago. HERE houses experimental theatre makers of all stripes: puppeteers, multimedia artists, dance-theatre makers, composers, and devisers. It provides space for artists to try new ideas and show unfinished works to small audiences.

Marting's 2018 piece, *Assembled Identity* started with a conversation at a bar between Marting and two of her long-time collaborators, actors Mariana Newhard and Purvi Bedi. Newhard is from the Philippines and Bedi is from India, but they discussed how they are often called in for the same roles. Sometimes they are even mistaken for sisters, even though they don't really look that much like each other. Toasting each other, the three women decided to make a play about identity.

When they first met to generate ideas, they read and discussed material about twins, ethnic ambiguity, and clones. Marting and her collaborators decided to create a play where Newhard and Bedi discover they are genetically engineered doubles.

Then, for three months, they met once a week and experimented with creating material. Marting told me about the company's first exercises during a phone interview:

> We would each bring in exercises, and we would try shit. We had no structure; we did not know what the show was. Bringing in text that we wanted to stage and somehow get on its feet. Somebody brought in an interview, somebody brought in a film exercise…we just all brought in shit. And then we would videotape stuff that we thought was useful, and our assistant director Drew was with us and he would notate what we were doing.

They composed songs, adapted scenes from the television show *Black Mirror*, created scenes about twins who didn't know each other existed, and played with dramatic material by Caryl Churchill.

They were searching for an elusive target—a through line.

Movement Leading the Way

Lucky Plush productions sometimes feel like a quirky contemporary play where a breathtaking modern dance breaks out in the middle. Or perhaps an athletically choreographed movement piece with characters who speak like normal people. They create arresting hybrid theatre.

As the artistic director and lead choreographer, Julia Rhoads almost always starts with movement vocabularies that grow out of themes or ideas. As she and Buxbaum started working on *Rooming House*, Rhoads had the ensemble create simple pieces around the themes that interested them from the Eurydice and Orpheus myth. Dancers explored the atmosphere of the underworld or the mechanics of looking backward. Her ensemble employs a system for generating new material called *writing a dance in real time*.

An ensemble member makes a short proposal for a movement phrase, something easy to repeat. Another ensemble member might propose an addition or a change, but they must incorporate the first part. Then the first person, or someone else, adds on. The ensemble crafts and refines as they go. As an ensemble of trained dancers, they have many compositional tools they can employ. Rhoads suggests they might call on one of the three Cs:

> Compliment, contrast, copy. Compliment might be someone is moving distally (digits, fingers, toes) and the other person is going to follow their pattern but move from the core. Copy might be to do exactly what they're doing in unison. Perhaps you're copying the head of what they're doing but your feet are doing something else. Contrast would be going with something totally different than what they're doing.

As the company generated material a few times a week for a period of months, co-directors Rhoads and Buxbaum searched for an anchor. They'd had great success in the past with their company-created pieces when they discovered some sort of framing device to hold all of the material they had generated as a group. When they worked on *The Better Half*, a piece that explored the complexities of a long marriage, they discovered that the melodrama *Gaslight* helped ground their improvisations. When they worked on *The Queue*, a performance about making and breaking personal connections, the piece fell into place when they decided to set it in an airport lounge.

Rhoads remembers struggling to find a similar device for *Rooming House* and calling Buxbaum on the phone to discuss their progress:

> And I said, *I think, we need some kind of game structure like Clue or something*. Leslie said, *Yeah!* I was kind of throwing that out as an example. But Leslie said, *No I'm serious we need to do that*. I said, *Okay I have it I'll bring it into a studio*. So, we played Clue the actual board game for one full rehearsal. And then the next several rehearsals we tried to populate stories inside of the Clue game where each room was a process in decision making.

As you may remember, the original Hasbro game board features several rooms in a mansion. The premise is that one of the guests has killed someone, and players move about the house asking each

Figure 4.2 Rooming House co-created by Julia Rhoads and Leslie Buxbaum Danzig. Devised in collaboration with an ensemble of six performers: Kara Brody, Michel Rodriguez Cintra, Elizabeth Luse, Rodolfo Sánchez Sarracino, A. Raheim White, Meghann Wilkinson for Lucky Plush Productions. Foreground: L–R: Kara Brody and Michel Rodriguez Cintra, Background: Ensemble. Lighting: Alexander Ridgers; Sound: Bradford Chapin, Dennis Huston; Original Music: Michael Caskey. Photo Credit: Benjamin Wardell.

other questions. By process of elimination the winner is able to solve the crime: i.e., Professor Plum, in the kitchen, with a lead pipe.

Rhoads and Buxbaum determined the different rooms of Clue could correspond to the different parts or *rooms* of myth or storytelling. They Googled elements of decision making and discovered that people often followed patterns when they decided to tell a story. Key elements include backstory, character, the event, and disruption.

So, they played games of Clue, but rather than solving a mystery, they were telling the story of Orpheus and Eurydice. Instead of wandering into a kitchen or a library, they entered the backstory or the event. The ensemble members set off on an exhausting journey to play this made up game of Clue.

They were letting the rooms speak to them, telling them what the eventual piece wanted to be. Most devisers work with the large blank canvas of empty rooms, but some bring objects in for inspiration.

Letting Objects Speak

In their book *Moment Work*, the Tectonic Theater Project describes their devising method. Rather than starting with a script or even an outline of how they will create a performance, company members begin by creating short performances, or Moments. Anyone can create a Moment: actors, designers, directors, or dramaturgs. These short pieces can utilize props or lights or music, or just bodies. Moments need to have a beginning, middle, and end.

Someone may come in with a rope and twirl it in a way that no one thought possible. Or a couple of actors could slowly reveal themselves by turning on more and more lights. A corner of the rehearsal hall could become more potent if one actor sat there for an extended period of time.

Leigh Fondakowski was the head writer of *The Laramie Project* and has created many of her own projects based on extensive periods of research and interviews. She always starts with Moment Work and objects that inspire her. In a phone interview with me Fondakowski shared her personal take on Moment Work:

> *Do something with this until you're surprised.* So, you're playing along, you're playing along, you're playing along, and then you have an ah-ha moment. Moment Work pre-supposes that every object, every space, every costume piece has its own kind of language—its own way of speaking. A density, shape, color. And sometimes, a story.

When she started working on *The People's Temple*, a docudrama based on the Jonestown Massacre, she didn't know what form the play would take. The story of Jim Jones's cult, which ended in tragedy when almost one thousand members died from drinking cyanide-laced Kool-Aid, called out to Fondakowski. She and her ensemble talked their way into the basement storage room of the California Historical Society. They encountered hundreds of boxes of interviews, documents, and physical artifacts.

One member took down a box and found Jim Jones's ceremonial robe, another his bulletproof vest, a third found internal documents of the People's Temple or news clippings. She noticed how reverently her ensemble treated the boxes. In her essay as a part of

Tectonic Theater Company's *Moment Work* book, Fondakowski reveals the breakthrough moment:

> I realized that the archive itself could be the storytelling form for the play. I had a hunch that our time in the archive could become the theatrical event of the play. The simple action of taking an object out of the box could be a way to tell each small piece of the story, with the archive itself becoming the theatrical container for all the stories.²

She gathered bankers' boxes in her studio and let her ensemble play. They were able to treat the boxes imaginatively and theatrically, creating specific locations with the boxes or using them to make podiums. They stood in for the autopsy room.

When I spoke to Fondakowski she had been in workshops for a few years on a piece called *Casa Cushman*, about a famous 19th-century actress named Charlotte Cushman, who was known for being in a gay marriage for forty years. Fondakowski had been doing research on Cushman's life, speaking to her biographers, and digging into theatrical archives.

I asked Fondakowski why she didn't use her research and write a script. She says she doesn't think like that. She always has to ask herself why something is stage worthy. Why not just write a novel? Why is theatre the best way to tell that story? She told me more about her process during our interview:

> I have to actually see it happen. I actually have to discover it in the room. For this workshop I have coming up: I'm going to have a handheld candelabra, I'm going to have black hoop skirts, dress forms, and I'm going to have a series of white tables and white textbooks of all kinds of shapes and sizes. So, we're going to begin to put the thing on its feet to see what it is. I don't know what the play is about. I literally am gleaning the information from the studio work about what it is that I'm thinking.

She's been in and out of workshops for over two years on the piece. She and her actors have played with ornate gowns, corsets, dress forms, black and white clothing, long white tables and myriad other objects.

She's waiting for the right theatrical elements to emerge, and then she'll fashion a story.

Writing as a Group

The group of artists who would eventually be called PigPen Theatre Company started creating original plays together as Carnegie Mellon students in 2007. Each of the seven men act, make puppets, play multiple instruments, compose original songs, write plays, and work together as a tight ensemble. Their plays feel like Mumford and Sons' roots-infused concerts with a story: organically homegrown, imaginative, theatrical, and saturated with original music.

The ensemble credits Kansas City Repertory Theatre artistic director, **Stuart Carden,** with inspiring their collaborative way of working during a class he taught in their sophomore year. Many years later, after Carden had moved on from Carnegie and was focusing on freelance directing, he got a call.

PigPen was opening up *The Old Man and the Old Moon* in New York and wanted Carden's opinion. Their play was a puppetry infused, tuneful tale about an old man who must abandon his duties of filling up the moon with liquid light to search for his missing wife. Carden loved every minute, although he thought they would have a richer work if they deepened their central myth and cut away other storytelling threads.

Carden suggested he could help them focus their storytelling and hone their sprawling epics. PigPen agreed and they joined forces. In 2013, Carden brought the group to Writers Theatre in Glencoe, IL, where *The Old Man and the Old Moon* was such a huge success that Writers immediately commissioned them to create a new work.

The ensemble had an idea for a story called *The Hunter and the Bear*, in which a logger in the Pacific Northwest investigates the loss of his son after a bear attack. They had a general outline of the entire story but weren't sure how to create the world of the play or the details of the narrative. Writers Theatre agreed to host a two-week workshop.

The artists asked for numerous flashlights, pieces of cardboard, bundles of kindling, backpacks of different sizes and shapes, and large canvases. Ensemble members wrote snatches of songs. They started experimenting with puppets—knowing they wanted to work with marionettes to represent the son who gets lost, and his ghost. PigPen loved shadow work and started trying to create a negative shadow puppet—where the main image was created by darkness rather than light. They played.

I asked Carden why they didn't start writing scenes of a play if they had the general outline? He said it was because PigPen doesn't believe in telling stories only through dialogue. They hope that a song, a sound effect, or a shadow puppet sequence can spin a yarn forward:

> We didn't want to get into a situation of locking ourselves in a room and writing the piece and trying to solve all the problems and find all of our inspiration just through a text based, verbal based storytelling. And so, some of that early work was about getting the other vocabulary in the room so that we had touchstones to go back to and say, *Oh, that element we were exploring through the puppetry, that can play out here. We can tell that part of the story non-verbally. We don't have to solve it through the text.*

Next, the ensemble and Carden undertook a second workshop in a cabin in Idaho to hammer out an outline and start writing. PigPen works by what Carden calls a *Quaker Consensus*, meaning they can't move forward unless there is unanimous agreement. They agreed quickly on the inciting incident, the rising action, the turning point, the climax, and the denouement. They labored to detail the journey from one node in the story to the next.

The group made storyboards and outlines and argued over the details until they agreed on a general flow of the story. Then they set to work writing scenes. Sometimes they would work by creating a Google document—something they could all edit at the same time.

Other times they would create three-person writing teams, each tasked with writing the same scene. They'd write separately, then convene to discuss and hash out next steps. Perhaps they liked team A's form, team B's climax, and team C's dialogue. Other times one group really captured the scene and was assigned to keep refining. Occasionally one ensemble member would step forward and say—*Hey, give me all three versions I can weave the threads.*

Thinking back to my work on *The Revel*, I definitely had collaborative moments with different artists along the way, but that work was spread out over years. Whenever I got a comment or an idea, it was up to me to implement the change.

My first draft of the play was just a light edit of the original *Bacchae* with some bluegrass songs thrown in. The readers hated the original play and suggested I rewrite it. Who was the main character? Is it the mother who kills her son? Let's meet her in the first five minutes not the last. And if you're going to use that country bluegrass music, your character better sound like they come from Appalachia.

The next draft started to bring the mother into focus but didn't feel personal enough. Someone suggested adding a daughter character. Others asked where the husband was. Was he dead? What was he like? What was that backstory?

What if I'd been collaborating with a composer from the beginning? Would the music drive the narrative? What about actors and musicians? What could we learn about the nature of a chorus before writing scenes? If we follow some of the examples in this chapter, we'd look for some objects that seem connected to the story. I can imagine us working with banjos, whiskey jugs, and religious garments to see what inspirational moments we could devise. Perhaps we would just work on different forms of ecstatic dances from various religious groups. Just trying out the different ways that a Greek-style chorus could operate—in unison, as separate individuals, in mask—could spark new discoveries.

As it turned out, I was on my own as a playwright. After many years in a singular struggle I finally created a cogent draft. I was ready for rehearsal.

REVISING AND REHEARSING

As Carden and PigPen dove into final preparations for *The Hunter and the Bear*, they convened a third workshop to marry the world building of their first workshop and the script writing of the second. Actors, director, and designers collaborated on inserting puppetry, songs, spectacle, and movement into the play.

I asked Carden if the rest of the rehearsal period felt more like a new play process, but Carden said no. Half of their time was still spent in devising mode. Perhaps in the morning they would refine scenes—learning and practicing music, staging moments, beat

Rehearsing a Play Without a Script 153

Figure 4.3 The Hunter and the Bear Created and performed by PigPen Theatre Co. - Alex Falberg, Ben Ferguson, Curtis Gillen, Ryan Melia, Matt Neurnberger, Arya Shahi, Dan Weschler. Directed by Stuart Carden for Writers Theatre, Center: Ben Ferguson, Background L–R: Curtis Gillen and Arya Shahi and Ensemble. Set: Collette Pollard; Lighting: Bart Cortright; Costumes/Puppetry: Lydia Fine; Sound: Mikhail Fiksel Properties; Master: Scott Dickens. Photo Credit: Michael Brosilow.

work. But in the afternoon they would try to resolve the climax of the play or work their puppetry technique. Or just play:

> Play with PigPen is crucial. Giving them the space and permission to goof off and test stupid ideas is really crucial to devising work with them. And so, one of the things that I felt like I needed to do was to give them a larger portion of undirected free time. Because so much of their most genius ideas come from a moment of just goofing off and saying, *What if?*

Late in the rehearsal process, as tech was approaching, an actor was just messing around with the tail from a coonskin hat and two sticks. Eventually he figured out a way to really make it look like a cute woodland creature. His little animal didn't contribute to the main thrust of the story, but it sure was adorable. The imaginary rodent gave the play some much-needed laughs in the early moments.

Directors of devised works are always on the lookout for the unexpected. Some find it through the bodies of their performers.

Finding Form in the Physical

As Kristin Marting, Mariana Newhard and Purvi Bedi continued work on *Assembled Identity*, they gravitated toward a futuristic science-fiction narrative. They imagined some mysterious laboratory where clones were being gathered for genetic testing. The lab became a character.

Marting's long-time collaborator, video designer David Bengali, joined the process. He was eager to find ways to create the presence of the nefarious facility through projections and live video. Lighting designer Christina Tang and sound designer Drew Weinstein added their own ideas about how to personify and identify the rooms of the laboratory. Marting told me about why she loves creating multimedia performances:

> I just feel like I can see characters more deeply when I see them through these different filters. It's not just using words but using music, using dance, gives me multiple access points to characters. And the video also provides different ways to get into the character's head depending on how you're approaching it dramaturgically.

Once they compiled a first draft the team gathered for rehearsal. For scenes that have been through a few rounds of edits, Marting likes to get physical quickly. First, she'll discuss the emotional vibe of the scene or the themes of the play. Then, she leads the actors through composition work. She'll give the cast an assignment to create a movement piece in a short amount of time with a set of ingredients. She explained some typical ingredients for a composition:

> A revelation of space, a slow walk, one entrance and two exits, an embrace, and then it might be a moment of rage…a rejection…and a laugh. Something like that. It's always a combination of the purely physical and the emotional. And sometimes I'll title the composition.

Marting uses movement work to unlock scenes indirectly. Her title for the composition might reference the subtext of the scene or hint at theme. She assigns emotions related to the character dynamics and relationships. When they create the composition, the actors don't use the text of the scene, only movement. She'd leave the actors alone for seven to ten minutes and then come back to see what they created:

> Sometimes I'll just take what they actually made, and I'll throw the words on top of it, and see what that does for the scene. Because maybe that move has to go with those words.

Working the text and the movement separately can provide surprising results. A scene you assumed would be played intimately suddenly makes perfect sense when the actors are distant. When someone says, "I love you," perhaps they should be backpedaling away from their partner. Movement can contrast rather than underscore the text. By creating a movement pattern that only indirectly connects to the text of a scene, Marting can sometimes unlock hidden potential.

How should you choose which movement unlocks the text best? What's the problem to solve?

Setting the Rules

As Madani Younis and Omar Elerian began assembling interviews and research for their site-specific production *The Mill*, they craved structure. They knew the mill would be a character in the play and audiences would move from room to room in the massive factory. They had scads of research on the mill, but they weren't sure how to structure it into a performance.

Eventually they decided to create a chronology of the factory, so that each act would cover a decade or a couple of decades. As the audience walked deeper into the mill, they delved further into the history of its inhabitants. Younis remembers when the guiding principles clicked into place:

> I think once we understood what was fixed and what was free—that's a really important model that Omar and I use— by giving ourselves structures in any creative process, then the language becomes easy for us. Here's the truth: Our company

will be no bigger than thirty actors. This show will have to take less than ninety minutes as an experience. We will only be able to use sound, kind of like PA sound in like two of the seven spaces—we came up with some of these obstructions, and some were just given. You could bend the rules of course, so far as you could bend any rule. But it meant each artist knew what the fuck we were talking about.

With a group of professional performers and some actors from the community, Younis and Elerian got to work creating their scenes. Younis said at times they felt like Motown song writers, working in a creative factory. He would write a scene with actors in one room—improvising around their research and interviews. He sent performers along to Elerian who put the material on its feet and rehearsed.

Setting creative rules unlocked their writing process.

Leslie Buxbaum Danzig started as a performer with devised theater companies in New York and remembers sitting through many rehearsals she found boring and tedious. She hung around for a very long time not knowing what show she was rehearsing. It took patience, faith, and confidence in the directors:

> Everybody wants to solve a problem. That's a very energizing thing to do. And so, with a play—the play is on the table. That's the whole problem to solve in a sense and it's very exciting to work on it together. With a devised piece, it's hard to know where the problem is. And it's hard to articulate in an energizing way—rehearsal after rehearsal, for day after day in the studio, what the problem is. And so, the worst feeling that performers have—is they are not making meaningful contributions.

Julia Rhoads agrees with Buxbaum. She knows her ensemble of dancers have patience for wandering around in *the muck*, but even they can get antsy after a while. When they were working on *Rooming House*, the co-directors pushed their ensemble for months without much of a structure and Rhoads sensed they were at a breaking point:

> Things got a bit tense after weeks of playing that live version of Clue because it's exhausting, it's relentless, it's hard, and I could sense everyone thinking, *When are we gonna set*

something you know? And I remember saying to Leslie, *I think we're getting an ensemble fatigue right now we should probably change gears and start focusing on movement for a while.*

Rhoads intuited that her ensemble was tiring of improvised *walking and talking* exercises and needed to flex a different muscle. Lucky Plush requires a high level of dance from performers who love to move, so they can't spend too many rehearsals in a row without creating some form of choreography. Even though the directors didn't know what the piece was about yet or how to frame the evening, Rhoads figured creating some movement sequences, even if they might seem random at first, might shake something loose.

The conundrum remained for the collaborators: how can we generate material if we don't know the form we are filling? How can we make movement when we don't know why we're moving?

Finding the Form

As Leigh Fondakowski continued work on *Casa Cushman*, she'd been fascinated with letters between Cushman and her lovers but stumped by the gaps between the epistles. In her Moment Work she'd experimented with a chorus of women who could help move the story along. She'd played with dress forms and corsets, uncovering ideas about female sexuality and the male gaze.

Finally, she'd started writing the inner thoughts of her main characters. The two halves of her creative self were at work. Fondakowski elaborated about her process:

> The playwright has been kind of a few steps behind the director in me—in a fog wondering what the hell to do with all of this beautiful stuff and how to do this giant story. But the playwright is catching up. The playwright is coming out of the fog and is ready to get in there.

Fondakowski flips the typical hierarchy on its head in her devising work. In a new play process with a single writer, the playwright spends many months or years writing and rewriting a narrative. They come into a rehearsal with a sense of the play and the director has to catch up and figure out how to put their words on stage.

I remember how relieved I was when *The Revel* finally went into rehearsal. As the director, actors, and the composer started collaborating, the script leapt to life. Ideas came from everywhere. Now we were devising a play as a group. If an actor wanted to improvise the lines to a new joke, we'd let him. A chorus member tried out a novel approach to a song as we listened.

When an actor accomplished a moment with a look or a physical gesture, I cut language. When a dance erupted that captured the joy of a scene, I made rewrites to match the mood. I didn't have to solve a problem with dialogue, better if I could just get out of the way. Rehearsal was the closest the many years of working on *The Revel* came to a devising process. Even as we finished teching the show I made slight adjustments to the script based on collaborators' suggestions and proposals.

I braced myself for previews. What would I learn from audiences?

AUDIENCE FEEDBACK

Leigh Fondakowski holds public showings at the end of each workshop period. She hungers to know what audiences remembered:

> I ask people literally what struck them. So, *When that light hit that curtain space or when she crawls down there*. And I kind of keep a mental record of the things that strike people. And then I ask them, *What questions do you have?* And then, if I'm feeling brave, I ask, *What did you not like?* If I'm feeling tender or vulnerable, I don't ask that. But if I'm really happy with it and I feel really solid, then I'll let them tell me what they didn't like.

Fondakowski has been working in the field of devised work for decades and has developed her own method of soliciting feedback. It's modeled after Liz Lerman's Critical Response Process, a way of soliciting observations that the choreographer developed over time to help protect and feed the artistic needs of art makers. Lerman's Critical Response Process takes an audience through a series of specific questions, starting by asking what moments they remember, and proceeding to what they liked about the performance. Next the artist asks the audience questions, and then audience members can ask neutral questions. Each step of the process is designed to protect the artists and filter information from the viewers.

Fondakowski brushes off advice on how to rewrite the play but notes what sparked interest. She can sniff out hidden writing tips in a rhetorical question but leans closer when an audience member

seems confused about a moment. If someone's lost, does she need to fill a gap in the narrative or clarify her intentions?
She's looking to find the signal within the noise.

Knowing When to Listen to Audiences

In their search for a form for their musing on regret, myth, and storytelling, *Rooming House*, Leslie Buxbaum Danzig and Julia Rhoads knew that they needed to stop spinning their wheels and put something, anything, in front of a new set of eyes.

They identified all the short sequences they'd been generating in rehearsal that sparked passion. Trusting their instincts, they sequenced material: put this scene here, this dance moment there. They didn't expect the piece to make narrative sense, just hang together. Rhoads told me she trusts her instincts:

> You find a reason—there's some logic that starts to connect these things. And you start to build through lines. So, we did that with a bunch of material, just to sort of see what started to resonate with people. And usually the question we have at the end of such early showings is, we just ask the audience: What do you find yourself caring about? Because it's too early to ask about: does this all make sense?

Rhoads and Buxbaum have a strong aversion to theatre that tells an audience what to think or is too obvious. Their work is complex and multidisciplinary, so it's not surprising that early drafts of material can confuse an audience. Rhoads knows she is walking a fine line:

> The last thing that I want is for audiences to see my work and feel alienated or confused by it. We are always talking about how to give audiences anchors or how do we help them to assemble meaning when the storytelling isn't always linear, or the vocabularies move into abstraction?

Rhoads and Buxbaum showed twenty minutes of material in front of a small group. The audience hooked into one relationship in the show and wanted more. The co-directors were uneasy about that suggestion but noted the desire. Buxbaum and Rhoads heard that the show was too Orpheus centered. One comment drew them up short: *you're skating on the surface of this material. Go deep.*

While it was early in the process, the comment resonated with the co-directors. Turning a myth into a board game was an interesting intellectual exercise, but it didn't grab the audience emotionally. They got back into rehearsal and asked their ensemble members if anyone had a personal story about regret or loss they were excited to share publicly.

Some company members came forth with touching autobiographical anecdotes, which charged the rehearsal room. The ensemble worked for months generating new material and sequencing a performance before showing their next draft to another group of people. They had developed a show where they stayed with the Orpheus and Eurydice myth for the first third of the show and then veered into personal stories. Buxbaum remembers listening to audiences' responses after the second showing:

> And we were getting feedback, *Oh, it's the personal stories! That's the part! Give us more, give us more, more, more of that!* And I hear that, but my more experienced self says, *You think you want more of that, but I think the reason that you were loving that so much is because it took twenty-five minutes to get there. And if we give you what you want out of the gate, it's not going to actually be what you want.*

Buxbaum knew that the personal story would only resonate if they delayed the event. She wanted to create a pressure cooker that released at the right moment. The collaborators continued on their path of creating narrative signposts and emotional hooks for the audiences to follow without revealing too much too soon. They balanced listening to their audience with trusting their instincts and craft.

Watching *Rooming House*, I started out intrigued, perplexed, and delighted by this odd combination of a retelling of the Orpheus and Eurydice myth and the classic game Clue. Then, when one of the cast members started telling the story of his immigration to America, uncovering and exploring his life story in the same manner as the myth, I was touched.

Thinking Long Term

Stuart Carden and PigPen Theatre have produced *The Old Man and the Old Moon* in Williamstown, Los Angeles, Chicago, New

York, Boston, and other places. With each production, Carden and the ensemble listen to a new audience, gauge how certain sections are landing, and look for possible changes. Knowing a show will have a second production takes pressure off Carden to *get it right* the first time. Because PigPen's work is intertwined with design and feeds off of audiences, they won't really know what they've created until opening night of the first production. As Carden approaches opening night, he's not stressed about serving some ideal version of the play. That ideal doesn't exist. Carden told me that how he watches plays has changed:

> The piece is revealing itself every single day. My stress comes from trying to listen as deeply as I can to the piece as it intersects with an audience, hold on to all the elements that are telling the story, and understand, *How well are we telling that story?* And then marshaling the time and the team, with each revelation through the process, to take a step towards what is being revealed. What the story wants to be.

Devising taught Carden how to collaborate, how to listen, and how to rehearse a play. He used to worry about crafting every moment of a play perfectly and serving his own vision. Devising has encouraged him to let ideas come late, and to allow these discoveries these discoveries to inform inform how he tells the overall arc of the story. He values his time with PigPen for what it has demanded of him:

> Working with them has improved my ability to work simultaneously. In multiple ways. I can be thinking about the breath of a puppet while also listening to a harmony while also thinking about the structure of the story. And it has asked me to pay attention in different ways and also let me—given me permission to not feel like I have to solve everything at the same time.

Carden has been directing plays for decades, working with new writers, creating musicals, and teaching collaboration to students. He's still learning on the job and found that working with PigPen pushed him in directions he hadn't expected. It encouraged him to ask basic questions.

Figure 4.4 The Revel by Damon Kiely. Directed by Leslie Buxbaum Danzig for The House Theatre of Chicago. Foreground: Andy Lutz, Jeanne T. Arigo, Background: Ensemble. Set: Grant Sabin; Lighting: Lee Keenan; Costumes: Izumi Inaba; Sound: Kevin O'Donnell; Composer/Co-Lyricist: Jess McIntosh; Music Director: Matthew Muniz Fight Choreography: Matt Hawkins; Clogging Instructor: Barbara Silverman; Dialect Coach: Christine Adaire. Photo Credit: Michael Brosilow.

What is a director? How do you inspire collaboration? What does listening to a play mean? How can you tell a story? How else? How do you rehearse a play?

HOW TO REHEARSE A PLAY

Listening to actors read *The Revel* during workshop readings didn't prepare me for watching the show with a group of strangers in attendance. When audience members filed in for the first preview, I remember thinking, *What a terrible idea. Who thought it was a good plan to let anyone see this?*

I was relieved to hear people laugh, see them groove to the music, and watch their shocked reactions when the lead character burst in covered in her own son's blood. But I also noticed when they seemed lost, confused, and bored. We looked for more humor, cut a major song, and tightened dance sequences.

Finally, we opened to generally positive reviews from patrons and critics.

Would the show have grown more if we'd shown it in stages to audiences? What if we performed a concert of the music at some point? Could we have shown an evening of the dances? What about the religious arguments in the show? Would they have strengthened if we'd tried them out several times over several months?

Directors who devise plays with an ensemble of designers and actors in a room embrace chaos. Without a set script to come back to, anything and everything can change. The ensemble starts to trust their hunches and instincts on what should stay and what needs to be cut. Set pieces of choreography, staging, movement, and text become the anchors for the show. As they build around these anchors hopefully they can show their progress to audiences and home in on the heart of their productions. A devised work should fit the actors like a bespoke outfit—it was made specifically with their talents in mind.

Directors who work on establish plays can learn great lessons from the world of devising. Hopefully when a director picks up a play for the first time they can experience the same type of spark that devisers encounter when they begin a project. During an initial research period, directors can dig into historical archives, interview primary sources, and connect their play to current events. Many plays benefit from workshop periods well before rehearsals begin. During a workshop a cast could explore style, experiment with different ways to speak the text, or learn music and dances.

During rehearsals, directors of established plays could take a page from devisers and generate more material than they need. Just because a scene has been staged, perhaps you want to stage it three or four times in different ways. While the text may be set, what is still in flux? Can you try out different approaches to character development, relationships, use of given circumstances? Can any of the design still change before and during technical rehearsals? Finally, how can you listen to an audience with flexibility? Can you tell part of the story with movement? With gesture? With stillness?

To rehearse a play a director needs to ask: Why do we rehearse? How will we work together? What steps will we take to get to opening night? In the following workbook, I've assembled twenty-one prompts that help guide the planning process.

NOTES

1. Moisés Kaufman and Barbara Pitts McAdams, *Moment Work: Tectonic Theater Project's Process of Devising Theatre* (New York: Vintage Books, 2018), 177, 179.
2. Leigh Fondakowski, quoted in *Moment Work*, 278.

Chapter 5

Rehearsal Workbook

I've interviewed over fifty working directors at the top of our field. Each recounted a different outline for their rehearsal process. The question remains: how do *you* like to rehearse a play?

You might change your process based on the type of play you are working on. Are you delving into Shakespeare? Maybe spend ample time at the table to unravel the complicated rhetoric. Is it a highly physical play? Should you start staging immediately? Are there dance numbers? Songs? Fights?

Are you a visual learner? Maybe you should make a quick and dirty sketch. Do you hate mess on stage? Perhaps you should stage slowly and meticulously, holding off full run-throughs until the last possible moment.

What about the cast of actors? If you already know their strengths, how can you play to them? If you are working with them for the first time, what can you deduce about their learning style as a group? Do they seem more interested in working as an ensemble to create the world or do they want to jump into scene work? Do they want freedom, structure, or perhaps some combination?

This chapter outlines the endeavors every director engages with: reading and analyzing before rehearsal, launching the journey, exploring the text, creating a world, crafting staging, and detailing scene work. I finish with an exercise around creating a rehearsal schedule.

For each exercise I start with a simple explanation of the task and then follow up with a deeper exploration of the prompt. I delve into why a particular job is important and how you might employ these ideas in rehearsal. Here's the breakdown.

PREPARING FOR REHEARSAL

1. The first read
2. Given circumstances
3. Events that occur between scenes
4. Events within the play
5. The Moment Chain

LAUNCHING THE JOURNEY

6. Opening day speech
7. Ground rules
8. Initial practical work

EXPLORING THE TEXT

9. Reading from event to event
10. Some questions to ask at the table
11. Dramaturgical reports

CREATING A WORLD

12. Etudes
13. Character webs
14. Mapping space

SHAPING THE STAGING

15. Run with no rehearsal
16. Preparing for staging
17. Some questions to ask your staging

DETAILING SCENE WORK

18. The laws of attraction
19. Coaching actors
20. Troubleshooting scenes

CREATING A REHEARSAL SCHEDULE

21. Planning your time

These activities often overlap. Can't figure out a scene on its feet? Try sitting back down and conducting table work. Building a world often overlaps with working on scenes. Having trouble with a character arc? Maybe look back at your first day address for inspiration.

I encourage you to investigate your rehearsal process until you find something that works for you. I wouldn't suggest trying every exercise on one show—you'd probably drive yourself crazy. Investigate ideas that intrigue you.

What prompts spur your imagination?

PREPARING FOR REHEARSAL

In my first book, *How to Read a Play*, I outlined twenty-one exercises to help directors prepare for casting, design meetings, and rehearsal. Here are five of my favorites.

1. The First Read

Clear your schedule, turn off your cell phone, find a cozy spot and read your play straight through. If your play has an intermission, take a ten-minute break, then sit back down and read to the end. If you have a three-act play, take a second break.

Pull out a notebook and write down any first impressions. Did you have any expectations at the end of the first act? Were they fulfilled or dashed by the climax? Any characters you were initially drawn to? Repelled by? Did the play inspire questions? How did it affect you emotionally?

Don't worry over elegant writing, simply jot down what comes to mind. Hold these notes in a special place.

Reading the script for the first time is your chance to experience the play the way an audience will: straight through. Assuming you love the play, you'll uncover the seeds of your attraction.

Deep in the process, a design element or an actor's performance can muddy your vision of the show. When you're bogged down in a scene that doesn't work, returning to your first impressions can lead you back to the light.

2. Given Circumstances

Read your play slowly page by page. Amass a list of facts about the events that happened before the play began or places that exist. Also write a list of questions.

Some facts about places that exist and events that precede the first scene of *A Streetcar Named Desire*:

> *Blanche and Stella grew up on a plantation in Laurel, Mississippi*
> *Stella left her ancestral home and her sister years ago*
> *Stella and Stanley live on the first floor of a two-story walk up*

Some questions:

> *When exactly did Stella leave? Why?*
> *Where did Stella and Stanley meet? How long have they been married?*
> *How small is the two-room apartment?*

Be wary of opinions. Just because Stella says that Blanche is unreliable—that's an opinion she's stating. Not a fact. When Stanley says Blanche is lewd, again, this is only one character's impression.

In her book *The Director's Craft*, Katie Mitchell introduced me to this particular method for amassing given circumstances. Anything that we can determine is absolutely true based on a reading of the script goes in our fact column. Anything we have doubts about we should write as a question:

> Organizing information from the text about what exists before the action of the play begins will help you to map the physical, geographical, and temporal certainties of the play—and help create a picture of each character's past.[1]

During every rehearsal process, actors will inevitably ask questions about things that happened before the play began. Best to have a list at the ready. (See pages 92–94 for a more thorough investigation of facts and questions.)

Why does Blanche lie to her sister and her brother-in-law from the very first moment she sees them? Look to the recent tragedies in her life that she's desperate to cover up. Why is Stanley insistent on exposing Blanche's lies? Examine the difference between Stanley and Stella's upbringing.

I like to assemble my assistant director and dramaturg a few months before rehearsal and divide up any questions we discover. Anything that could be answered by research I assign to the dramaturg:

> *How long is the trip from Belle Reve to New Orleans?*
> *What would a master sergeant in the Engineer Core do in World War II?*
> *How does someone lose a property by defaulting on loans?*

I assign questions about backstory or timeline to the assistant director.

> *When did Stella leave Belle Reve?*
> *How far along is Stella's pregnancy in the first scene? In the fourth scene?*
> *When did Stanley start talking to Mitch about his suspicions about Blanche?*

I assign character secrets, motivations, and key events to myself.

> *Is Stanly attracted to Blanche? Is she attracted to him?*
> *Does Stella believe Stanley's story about Blanche's past?*
> *Why does Mitch fall for Blanche?*

I meet with the assistant director and dramaturg a few times before rehearsal begins to hash out what we've found in the library or deep in the script. Some questions stay in the unanswered pile: we will clarify them with the actors in rehearsal.

3. Events That Occur between Scenes

Read the play again and now look for events that happen *between* scenes.

Scene one is at the end of a workday for Stanley. After arriving unannounced, Stella and Stanley welcome Blanche into their small apartment. Scene two is twenty-four hours later. Some facts about things that happen between scene one and scene two:

> Stella made a cold dinner for Stanley and arrangements for her and Blanche to go out.
> Stanley has been to work and is expecting his friends for poker night.
> Blanche has decided to take a bath (one of many in the play!)

Some questions about the time passed:

> How did everyone sleep last night?
> What did Stella and Blanche do during the day?
> Where did all of Blanche's belongings get put?

Many juicy interactions ensue in the twenty-four hours between scenes to spur actors toward strong actions and deep characterizations. Blanche and Stella and Stanley slept in the apartment together for the first time, Blanche on a pull-out bed in the kitchen. Blanche started to unpack her trunk. Stanley worked all day, expecting a long rambunctious game of poker with his friends. It's only been one day—but the atmosphere has changed in the apartment.

Events between scenes reveal how characters change over the course of the play and reveal the action map. When Blanche arrives she's a disgraced schoolteacher trying to hide her past. Over the course of the play she moves into the apartment, has fun with her sister, spends an evening apart after a huge fight, starts to date Stanley's best friend Mitch, lies to him about her age and her background, prepares for her birthday, and hatches an escape plan. Over the course of the play Blanche morphs from disgraced teacher to desperate schemer.

4. Events Within the Play

When a character makes a decision that affects every character on stage, home in on that event. Whenever a character enters or exits the stage, make a line in your script. When characters change conversation topics don't mark an event. Only make a mark when the scene takes a turn.

Identify all the events in the play. Name each decision-making turn simply, based on the action of the moment rather than something poetic. Think *Stella rushes from the room in shock* rather than *Collapsing Columns*.

In the first scene, Blanche shifts topics of conversation often, but these moments of repartee don't represent events. For example, Blanche asks where Stella met Stanley and then complains about the mess in the apartment. Blanche is lightly upbraiding Stella about her current living conditions. (See pages 49–50 for more on events.)

When Blanche asks Stella if she has a maid she causes an event that changes the course of the scene. Stella says she doesn't have help because she only has two rooms.

Blanche: What? Two rooms, did you say?
Stella: This one and—
Blanche: The other one? *(She laughs sharply. There is an embarrassed silence.)* I am going to take just one little tiny nip more, sort of to put the stopper on, so to speak.[2]

The decision-making moment above happens in the embarrassed silence. The sisters now have to deal with a new reality: they, along with Stanley, will have to live in cramped quarters together. At this moment the play could take an infinite number of turns. The sisters could have a frank discussion about how long Blanche needs to stay. Or Blanche could confess to Stella why she's really run from Laurel. Or Stella could more aggressively defend her life choices.

Blanche takes a drink. They decide to carry on as if everything will work out fine.

5. The Moment Chain

Make a list of key moments that played in order tell the emotional and narrative story of the play. List approximately twenty-four for a two-act play, fewer for a ninety-minute one act, more for a three-act play.

A play will contain hundreds of events—but only a handful of key moments. As you pare down your list, home in on decision points. Blanche's entire date scene with Mitch isn't a moment. When they kiss at the end of the scene clearly is.

If everything is important, then nothing is important. Directors need to guide an audience through a play: highlight key relationships, spring plot twists, and create theatrical moments that underscore the themes of the script. While twenty-four moments for a two-act play is somewhat arbitrary, this number typically allows enough time to pass between moments for each node point to make an impact.

Jon Jory introduced me to this crucial idea in his book *Tips: Ideas for Directors*. He elucidates one of the most essential tasks for directors, "The director is eternally on the hunt for the moments that illuminate or contain the seeds from which the play grows. We want the key moments of story and character to detonate and resonate."[3]

The moment chain guides me through every part of the rehearsal process. I use it to organize my table work, drawing actors' attention to key turning points of the story. As I rehearse, I spend more time on the key narrative junctures. As I approach run-throughs, the moment chain serves as checklist for places that need attention. (See Appendix 3 for my moment chain for *Streetcar*. I found twenty-eight for the three-act play.)

LAUNCHING THE JOURNEY

At the inaugural meeting with the cast a director has a chance to inspire the team, set some ground rules, and perhaps even start working. *You don't get a second chance to make a first impression*, is a cliché for a reason. There are an infinite number of ways to launch a production, so take some time to craft your plan of attack.

6. Opening Day Speech

Write out a speech to give on the first day of rehearsal with the actors. Be sure to tell the story from your point of view. Inspire

your collaborators. Why this play? Why now? Why this team of artists?
Read this out loud to a colleague or a friend. What resonated for them? What fell flat? Revise and repeat.

In his seminal book, *Start With Why*, Simon Sinek argues that companies are successful when leaders have a clear *why statement* that resonates with their customers. He argues that people connect first with why, then with how, and finally with what.

> We are drawn to leaders and organizations that are good at communicating what they believe. Their ability to make us feel like we belong, to make us feel special, safe and not alone is part of what gives them the ability to inspire us.[4]

Why did you gather these actors and designers? Why start this complex journey? What is the story of the play from your point of view? How can you shine a light on the dark path from first rehearsal to opening night?

Some questions you might ask yourself to help drive a first day speech:

- Why does this play need to be seen now?
- What gives this play beauty?
- Why will this production resonate with this specific audience?
- How do you personally relate to the play?
- Is there a myth that resonates within this play?
- What type of play is this? Comedy? Tragedy? What kind specifically? Political comedy? Family Tragedy?
- What question burns at the center?
- What will be your measure of success?
- What excites you as a director?
- Why are they the right cast for the show?

Speeches don't need to be long to inspire. Lincoln's Gettysburg Address was 272 words. You might not want to read a letter to the company but improvise from notes. Perhaps you don't want to say much of anything before a first reading of the play, but instead lead a discussion afterward that weaves in the ideas you've developed about the play.

Why have you gathered the actors? It's your job to endow them with a sense of purpose.

7. Ground Rules

How do you want to conduct rehearsal? Ask yourself a series of questions about the process. These might include:

- Will you slowly work through the play from the top or throw it together quickly and revisit?
- What do you prize in rehearsal? Expertise? Experimentation? Enthusiasm?
- Should people leave their personal troubles at the door or bring them into the work?
- Is it a new play? How do you see rewrites coming in? When?
- Is there intimacy or violence in the play? How will you rehearse that?
- How will you deal with politically or socially sensitive material?
- Do you know what kind of culture you want to create in the room, or do you want to collaborate on that with your cast?
- Do you want to set an off-book date?
- How do you want to address the basic tenets of professionalism? (Being on time, communication, respect for others)

How do you want to communicate these guidelines?

When working with a cast of student actors, I set guidelines for behavior. Ideally we collaborate on a contract covering when actors should get off book, how to handle lateness, how people will speak to each other, and what collaboration looks like.

I wonder if professional companies might benefit from the same process. While unions cover some of the ground rules, much is left to the discretion of the director. Often I think seasoned actors assume we are all following a set of established norms, but not everyone shares the same beliefs about process. You might ask if the theatre has a set of protocols.

If you express clear expectations, actors are more likely to meet them. It may seem too formal to set guidelines on the first day. Perhaps you'd rather lead by example and hope the company adopts your attitudes.

On the first day at the very least I outline the rehearsal schedule. I let actors know when we are working, when we will run the play, and set the framework for our time in the room.

8. Initial Practical Work

What do you want to accomplish on the first day? Ask yourself a series of questions:

- Does the theatre company have any expectations you need to meet? Do you understand them?
- How do you want everyone to introduce each other? Name and role in the production? Pronouns? Hometown?
- Are you going to do a first read-through? Are you sure? Is this for the entire theatre company or only the actors?
- Will the team present the design concepts? How?
- Do you want to get to table work the first day?
- Is there music to learn? Dances to start working on?
- Are there world-building exercises you want to try?
- Look ahead to the first two weeks—what must be done on the first day to start the process off right?

The most traditional version of a first day goes something like this:

- Meet and greet with the assembled company, which likely includes designers, but may include the theatre's staff
- A speech by the director about the show
- A design presentation of models, sketches, sounds, music, slides
- A read-through of the entire play
- A dramaturgical presentation of research
- The beginning of table work

This traditional version of a first day offers many benefits. The actors and designers come together for the first time, and often the last time until technical rehearsals. The actors learn about the world the designers created and start to contemplate their own creative journey. By starting with a read-through and table work, the director signals that the script is our starting place for investigation.

Barring any dictates from the theatre, you might skip any of the above. Perhaps you feel that a first read-through for producers and designers puts too much pressure on the actors. Maybe you want to delay designer presentations until after the first read-through or even later. Maybe dancing or singing the first day better serves your production.

How will you know if you want to follow the traditional model or devise an alternative? Only by asking yourself rigorous questions. Own your rehearsal process.

EXPLORING THE TEXT

Some directors like to spend time poring over their scripts with the cast and creative team. For these directors, solid sessions at the table lead to quicker, more secure work on their feet.

9. Reading from Event to Event

Start reading at the top of the first scene. Stop when you hit an event. Remember every entrance and exit is an event. Every major decision is an event. (See pages 49–50 for more information on discovering events.)

At first you may need to stop the actors to let them know where events occur, but eventually they will start to find them on their own.

Discuss the section you just read. Why does the event happen? What happens between the characters? What changes in that section?

Reading event to event organizes my table work. I can engage the entire team in looking for turning points. The ensemble celebrates each discovery as a successfully completed task.

Reading event to event emphasizes the importance of every entrance and exit. When someone new enters the room, the occupants inevitably change course. Events highlight where characters make decisions and encourage actors to change tone and attack. As a group, we discover the rhythm of scenes.

What does it mean if a scene starts with an event every two pages and then all of a sudden accelerates to three or four shifts per page? Why do many characters enter and exit in a scene? Or none?

Some ensembles really dig into this work, becoming a crack team of investigators. Others may find it too stifling and academic. Read your room to see what method of breaking up table work will jazz your company. Maybe you want to only stop when the playwright indicates a scene break? Perhaps you want to stop anytime anyone has a question. Figure out what works for your ensemble.

10. Some Questions to Ask During Table Work

Almost any question can bear fruit during table work. Here are some basic ones to stir discussion:

- Who's in this scene? How are these people connected? What's their relationship like? How long have they known each other? How old are they?
- Where are we? What's in this place? Why are we in this place?
- What's the weather like? What time of day is it? Time of year? How does that affect the scene?
- How is this scene different from the last one we read?
- What changes in this scene?
- What's the basic situation? Is someone coming soon? Or leaving soon? Are we preparing for something? Dealing with new information? Is the situation brand new or something more habitual?
- Why does she speak? Why does he listen? Why are they attacking them?
- Who is chasing whom? Who is driving the scene?
- What does she want? What is he fighting for? What is their action?

Questions spur actors to discover what they are doing and why. By asking lots of questions you encourage all the actors to study the text for evidence. You teach actors that you don't have all the answers.

When I ask questions, I try to engage the entire ensemble at the table, rather than having a private discussion with the actors in the scene. I'm just as happy to hear from the actor playing Pablo about Stanley and Stella's marriage as from the lead actors. You never know what someone has to offer.

The actor playing Stanley may dispute Pablo's assessment of his relationship with Stella, but a healthy discussion over a plot point leads to a creative room. By allowing disciplined disagreements over the script you signal that the text is complex, making a play is a group effort, and there is more than one way to answer a complex question.

11. Dramaturgical Reports

A few weeks before the first rehearsal, send each of your actors on a fact-finding mission. Their task is to research a topic that informs the play and create a short presentation. You may also assign topics to assistant directors, dramaturgs, and anyone else in the room game for an adventure.

Some possible topics for *A Streetcar Named Desire*:

- Southern Plantation life between the World Wars
- New Orleans neighborhoods in 1947
- Louisiana Immigration in the early to mid-1900s
- The role of the Engineer Corps in World War II
- Life of Tennessee Williams
- Work of Tennessee Williams

Encourage your cast and crew to deliver creative and brief presentations. Bring in music or food. Tell a story from their character's perspective. Sit for an interview as a historical person.

What will feed the production? Want to understand Blanche's mental condition at the end of the play? Have a cast member talk about about Williams's family hospitalizing his sister, ordering shock treatments for mental illness.

How far has Stella fallen from the upbringing of her youth? Demonstrating manners of a Southern afternoon tea party or receiving a gentleman caller will spark imaginations.

Mark Wing-Davey first assigned me this task when I was his assistant on *36 Views* by Naomi Iizuka at Berkeley Rep Theatre. The play depicted the conflict between a macho art dealer and a prim scholar of the history of Asian American artwork and poetry. Wanting to impress, I orated a thirty-minute presentation about the history of Japanese fine arts over the centuries. Mark was polite—but made it clear that my presentation was overdone, academic, and unlikely to stick. Encourage creativity and brevity.

CREATING A WORLD

While reading the play over and over, some directors engage the cast in physical work that fleshes out the universe of the play. Often these ensemble exercises are performed in tandem with script analysis at the table. Some create games that help reveal hidden forces at work.

Can you physicalize past events? Are there corporeal ways to reveal character? How can you lead a cast to clearly imagine the settings of the play?

12. Etudes

Actors create etudes by performing structured improvisations around a theme, an event, or a situation. Starting with a clear set of rules delivers the most fruitful improvisations. Some examples: Improvise key past events that impact the present moment of the play. Recreate moments where characters are alone doing some sort of work. Act out a character's worst nightmare.

The ingredients for a successful etude are:

- A specific character or set of characters
- A precise place, time of day, and event
- A definite intention from each actor
- An event or turning point
- A new intention from each actor

Give actors time to create these etudes on their own. Then view them as a group. Discuss what you learned and how these discoveries might inform the playing of the script.

Etudes are a central part of the Russian system of training actors. Actors create short pieces and teachers comment on the students' ability to creatively and truthfully live within imaginary given circumstances. Some directors use etudes to create physical and imaginative staging.

In rehearsal, etudes can help actors ground themselves in the unseen events that drive behavior on stage. If you were going to create a set of etudes for *Streetcar* you might ask actors to invent structured improvisations around:

- The day that Stella left Belle Reve
- The day that Blanche left Belle Reve herself
- The first time Stella and Stanley met
- Mitch sitting with his dying mother
- Some moments from the date between Blanche and Mitch

By acting out these moments, actors will share a physical memory of an incident. If the actor playing Blanche viscerally experiences being abandoned by her sister, she may be able to access her pain more easily.

One could go further and use improvisations to explore characters' hopes and fears. You might ask Blanche to stage a nightmare of herself homeless in the streets of New Orleans. Stella could create both a dream of a happy home with her new baby—and one where she's trapped in an abusive relationship with Stanley.

13. Character Webs

Ask your actors to describe the current state of their relationship with every other character.

Name the literal relationship: son, mother, former lover, teacher. Now, describe why they love the other person. What drives them crazy? What past common experiences do they share? What problem are they trying to solve with the other person?

You may use these character webs in a number of ways:

- Discuss as a group
- Discuss one-on-one with each actor
- Create a group craft project
- Fashion a movement exercise
- Let the actors keep their results a complete secret

The more actors in the cast, the more lines between characters, and the more complicated the web of relationships.

Some actors will naturally treat every other character on stage differently. Others need inspiration. (See 86–88 for the importance of channel work.)

You may want to wait to ask questions about relationships until you are working on scenes with actors. *What's your relationship like with this person now? What do you dream about them? What do you think your current status level is with them? Does that change in the scene?*

You might want to conduct group discussions about shared history and family lines. If you have a crafty cast, create a physical web. Write all the character names on a large piece of paper and connect each name with a line. Above the line write out the most obvious givens: ex-lover, not seen each other in fifteen years, parents. Beware! For a play like *A Streetcar Named Desire* there are ten plus characters meaning almost one-hundred lines to draw.

If your cast learns physically turn this work into a physical exercise: get your cast walking around the room with some vigor and then ask them to move according to their relationships. Head toward people you're attracted to and away from those who repel you. Now, create alliances. Next, move according to relative status.

14. Mapping Space

Divide the cast and creative team into at least three groups. Each group homes in on the specifics of place in an expanding geographical radius. The first group focuses on the home or rooms central to most scenes, the second group concentrates on the surrounding neighborhood, the last examines the entire globe. (See page 64 for an example of running this exercise for *A Streetcar Named Desire*.)

Give each group twenty minutes to comb through the play for clues about geography, create a diagram or map, and present findings to the ensemble.

By asking the group to focus on the specifics of geography, you stimulate actors' imaginations about the world of the play.

I often see student actors enter a scene without having imagined where they are coming from or where they are going. They seem like an actor who has come from off stage, and now is on stage. They don't seem like people existing in a world.

Through effective place work, actors ground themselves in specifics. Imagine a best-case scenario: an actor walks on stage from an unseen fictional part of the house. They bring with them memories of that room and who was in it. When they enter this room they know it well, know what's happened here, how it's typically used. When speaking to a scene partner they connect over some place in the nearby vicinity they've imagined deeply. Finally, the character tells a story about some far-off place the other person has never experienced—bringing the geography to life with sparkling detail.

Hidden worlds lurk just offstage; actors bring them to life through imagination.

SHAPING THE STAGING

After digging into the text and working as a group to create an imagined world, it's time to put some sort of framework on the scenes of the play. How to make the transition from sitting to standing, walking, and interacting? What should directors focus on in their blocking?

15. Running with No Rehearsal

This exercise works best if you surprise the cast.

Either in the afternoon after finishing up table work, or at the top of day, announce that you'll be running the play from top to bottom.

Set up a few guidelines so the ensemble can run without stopping, figuring out challenges in the moment:

- If there's any intimacy, tell the actors to hug each other or make eye contact
- If there's violence, simulate the fight without actually touching
- No speaking except for lines from the play
- Actors may enter and exit from anywhere
- Indicate a general playing space

- People may bring on simple furniture and props or mime the essentials
- Have Fun!

Typically, some folks will be confused, others excited, and a few completely terrified. I encourage you to rip off the Band-Aid and say: "Okay, let's go!" (See page 73 for my experiences with this technique.)

I don't recommend taking too many detailed notes on this run, and I definitely wouldn't give any prescriptive notes afterward. Here's what I watch for:

- What areas of the stage do people gravitate toward? Ignore or avoid?
- What relationships are clear right off the bat? Muddy?
- What scenes felt like they already played clearly? Which were completely confusing?
- What did we learn about pacing? Where was it exciting? Where did it lag?
- Who came ready to play? Who was flummoxed? Who did their homework?

Remember, this isn't a final performance. Actors, like students, learn differently and at different paces. Someone who's hot out of the gate may stall out. An actor who is timid at the beginning might develop a layered performance over time.

Afterwards I like to start a ritual: the post-run-through check in.

All the actors and creatives circle up and I ask, *How did it go?* People are encouraged to give a brief one- or two-sentence report. People hear that some ensemble members loved the run, while others were stymied. We perform this ritual after every run, checking in with each other on our progress.

16. Preparing for Staging

Before working on a scene for the first time ask yourself questions about the structure and purpose of the section:

- Who's in the scene?
- Where are they? When does the scene take place?

- When did they last see each other?
- If they are entering—where from?
- If they exit—where to?
- If they start on stage—how long have they been there? Doing what?
- What's the tone? How is it different from the scene before and after?
- Where does this scene take place in the arc of the play?
- Where are the major events or beat shifts?
- How is the beginning of the scene different than the end?
- Do you have clear images or hunches about how people relate to each other and the space physically?
- Does the dialogue of the scene indicate any specific physical business or behavior?
- Have you investigated the author's stage directions?

Read the scene over once or twice. Try to visualize it but leave space for new choices the actors will bring.

As actors transition from the table to their feet, directors provide structure.

At first blush, the initial meeting between Stella and Blanche seems daunting to tackle. Approximately twenty minutes long, the scene brims with exposition, seemingly repetitive behavior, and static dialogue. Without understanding how the scene works the beginning of your play could drag.

Beginning: Blanche alone in the dark trying to get a hold of herself. Stella bursts in and embraces her warmly.

Ending: Stella runs from the room in despair and shock.

Major events:

- Blanche criticizes Stella's apartment
- Stella tells Blanche she only has two rooms
- Blanche reveals that their ancestral home Belle Reve was lost
- Blanche berates Stella for having left her alone

Known physical actions:

- The sisters hug
- Stella turns on a light, and Blanche commands her to turn it off immediately

- Blanch grabs a bottle of liquor, Stella pours for them
- Stella shows Blanche Stanley's picture
- Stella runs off into the bathroom to escape

Finally, consider the stage directions. On a new play with a playwright in the room, have a conversation about the stage directions. How much does the writer value them specifically? Do they want them enacted completely, or should we experiment? If you're working on an established play, know that some stage directions are actually notes the stage manager recorded during the first production. These movements and staging ideas worked for that production, on that set, with those actors.

If I'm dealing with an established play and I'm confident that the playwright wrote the stage directions, I've started to consider these as *proposals* from the author. When these proposals are helpful, I follow their intentions. But sometimes stage directions dim a scene's potential by overprescribing the final result. I love stage directions I don't fully understand but provoke my imagination.

Right at the top of the scene Williams proposes that the sisters, "*catch each other in a spasmodic embrace.*" When I was directing the play, we tried to embody that direction. They hugged and released, hugged and released, setting the tone for an uneasy sisterly encounter.

17. Some Questions to Ask Your Staging

Ask these questions as you prepare to stage the play, after your first sketch, and before heading into technical rehearsals.

- Have you used every part of the stage or are you stuck center stage too often?
- If you turned the sound off on your play could you understand it?
    - Would you recognize relationships?
    - Does status come across?
    - Do you know where you are?
    - Does the story progress physically as well as emotionally?
- Have you placed each scene in the most effective part of the stage?
- Have you highlighted the most important moments?
- Are you spending too much time on non-essential business?
- Do you recognize your staging as truthful?

- Have you created beauty? Metaphor?
- Can you simplify?

Give this list to a dramaturg or assistant director. Embolden them to check your work.

I encourage you to evaluate your staging using two tools: a ground plan or model and the moment chain.

Take the time to understand what you're looking at on a ground plan. How wide is the stage? Where are the entrances and exits? Where are places to sit, move, or create business? Imagine groupings of actors, movement across the stage, and transitions between scenes.

See Exercise 5 for Jon Jory's insights on the moment chain—a list of the twenty-four or so most important events in your play. Armed with your moment chain, march through your play point by point and plot where each situation plays out. Have you staged three important events in a row at the same place on stage? Can you change one? Where's the most crucial event of each act happening? Way up in a corner? In the audience's lap?

DETAILING SCENE WORK

If you've done a first pass on your play, creating a bare bones sketch, now is the time to dig into each scene and unlock it's dramatic, comic, and human potential. How can you help actors create lively, surprising scenes they can perform every night?

18. The Laws of Attraction

In their simply readable book, *Notes on Directing*, Terry Hauser and Russel Reich propose two simple rules that put together can solve almost every scene:

> Every scene is a chase scene...Usually, when someone chases someone else they move toward their object, and the object, feeling the pressure, moves away. Blocking, that obscure mystery, is simply that.
>
> Ask: Is it nice or nasty? Big or little?...If it's nice, you tend to move towards me, however slightly. If it's nasty, you move away. If you don't move at all, you're dead.[5]

Watch your scene. Who is chasing whom? Who is evading? Who thinks someone is nice? Nasty?

Several colleagues told me they directed entire plays using these two simple ideas.

By imagining every scene as a chase scene, you simplify Stanislavski's ideas about action, task, and obstacle. Character A wants something from Character B. Character B doesn't want to give it up—so we have dramatic conflict. Directing scenes with the whiff of a chase adds suspense and dramatic tension—will Character A get the prize? Will Character B give in? Every time Character B evades or dodges the advances of Character A, they must try a new tactic or approach. A never-ending chase with twists and turns leads to variety of action. Does flattery work? No? How about guilt? Berating? Sheer Force?

If you look at Blanche and Stanley's second scene when he grills her about the loss of Belle Reve, the chase switches directions at least twice. At first, Blanche chases Stanley by shamelessly flirting with him, trying to keep him off the subject of her past troubles. Stanley demurs, then questions Blanche, and eventually yells out: "Now let's cut the re-bop!"[6]

Now Stanley goes on the hunt. He wants answers, papers, and proof of what happened to an estate he had a financial stake in. His chase moves are more direct and blunter and eventually lead him to grab the papers he wants.

Using the laws of attraction, Blanche sees Stanley as *nice* during the first part of the scene. The language indicates that she's constantly approaching him, flirting with him, and closing in. Stanley definitely views Blanche as *nasty* and evades her again and again.

19. Coaching Actors

As you delve into the details of scene work, here are some questions to ask your actors:

- What is the current state of your relationships?
- What do you want from the other person? What obstacle stands in your way? What does winning look like? What will it cost you if you lose?
- What's the time of day? Season? Time of year?
- How are you affected by this space? Is it a place you know?

- What's happened in the last twenty-four hours?
- What are the key given circumstances that affect the scene?
- Where are the key decision points in the scene?
- Are you carrying any secrets?
- Are there opportunities for humor?

Read the scene with these questions in mind. You may want to keep a list of key given circumstances at hand.

Coaching acting and helping each cast member build a performance is an ongoing job that starts from the first audition and continues after opening. Sometimes actors attack a scene from the beginning and know exactly what to do. Best to stay out of their way. Most of the time, actors need help.

After a first sketch of a scene, start to home in on discreet moments. Look at the structure of each beat. What is the beginning? What is the end? How does it change? Asking these questions helps your actors specify their performances. Focusing on tiny beats builds moment to moment life.

Concentrate on a tiny moment in the interchange between Blanche and Stanley at the end of scene two: we see Stanley digging through Blanche's trunk for legal papers but finding love letters instead.

(He rips off the ribbon and starts to examine them. Blanche snatches them from him, and they cascade to the floor.)
Blanche: Now that you've touched them I'll burn them!
Stanley: What in hell are they?
Blanche: Poems a dead boy wrote. I hurt him the way that you would like to hurt me, but you can't! I'm not young and vulnerable anymore. But my young husband was and I—never mind about that! Just give them back to me!
Stanley: What do you mean by saying you'll have to burn them?
Blanche: I'm sorry, I must have lost my head for a moment. Everyone has something he won't let others touch because of their—intimate nature ...
(She now seems faint with exhaustion and she sits down with the strong box and puts on a pair of glasses and goes methodically through a large stack of papers.)[7]

These two stage directions and five lines pack in as much action as some entire plays. We start with Blanche hysterically pawing at her papers, attacking Stanley savagely. In the middle she accuses him of wanting to destroy her, then she settles into the mundane task of digging through legal documents. Their relationship has altered now that she's named Stanley as dangerous and herself as vulnerable. All in the space of thirty seconds.

Questions you can ask actors to help guide specific choices: What does she want? What's the obstacle? Where is she? What do those papers mean to her? How does Stanley affect her?

Start asking these questions and you can carve out a specific moment of drama. Craft hundreds of moments and your production will sparkle with life.

20. Troubleshooting Scenes

You view a scene. You know it's not working. What can you do? Here's a list of questions:

- Should you try changing where characters enter from? What about the exit?
- Are the status roles clear? Do they change?
- What happening at the beginning of the scene? The end? Are they different?
- Is the pace off? Are people rushing their decisions? Or slowing down where they should be driving?
- Is every moment of the scene given the same weight? How can you find variety?
- Is the scene playing the same as the scene before or after?
- Have the actors forgotten a key given circumstance?
- Are the actors playing for emotion rather than action?
- Do the actors understand what they are saying and why?
- Do they need some sort of physical business?

Don't be afraid to use the same tools over and over. Or to surprise yourself with new diagnostic techniques.

When I was speaking with Anne Bogart she related a story about Broadway director Jack O'Brien visiting one of her classes. He was speaking to a group of MFA directors:

He said, *You know what a director's job is? Fix it. Just fix it.* I thought, *Oh fuck you, that's so true.*

For my Chekhov scene study class, I ask MFA directors to tackle half of an act of one of the Russian modernist's classic plays. First, they analyze the scene, identifying given circumstances and events. Next, they rehearse for a few hours to create a rough draft. I'll watch the showing, give a few notes, then start to work on the scene myself, using the same actors.

I always tell my students not to be impressed if I happen to unlock some of the dramatic tension in the scene or help the story make more sense. Working on a scene is like trying to open a stuck pickle jar. The student director has tried to unscrew the lid for hours and I come in in the last moment and open it up. They did the hard work, I just moved it one more millimeter.

I rely on some techniques over and over:

- Trust Chekhov's rhythms and don't put in pauses except where he indicates
- Follow Chekhov's cues about stakes—usually scenes are time-compressed for a reason
- Every entrance and exit completely changes the world
- People almost never get what they want, but they also never give up
- Know the problem but play the solution

But what's also true about this work is what's true of most scene work. You don't actually know what will unlock a scene until you try it. What worked one day with one actor most likely won't work the next time with a different actor.

Trial and error: another definition for rehearsal.

CREATING A REHEARSAL SCHEDULE

You should collaborate with your stage management team, but ultimately the director chooses how to spend their time in rehearsal. What you do with your limited time in the room determines the kind of show you'll create.

21. Planning Your Time

Look at the amount of time the theatre has given you. Examine your play. How will you get from the first rehearsal in the room to the first technical rehearsal?
- Are there special circumstances in your play that will take extra time? When do you want to work on them? How long will they take? For example:
  - Music
  - Dance
  - Fights
  - Intimacy
  - Large crowd scenes
- Does your play have complicated language? Do you want to unravel the intricacies up front or as you go?
- Do you want to build slowly or make a few passes through the play?
- When are designer run-throughs? How many does the theatre require?
- How much of the play can you discover in the rehearsal room and what will you need to leave for tech?
- Where can you build in flexibility?

Make a draft with your stage management team. Show it to a producer or an assistant director—did you leave anything out? (See Appendix 4 for a Sample Rehearsal Schedule)

For student directors, this is one of the most important skills to develop—how to use time effectively. I see directors falter on both ends of the spectrum: some plan to the minute and others blunder forward hoping it all works out.

Those who plan too closely end up treating every scene with the same weight. They divide the hours allotted by the number of pages and march forward. While this makes some sense, inevitably directors discover that some scenes need twice as much time as others. Typically, directors can't predict which moments will work after one pass, and which will need countless hours to unlock.

More often, I see directors panic as they head into tech behind schedule. They show up each day and keep working forward without a plan for how to assemble their show before technical rehearsals.

These days I try to find a balance between the two. I create a schedule that allows us to get to a run quickly. I leave the rest of the time flexible. Once I see a run-through, I'll know how to allot the rest of my hours.

I've put this prompt last because I hope you'll take some time to examine your rehearsal process before you create a schedule. Do you want to move quickly or slowly? Are you going to spend more time analyzing the script or staging scenes? What kind of room do you want to run? How will you achieve that atmosphere?

How do you rehearse a play?

NOTES

1 Katie Mitchell, *The Director's Craft* (New York: Routledge, 2009), 12.
2 Tennessee Williams, *A Streetcar Named Desire* (1947. Reprint, New York: Book-of-the-Month Club, Inc., 1994), 113.
3 Jon Jory, *Tips: Ideas for Directors* (Hanover: Smith and Kraus, 2002), 247.
4 Simon Sinek, *Start with Why* (New York: Penguin Books, 2009), 55.
5 Terry Hauser and Russel Reich, *Notes on Directing* (New York: RCR Creative Press, 2003), 33, 35.
6 Williams, 138.
7 Williams, 115.

Appendices

APPENDIX I

Brecht's Phases of Production[1]

In 1952 Brecht's Berliner Ensemble published *Theaterarbeit* or *Theatre Work*, an account of their productions from 1949–1951. The book emphasizes the practical over the theoretical, including Brecht's outline of the stages necessary to create a play. Below I've presented his outline, paraphrasing and simplifying his language.

1. Analysis of the play
    a. Summarize the script in half a page. Divide it into easy to understand episodes and identify the key events of the narrative. How can you easily tell the story and emphasize the social significance?
2. First discussion of the setting
    a. Create sketches for each scene, emphasizing the stage pictures. What kind of set will you need to accommodate these pictures?
3. Casting
    a. Choose reality over theatrical convention. Hopefully you can re-cast the play if you make discoveries in rehearsal.
4. Reading rehearsal
    a. Actors read the script with no emotion, just to familiarize themselves with the story. Hand out the director analysis.
5. Positioning rehearsal
    a. Actors and director try out different ideas for groupings, stage pictures, gestures, and movement. Actors may start to make specific character choices.
6. Set rehearsal
    a. The work from the positioning rehearsals helps the set designer refine their designs. Now actors use doors, props, tables, and any other necessary set pieces in rehearsal.
7. Rehearsal of details
    a. Actors fill in character specifics, staging details are rehearsed. Pacing is ignored for now.
8. Run-throughs
    a. The focus of the run-through is continuity and balance, not speed.

9. **Discussion of costume and masks**
    a. Now that character specific choices have emerged in rehearsals, costume designers begin the work of creating clothes.
10. **Checking rehearsal**
    a. Make sure the social significance of each event is coming across. Polish and refine.
11. **Tempo rehearsals**
    a. Conducted in costume, the pace is finally set.
12. **Dress rehearsals**
    a. All the technical elements are incorporated.
13. **Speed throughs**
    a. Gestures are indicated, all the lines spoken very quickly.
14. **Previews**
    a. Watching the audience and hopefully discussing with them afterward. More revisions based on what was learned.
15. **Opening**
    a. The producer is not allowed to attend so the actors may feel free and not judged.

NOTE

1 Bertolt Brecht, *Brecht on Theatre: The Development of an Aesthetic*, edited and translated by John Willet (New York: Hill and Wang, 1964), 240–242.

APPENDIX 2

Kimberly Senior's List of Run-Through Targets: An Edited Selection

- No judgment of your own character
- Activate the language
- Love your scene partner
- Find access to joy
- Connect the dots of thought for your character
- Who has the status in every moment of the play?
- Who is your line intended for?
- Simplify
- Play to win
- Spend it all—to raise the stakes
- Defend your ideals
- Precision of beats and language
- Pay attention to details
- Going *bigger*—Big Nice or Big Nasty (see Exercise 18 for Reich/Hauser on this idea)
- Today is the day
- Find the opposites (both within your character and in your intentions)
- Generosity: share the play with the audience
- Stay on task no matter what
- Seek the obstacles
- Keep your secrets
- Use the right tool for the job
- When in doubt, choose love
- Be the best attorney for your character
- Surprise your scene partner
- Form alliances
- Aggressive listening: find your next line in what just happened on stage
- 360-degree awareness: emotionally and physically
- Whose play is it? *Your* play. Place yourself at the center of the story.
- Find the danger
- The last scene of the play is the first of the next

- What do you drive into the scene with? What's the detour?
- Lean into the discomfort
- Hold on to optimism as long as you can
- Efficiency, economy of language, action, movement
- Crave intimacy

APPENDIX 3

A Streetcar Named Desire: Moment Chain

28 Moments Over Three Acts

ACT 1

1. Blanche arrives at the Kowalski's.
2. Blanche tells Stella Belle Reve is lost, blaming her for leaving.
3. Blanche flirts with Stanley—squirts him with atomizer.
4. Blanche gives Belle Reve papers to Stanley.
5. When Stella asks Stanley to break up card game, he refuses.
6. Mitch puts Blanche's lantern on the light bulb.
7. Stanley hits Stella.
8. Stella goes back to Stanley.
9. Blanche implores Stella to not hang back with the apes as Stanley eavesdrops.
10. Stella embraces Stanley in front of Blanche.

ACT 2

11. Blanche denies knowing a man named Shaw to Stanley.
12. Blanche tells Stella she can't turn the trick anymore.
13. Blanche kisses the young man.
14. Mitch asks Blanche how old she is.
15. Blanche reveals her first husband killed himself then crouches as train passes.
16. Mitch and Blanche kiss.

ACT 3

17. Stanley tells Stella Mitch won't marry Blanche.
18. Stanley smashes his plate, cup, and saucer.
19. When Stanley gives Blanche a ticket to Laurel, she runs to throw up.
20. Stella asks to be taken to hospital.
21. Mitch turns on the light to take a good look at Blanche.
22. Mitch tries to kiss Blanche.
23. Stanley says he's been onto Blanche from the start.
24. Blanche crouches as a locomotive passes and Stanley comes out in pajamas.

25. Stanley forcibly carries Blanche towards bed.
26. Blanche is pinned by the matron.
27. Doctor takes off his hat.
28. Stella cries while holding her baby as Blanche leaves.

APPENDIX 4

Sample Rehearsal Schedule

SUNDAY	MONDAY	TUESDAY	WEDNESDAY	THURSDAY	FRIDAY	SATURDAY
		May 1 First rehearsal Meet and greet	2 Table work Dance/Fights	3 Table work Dance/Fights	4 Table work Dance/Fight	5 Surprise Run-through! Start Staging
6 Continue Staging	7 **Day Off**	8 Continue Staging	9 Continue Staging	10 Run First act Review Dance/Fights	11 Continue Staging	12 Continue Staging
13 Review dance/fights **First Run**	14 **Day Off**	15 Detailed scene work	16 Detailed scene work	17 Review dance/fights Run First act	18 Detailed scene work	19 Detailed Scene work
20 Review dance/fights Designer Run	21 **Day Off**	22 Work Run Act 1	23 Work Run Act 2	24 Work Final Run	25 Work in theatre space	26 Tech
27 Tech	28 **Day Off**	29 Tech Dress Run	30 First Preview	31 Work time 2nd Preview	June 1 Work Time 3rd Preview	2 Work time 4th Preview
3 5th Preview	4 **Day Off**	5 Tech Day	6 Work 6th Preview	7 Work 7th Preview	8 **Opening Night!**	

Sample Rehearsal Schedule

This rehearsal schedule moves from first rehearsal to opening night in just about a month and is predicated on many assumptions:

- I imagined a set of fights and dances that could be worked in the first week and then reviewed in the weeks after. I chose fights and dances, but this could be time for dialect work, singing, specific movement exercises, intimacy, and so on.

- I assumed the director wanted a few days of table work in the beginning
- I threw in a surprise run-through!
- I assumed the theatre wanted a designer run-through a week before tech
- I gave a lot of time for previews and work during previews—this is quite generous. Many theatres would open by June 2 or 3 without a second week of work. I have found that on new plays especially, this second week is invaluable.

This is only one model of rehearsal and I purposely didn't put in rehearsal hours as either the union contract, university policies, or theatre practices will dictate when and how long you can rehearse.

Bibliography

Alfreds, Mike. *Different Every Night*. London: Nick Hern Books Ltd, 2007.
Aristotle. *Poetics*. Translated by Malcolm Heath. London: Penguin Books, 1996.
Ball, William. *A Sense of Direction*. Hollywood, CA: Quite Specific Media Group Ltd., 1984.
Bogart, Anne. *A Director Prepares: Seven Essays on Art and Theatre*. New York: Routledge, 2001.
Bogart, Anne and Tina Landau. *The Viewpoints Book: A Practical Guide to Viewpoints and Composition*. New York: Theatre Communications Group, 2005.
Brecht, Bertolt. *Brecht on Theatre: The Development of an Aesthetic*. Edited and Translated by John Willett. Frankfurt: Suhrkamp Verlag, 1957. Reprint: New York: Hill and Wang, 1964.
Brook, Peter. *The Empty Space*. New York: Touchstone, 1968.
Brook, Peter. "Lear Log," *The Tulane Drama Review*, 8(2) by Charles Marowitz. Winter, 1963.
Chekhov, Anton. *A Life in Letters*. Edited by Rosamund Barlett, 111–112. Translated by Rosamund Barlett and Anthony Phillips. London: Penguin Books, 2004.
Chekhov, Anton. *Chekhov: The Four Major Plays: Seagull, Uncle Vanya, Three Sisters, Cherry Orchard*. Translated by Curt Columbus. Chicago: Ivan R. Dee, 2005.
Dean, Alexander and Lawrence Carra. *Fundamentals of Play Directing*. New York: Holt, Rinhart, and Winston Inc., 1941.
Duke of Saxe-Meiningen, George II. "Pictorial Motion." In: *Directors on Directing*. Edited by Toby Cole and Helen Krich-Chinoy, 81. New York: Macmillan Publishing Company, 1953.
Fuegi, John. *Bertolt Brecht: Chaos According to Plan*. New York: Cambridge University Press, 1987.
Hauser, Terry and Russell Reich. *Notes on Directing*. New York: RCR Creative Press, 2003.

Jory, Jon. *Tips: Ideas for Directors*. Hanover, NH: Smith and Kraus, 2002.
Kaufman, Moisés and Barbara Pitts McAdams. *Moment Work: Tectonic Theater Project's Process of Devising Theater*. New York: Vintage Books, 2018.
Koller, Ann Marie. *The Theatre Duke: George II of Saxe-Meiningen and the German Stage*. Stanford: Stanford University Press, 1984.
Mitchell, Katie. *The Director's Craft: A Handbook for the Theatre*. New York: Routledge, 2009.
Sinek, Simon. *Start with Why*. New York: Penguin Books, 2009.
Stanislavski, Konstantin. *An Actor's Work*. Translated and edited by Jean Benedetti. Oxon: Routledge, 2008.
Stanislavski, Konstantin. *My Life in Art*. Translated by J. J. Robbins. 1924. Reprint: New York: Routledge/Theatre Arts Books, 1996.
Toporkov, Vasili. *Stanislavski in Rehearsal*. Translated by Jean Benedetti. New York: Routledge, 2004.
Williams, Tennessee. *A Streetcar Named Desire*. 1947. Reprint: New York: Book-of-the-Month Club, Inc., 1994.
Ziegler, Anna. *Boy*. New York: Dramatists Play Service, 2016.

List of Interviews

Bogart, Anne. Personal Interview. January 22, 2018.
Buxbaum Danzig, Leslie. Personal Interview. September 18, 2017.
Carden, Stuart. Personal Interview. June 3, 2019.
Chavkin, Rachel. Skype Interview. January 8, 2018.
Columbus, Curt. Phone Interviews: September 18, 2017 and November 4, 2017. Email interview: August 1, 2019.
Davis, Will. Personal Interview. November 9, 2017.
Ellis, Scott. Personal Interview. January 28. 2018.
Falls, Robert. Personal Interview. July 12, 2017.
Fondakowski, Leigh. Phone Interview. August 17, 2018.
Frecknall, Rebecca. Personal Interview. March 22, 2018.
Gaines, Barbara. Personal Interview. July 11, 2019.
Garcés, Michael John. Phone Interview. September 21, 2017.
Garrett, Nataki. Personal Interview. December 4, 2017.
Icke, Robert. Skype Interview. May 24, 2018.
Kauffman, Anne. Personal Interview. January 21, 2018.
Kramer, Daniel. Personal Interview. March 20, 2018.
Krymov, Dmitry. Personal Interview. June 24, 2017.
Kulick, Brian. Personal Interview: January 21, 2018. Email interview: August 1, 2019.
Luscombe, Chris. Personal Interview. March 20, 2018.
Marting, Kristin. Phone Interview. August 8, 2018.
Newell, Charles. Personal Interview. June 21, 2018.
O'Hara, Robert. Personal Interview. February 2, 2017.
Parson, Ron OJ. Personal Interviews. November 8, 2017 and July 1, 2019.
Portes, Lisa. Personal Interviews. August 10, 2017 and July 8, 2019.
Posner, Aaron. Personal Interview. April 11, 2018.
Rauch, Bill. Phone Interview. November 18, 2017.
Rhoads, Julia. Personal Interview. July 18, 2018.
Rubinstein, Kim. Phone Interview. July 9, 2018.
Sanders, Derrick L. Personal Interview. August 28, 2017.

Senior, Kimberly. Personal Interview: June 28, 2018. Phone interview: August 3, 2019.
Silverman, Leigh. Personal Interview. January 22, 2018.
Taichman, Rebecca. Personal Interview. January 22, 2018.
Thebus, Jessica. Personal Interviews. September 27, 2017 and July 17, 2019.
Van Hove, Ivo. Phone Interview. December 1, 2017.
Vargas, Jorge Arturo. Personal Interview. October 25, 2017.
Wing-Davey, Mark. Phone interviews. September 18, 2018 and August 1, 2019.
Yew, Chay. Personal Interview. August 8, 2017.
Younis, Madani. Personal Interview. March 21, 2018.

Biographies of Interviewees

Anne Bogart is the Co-Artistic Director of the SITI Company, which she founded with Japanese director Tadashi Suzuki in 1992. She is the Head of Directing at Columbia University and the author of several books, including *A Director Prepares*; *The Viewpoints Book: A Practical Guide to Viewpoints and Composition*; *And Then, You Act*; *Conversations with Anne*; and *What's the Story: Essays about Art, Theater and Storytelling*. Her work with the SITI Company includes *Persians*, *Steel Hammer*, *A Rite*, *Café Variations*, *Trojan Women*, *American Document*, *Antigone*, *Freshwater Under Construction*, *Who Do You Think You Are*, and *Radio Macbeth*, among many others. Bogart is the recipient of three Honorary Doctorates from Skidmore College, Bard College, and Cornish College. She was a recipient of the Doris Duke Performing Artist Award, the Richard B. Fisher Award, a USA Fellowship, a Rockefeller Fellowship, a Guggenheim Fellowship, and received the 2016 Alfred Drake Award from Brooklyn College.

Stuart Carden is the Artistic Director of Kansas City Repertory Theatre. He specializes in new plays as well as devised theater. He has worked with City Theatre Company, The Old Globe, Lyric Opera of Chicago, The Second City, The New Victory Theater, Williamstown Theatre Festival, Writers Theatre, People's Light, ArtsEmerson, Virgin Voyages, The Repertory Theatre of St. Louis, Philadelphia Theatre Company, and Chicago Children's Theatre. Stuart earned his BA in Theatre from Hanover College, USA, and his MFA in Directing at Carnegie Mellon University, USA.

Rachel Chavkin is the Tony Award–winning Director of *Hadestown*. She is also a dramaturg, writer, and the founding Artistic

Director of the TEAM in Brooklyn, NY. Since its founding in 2004, Chavkin has directed/co-authored all of the TEAM's work, including *RoosevElvis* and *Mission Drift*. Chavkin regularly collaborates with writers and composers on new work (including composer Dave Malloy, whose collaboration on the electro-pop opera *Natasha, Pierre, and the Great Comet of 1812* earned the two an Obie award). Chavkin is a New York Theatre Workshop Usual Suspect, an Artistic Associate at London's Gate Theatre, an alum of Soho Rep.'s Writer/Director Lab, The Drama League Directors Project, the Women's Project Director's Lab, and a New Georges Affiliate Artist. She has also taught directing and performance at NYU, Pace University, and other colleges, as well as workshops with the TEAM about their collaborative process.

Curt Columbus became Trinity Repertory Company's fifth Artistic Director in January 2006. He is also the Artistic Director of the Brown/Trinity MFA programs in Acting and Directing. His directing credits for Trinity include *Beowulf: A Thousand Years of Baggage*, *Middletown*, *Vanya and Sonia and Masha and Spike*, *The Merchant of Venice*, *His Girl Friday*, *Camelot*, *Cabaret*, *Blithe Spirit*, *A Christmas Carol*, *Cherry Orchard*, and the world premieres of *The Completely Fictional, Utterly True, Final Strange Tale of Edgar Allan Poe* and *Social Creatures*. Trinity has been home to the world premieres of three of his plays: *Paris by Night*, *The Dreams of Antigone*, and *Sparrow Grass*. Trinity has also produced his translations of Chekhov's *The Cherry Orchard* and *Ivanov*, as well as Feydeau's *A Flea in Her Ear* and Lope de Vega's *Like Sheep to Water (Fuente Ovejuna)*. His adaptation of Dostoevsky's *Crime and Punishment* (with Marilyn Campbell) has won awards and accolades at theaters around the United States, the United Kingdom, and Australia. His translation of Chekhov's *Three Sisters*, developed at the Arden Theatre Company in Philadelphia, is now published by Dramatists Play Service, as is his play, *Sparrow Grass*, and his translations of Chekhov's other major plays, *Seagull*, *Uncle Vanya*, *The Cherry Orchard*, and *Ivanov*. Curt lives in Providence, Rhode Island with his husband, Nate Watson.

Leslie Buxbaum Danzig is a Co-Founder of the Chicago-based 500 Clown, where she co-created and Directed *500 Clown Macbeth*, *500 Clown Frankenstein*, *500 Clown Christmas*, and *500 Clown* *and the Elephant Deal*. She is also a Collaborating Director with Julia Rhoads/Lucky Plush Productions, where she co-created the dance-theater productions *The Better Half* and *The Queue*, both of which received a National Dance Project Award and a National Performance Network Creation and Development Fund Award (2012 and 2014). She received her BA from Brown University, USA, and a PhD in Performance Studies at Northwestern University, USA. She trained in physical theater at Écoles Jacques Lecoq and Philippe Gaulier, Paris. She is the curator of The Richard and Mary L. Gray Center for Arts and Inquiry at the University of Chicago, a laboratory where artists and scholars experiment with forms of collaboration.

Will Davis is a Director and Choreographer focused on physically adventurous new work. Projects include *Men on Boats* by Jaclyn Backhaus for Clubbed Thumb's Summerworks, and a remounted version of that production for Playwrights Horizons. *Orange Julius* by Basil Kreimendahl, Mike Iveson's *Sorry Robot* for PS122's COIL Festival and two productions of *Colossal*, by Andrew Hinderaker for Mixed Blood Theatre and the Olney Theatre Center, for which he won a Helen Hayes Award for Outstanding Direction. Will has developed, directed, and performed his work with New York Theatre Workshop, the New Museum, the Alliance Theatre, the Playwright's Realm, the Fusebox Festival, New Harmony Project, the Orchard Project, the Ground Floor Residency at Berkeley Repertory Theatre, Performance Studies International at Stanford University, and the Kennedy Center. Will holds a BFA in Theatre Studies from DePaul University, USA, and an MFA in Directing from UT Austin, USA.

Scott Ellis is the Adams Associate Artistic Director of Roundabout Theatre Company in New York City. His Broadway credits include *Tootsie*, *The Mystery Of Edwin Drood*, *The Elephant Man*, *Harvey*, *Curtains* (Tony Nomination, Best Direction of a Musical), *The Little Dog Laughed* (Lucille Lortel Award nomination), *Twelve Angry Men* (Tony Award and Drama Desk nominations), *1776* (Drama Desk, Outer Critics Circle and Tony Award nominations), *Company*, and *Steel Pier* (Drama Desk, Outer Critics Circle, and Tony Award nominations), among many others. His Off-Broadway credits include: *Gruesome*

Playground Injuries, The Understudy, Streamers, and *The World Goes 'Round ... The Songs of Kander and Ebb* (Drama Desk Award and Outer Critics Circle nomination). Ellis was the Executive Producer for Showtime's *Weeds,* and has directed for *Modern Family, Nurse Jackie, The Good Wife, Hung, 30 Rock* (Emmy Nomination, Outstanding Directing For A Comedy Series), *Desperate Housewives, The Closer,* and *Frasier.*

Robert Falls is a Tony Award and Drama Desk Award–winning Director. Falls has served as the Artistic Director of Goodman Theatre in Chicago since 1986. At Goodman Theatre, he has directed more than thirty major productions and produced/co-produced more than 200 plays and 100 premieres. Broadway credits include *American Buffalo, Talk Radio* (Tony Award–nominated), *Shining City, The Night of the Iguana, The Young Man from Atlanta* (Tony Award–nominated), *Death of a Salesman* (Tony Award–winning, including Best Director of a Play), *Aida* (Tony Award–winning), and *Long Day's Journey into Night* (Tony Award–winning). Falls's work has been seen at Abbey Theatre, Lyric Opera of Chicago, Lincoln Center Theater, Metropolitan Opera Company, Manhattan Theatre Club, Playwrights Horizon, New York Shakespeare Festival, and Guthrie Theatre, among others. Robert was inducted into the American Theatre Hall of Fame in 2016.

Leigh Fondakowski was the Head Writer of *The Laramie Project* and is a member of Tectonic Theater Project. She is an Emmy-nominated Co-Screenwriter for the adaptation of *The Laramie Project* for HBO, and a co-writer of *The Laramie Project: Ten Years Later.* Her play, *The People's Temple,* has been performed under her direction at American Theatre Company, Berkeley Repertory Theatre, and Guthrie Theater, and received the Glickman Award for Best New Play in the Bay Area in 2005. Another original play, *I Think I Like Girls,* premiered at Encore Theatre Company in San Francisco under her direction and was voted one of the Top 10 plays of 2002 by *The Advocate.* Fondakowski is a 2007 recipient of the National Endowment for the Arts/Theatre Communications Group Theatre Residency Program for Playwrights and a 2009 Macdowell Colony Fellow. She was an Imagine Fund fellow and guest lecturer at the University of Minnesota in 2010 where she completed her play, *Casa Cushman*, about 19th century American actress Charlotte Cushman. She co-directed *The Laramie Cycle* at the Brooklyn Academy of Music with Moisés Kaufman and wrote and directed *Spill* at TimeLine Theatre Company.

Rebecca Frecknall is the award-winning Director of *Summer and Smoke* on London's West End. After training at Goldsmiths, LAMDA, and on the National Theatre Studio's Directors Course, she received a Jerwood Assistant Director Bursary to train at the Young Vic Theatre. In 2015 she won the acclaimed Regional Theatre's Young Directors Scheme Bursary at Northern Stage and in 2016 won the Michael Grandage Company Futures Bursary. Under the direction of Rupert Goold, she was the Associate Director and later the Resident Director for *Ink*, which appeared at both the Duke of York's Theatre and the Almeida Theatre. Other directing credits include *From Morning to Midnight* (Bridewell Theatre); *Educating Rita* (Durham Gala Theatre & Cinema); *Julie*; *What Are They Like?*; *Idomeneus* (Northern Stage); and *Three Sisters* at the Almeida Theatre.

Barbara Gaines is the longtime Artistic Director of Chicago Shakespeare. After an acting career that spanned two decades, she founded the theatre company in 1986. Since then, she has directed nearly sixty plays, thirty of them being Shakespeare's. Her honors include the 2008 Tony Award for outstanding Regional Theatre, the prestigious Honorary OBE (Officer of the Most Excellent Order of the British Empire) in recognition of her work in strengthening British-American cultural relations, as well as multiple Joseph Jefferson Awards for Best Production and Best Director. Gaines has directed at the Royal Shakespeare Company in Stratford-on-Avon, Lyric Opera of Chicago, and The Old Globe in San Diego.

Michael John Garcés is the Artistic Director of Cornerstone Theater Company in Los Angeles, where he has directed *Urban Rez* by Larissa FastHorse, *California: The Tempest* by Alison Carey, *Plumas Negras* by Juliette Carillo, *Café Vida* by Lisa Loomer, and *Three Truths* by Naomi Iizuka. He is a company member at Woolly Mammoth Theatre in Washington, DC, where he has directed *The Arsonists* by Max Frisch, *Lights Rise on*

Grace by Chad Bekim, and *The Convert* by Danai Gurira. New York directing credits include: BAMtheatre, Atlantic Theater Company, The Cherry Lane, INTAR, Repertorio Español. Regional credits include South Coast Repertory, A Contemporary Theatre (ACT), Hartford Stage, The Huntington Theatre, and The Children's Theatre. Michael is a recipient of the Rockwood Arts and Culture Fellowship, the Princess Grace Statue, the Alan Schneider Director Award, a TCG/New Generations Grant, and the Nonprofit Excellence Award from the Center for Nonprofit Management.

Nataki Garrett is the Artistic Director of Oregon Shakespeare Festival. She is the Co-Founder and Co-Artistic Director of Blank the Dog Productions, and co-created the Carolyn Bryant Project. She frequently works with writer Brandon Jacobs-Jenkin, and has directed three of his regional premiers: *Everybody* (CalShakes), *An Octoroon* (Mixed Blood Theatre and Woolly Mammoth Theatre), and *Neighbors* (Matrix Theatre Company). Garrett also directed the world premiere of *BLKS* by Aziza Barnes at Steppenwolf Theatre and the US premiere of *Jefferson's Garden* by Timberlake Wertenbaker at Ford's Theatre in Washington, DC. In 2008, Garrett received an NAACP Theatre Award–nomination for Best Director for *Black Women, State of the Union: An Evening of Plays by Black Women*. The former Associate Artistic Director of the Denver Center for the Performing Arts (DCPA), where she also served as the Acting Artistic Director during their eighteen-month leadership transition. Garrett was the 2005 recipient of the National Endowment for the Arts and Theatre Communications Group Career Development Fellowship for Directors and is a member of the Society of Stage Directors and Choreographers.

Robert Icke is an award-winning writer and theater director. He is currently Associate Director at the Almeida Theatre. From 2010 to 2013 he was Associate Director at Headlong Theatre, where he worked on all of the company's productions and directed three of his own. He was the Artistic Director of the Arden Theatre Company from 2003 to 2007 and of the Swan Theatre Company from 2005 to 2008. The director of *Oresteia*, Icke won Best Director at the 2016 Olivier Awards, and Best Director at both the Critics Circle and Evening Standard Theatre

Awards 2015. Director of *1984*, which appeared on Broadway, for which he won Best Director at the UK Theatre Awards 2014, Best Director at the Liverpool Arts Awards 2013, and was nominated for Best New Play at the 2014 Olivier Awards. Other credits include *Oedipus* (Toneelgroep Amsterdam); *Hamlet*, *Mary Stuart* (Almeida Theatre and West End); *The Red Barn* (National Theatre); *Uncle Vanya* and *Mr Burns, a Post-Electric Play* (Almeida).

Anne Kauffman is an Obie Award–winning Director who has directed for Soho Rep., Goodman Theatre, Playwrights Horizons, New York Theatre Workshop, Manhattan Theater Club, Classic Stage Company, The Vineyard, The Public Theater, Rattlestick Playwrights Theatre, New Georges, Clubbed Thumb, Woolly Mammoth Theatre Company, American Conservatory Theater, American Repertory Theatre, and the Guthrie Theater. She is a Program Associate with Sundance Theatre Institute, a New York Theatre Workshop Usual Suspect, a member of Soho Rep.'s Artistic Council, on New Georges' Kitchen Cabinet, an alumna of the Lincoln Center Directors Lab and The Drama League, a founding member of the Civilians, and an associate artist with Clubbed Thumb. Kauffman is a recipient of the Joan and Joseph F. Cullman Award for Extraordinary Creativity, the Alan Schneider Director Award, and several Barrymore awards.

Daniel Kramer served as the Artistic Director of the English National Opera (ENO) from 2016 to 2019. He is a Fellow of The Drama League in New York and previously served as an Associate at London's Gate Theatre (Notting Hill) and the Young Vic Theatre as well as Creative Associate at the Royal Shakespeare Company. Credits include *La Traviata* (Theater Basel); *Sadko* (Vlaamse Opera, Slovak National Opera); *Romeo and Juliet* (Shakespeare's Globe); *Dream Play* (Harvard University); *Tristan and Isolde* (ENO); *The Serpent* (Brown University); *Pelléas et Mélisande* (Mariinsky and Bolshoi Theatre, Golden Mask Awards); *Carmen* (Vlaamse Opera, Opera North); *Punch and Judy* (Grand Theatre Geneva, ENO – Outstanding Achievement in Opera, South Bank Award); *Bluebeard's Castle* (ENO, Mariinsky and Bolshoi Theatre – Golden Mask Awards); *Pictures from an Exhibition* (Sadler's Wells, Young Vic Theatre); *King Kong* (Regent Theatre, Australia); *Angels in America* (Headlong Theatre, Glasgow

Citizens Theatre, Lyric Hammersmith); *Woyzeck* (St. Ann's Warehouse, NYC); *Bent* (Trafalgar Studios, London); *Prick Up Your Ears* (Comedy Theatre, London); *Hair*, *Woyzeck* (Gate Theatre, Notting Hill); *Through the Leaves* (Southwark Playhouse, Duchess Theatre, West End).

Dmitri Krymov serves as the Founder and Head of The Dmitry Krymov Lab in Moscow. He is a Professor at the Russian Academy of Theatre Arts and the Head of the Experimental Theatre Project of the Union Theatre of Europe. In the 1970s and 1980s, Krymov scenic designed around 100 shows in Russia. From the late 1980s to the early 2000s, Krymov worked as a painter and his paintings hang in numerous museums and private collections around the world. Krymov made his directing debut in 2002 with a production of *Hamlet* at the Stanislavski Drama Theatre. His production of *Demon: The View from Above* received the Golden Mask Award for Experimentation in 2008. His productions of *Auction*, *The Cow*, and *Opus No. 7* have toured to numerous European cities. He is a recipient of Stanislavski (2006), Turandot (2007 and 2009) and Golden Mask (2008) awards, the highest theatre achievement awards in Russia.

Brian Kulick is a director, writer, educator, producer, and Chair of the Graduate Theatre Program at Columbia University, USA. From 2003 to 2017 he was the Artistic Director of Classic Stage Company (CSC), directing Lessing's *Nathan the Wise*, Shakespeare's *The Tempest*, and Ostrovsky's *The Forest*. He commissioned and co-directed poet Anne Carson's award-winning, *An Oresteia*. He developed CSC's popular programing of Shakespeare (directing *Richard II*, *Richard III*, and *Hamlet*), Brecht (directing *Mother Courage*, *Man's a Man*, *The Caucasian Chalk Circle*, and *Galileo*), and produced CSC's critically acclaimed Chekhov Cycle (*Ivanov*, *The Seagull*, *Uncle Vanya*, *Three Sisters*, and *The Cherry Orchard*). He produced the first major New York revival of Stephen Sondheim's *Passion* and Rodgers and Hammerstein's *Allegro*. Prior to CSC, Kulick was an Associate Artist and then Associate Producer for The Public Theater.

Christopher Luscombe is an English actor and director. He spent seven years with the Royal Shakespeare Company as an actor, and went on to appear at the National Theatre, the Old Vic, and in the West End. His directing credits in London include *Star Quality* and *The Madness of George III* (Apollo); *Home and Beauty* (Lyric); *Fascinating Aïda* (Harold Pinter – Olivier Award nomination for Best Entertainment); *The Comedy of Errors*, and *The Merry Wives of Windsor* (Shakespeare's Globe); *Nell Gwynn* (Shakespeare's Globe and Apollo – Olivier Award for Best New Comedy); *A Midsummer Night's Dream* (Regent's Park); *Enjoy* (Gielgud); *Alphabetical Order* (Hampstead); *When We Are Married* (Garrick–Olivier Award nomination for Best Revival); *Travels with My Aunt* (Menier Chocolate Factory) and *Spamalot* (Playhouse). He has directed several private entertainments for the Royal Family, including productions marking the 50th Anniversary of the Coronation and the Queen's 90th birthday.

Kristin Marting is the founding Artistic Director of HERE and a director of hybrid work based in New York City. She has directed nineteen works at HERE and also premiered works at BAM, 3LD, Ohio Theatre, and Soho Rep. Her work has toured to 7 Stages, Berkshire Festival, Brown, MCA, New World, Painted Bride, Perishable Theatre Arts School, UMass, Moscow Art Theatre, London, and Oslo. She has directed readings, workshops, and premieres for Clubbed Thumb, New Georges, National Sawdust, Playwrights Horizons, Prototype, The Public Theater, Target Margin, and others. Selected residencies include CalArts, LMCC, Mabou Mines, MASS MOCA, NACL, Orchard Project, Playwrights Center, Smack Mellon, Voice & Vision and Williams. She has also directed productions for CalArts, NYU, and Sarah Lawrence.

Charles Newell has served as the Marilyn F. Vitale Artistic Director of Court Theatre since 1994, directing over 50 productions. He made his Chicago directorial debut in 1993 with *The Triumph of Love*, which won the Joseph Jefferson Award for Best Production. He was awarded the SDCF Zelda Fichandler Award, "which recognizes an outstanding director or choreographer who is transforming the regional arts landscape through singular creativity and artistry in theatre." He has also directed at Goodman Theatre, Guthrie Theater, Arena Stage, John Houseman's The Acting Company, the California and Alabama

Shakespeare Festivals, Juilliard, and New York University. He has been nominated for sixteen Joseph Jefferson Director Awards, winning four times.

Robert O'Hara is an American theater director and playwright who directed *Slave Play* for New York Theatre Workshop and on Broadway. His first play, *Insurrection: Holding History* debuted at the Public Theater on October 11, 1996, and received *Newsday*'s Oppenheimer Award for Best New American Play. He received a 2006 Obie Award for his direction of the world premiere production of *In the Continuum*. He has directed at New York Shakespeare Festival, Kirk Douglas Theatre, Woolly Mammoth Theatre, Yale Repertory, Seattle Repertory, and Goodman Theatre, among others.

Ron OJ Parson is a Resident Artist at Court Theatre, former Co-Founder and Artistic Director of Onyx Theatre. Directing credits include *Gem of the Ocean* (Court Theatre), *Sunset Baby* and *A Raisin in the Sun* (TimeLine Theatre Company), *The Who & The What* (Victory Gardens Theatre), *Seven Guitars*, *The Mountaintop*, *Waiting For Godot* (Court Theatre), and *Detroit 67* (Northlight Theatre). Other Chicago theatres Parson has directed at include Black Ensemble Theatre, Congo Square Theatre, Writers Theatre, and Steppenwolf Theatre. Regional credits include Portland Stage, Studio Theatre, Roundabout Theatre Company, Actors Theatre of Louisville, Milwaukee Rep, St. Louis Black Rep, Signature Theatre (New York), Alliance Theatre, and South Coast Repertory. Parson is a proud member of AEA, SAG-AFTRA, and SDC.

Lisa Portes serves as the Head of Directing at the Theatre School at DePaul University, USA, and is the winner of the prestigious Stage Directors and Choreographers Foundation's Zelda Fichandler Award. Her work has been seen at California Shakespeare Theatre, Cincinnati Playhouse, Goodman Theatre, Steppenwolf Theatre, TimeLine Theatre Company, Playwrights Horizons, Soho Rep., New York Theatre Workshop, The Public Theater, the Flea Theatre, the Sundance Theatre Lab, the Cape Cod Theatre Project, the Santa Barbara Theatre Lab, and the Eugene O'Neill Playwrights Conference, among others. She is a founding member of the Latinx Theatre Commons (LTC) and co-produced the LTC Carnaval of New Latinx Work in 2015 and 2018.

Aaron Posner is a Director and Playwright, a Founder and former Artistic Director of Philadelphia's Arden Theatre Company, the former Artistic Director of Two River Theater, and an associate artist at the Folger Theatre in Washington, DC. His widely produced plays include *Stupid Fucking Bird*, *Life Sucks*, and *No Sisters* (all re-imaginings of Chekhov plays); *The Chosen* and *My Name Is Asher Lev*, both adapted from Chaim Potok novels; *Sometimes a Great Notion*, adapted from Ken Kesey; Mark Twain's *A Murder, a Mystery, and a Marriage*; and an adaptation of three Kurt Vonnegut short stories, entitled *Who Am I This Time? (And Other Conundrums of Love)*. He also has popularly adapted and co-directed two Shakespearian plays, *Macbeth* and *The Tempest* with Teller, of Penn and Teller. Posner has also directed nearly 200 productions at major regional theaters across the country. He has won numerous awards as both a director and playwright, including a Jeff Award, several Helen Hayes Awards, two Barrymore Awards, two Los Angeles Drama Critics Circle Awards, an Elliot Norton Award, The John Gassner Memorial Playwriting Award, an Outer Circle Critics Award, Theatre Bay Area Award, and more. Posner graduated from Northwestern University, USA, and is an Eisenhower Fellow.

Bill Rauch is the inaugural Artistic Director of the Ronald O. Perelman Performing Arts Center at the World Trade Center. He served as the Artistic Director for the Oregon Shakespeare Festival from 2006 to 2019, directing seven world premieres: *Roe*, *Off the Rails*, *Fingersmith*, *The Great Society*, *Equivocation*, *All the Way*, and *By the Waters of Babylon*. He Co-Founded Cornerstone Theater Company in Los Angeles, where he directed more than forty productions. He also served as the Artistic Director for Cornerstone from 1986 to 2006. In 2018 he received the Ivy Bethune Award from Actors' Equity Association for diversity and inclusion in hiring, casting, and producing.

Julia Rhoads is a director, choreographer, and the founding Artistic Director of Lucky Plush Productions. She has collaborated on many works with the company including *Punk Yankees*, *The Better Half*, *Cinderbox 2.0*, *The Queue*, *SuperStrip*, *Rooming*

House, and *Rink Life*. Many of these have toured throughout the United States. Julia graduated from Northwestern University, USA, with a BA in History and received her MFA in Performance from the School of the Art Institute of Chicago, USA. Rhoads is currently the Director of Dance at the University of Chicago's Department of Theater and Performance Studies. She has directed and choreographed for other companies including Redmoon Theater, Walkabout Theater, Hyperdelic, and the interdisciplinary collective M5. Rhoads has received a Cliff Dwellers Foundation Award for Choreography, a Jacob K. Javits Fellowship, a Chicago Dancemakers Forum Lab Artist Award, two Illinois Arts Council Fellowships for Choreography, and a fellowship from the Maggie Allesee National Center for Choreography.

Kim Rubinstein is an American theater director and a faculty member at University of California San Diego, USA. Previously, she served as the Long Wharf Theatre's Associate Artistic Director where she directed *Guys and Dolls*, *A Midsummer Night's Dream*, *Private Lives*, *Santaland Diaries*, and *The Cocktail Hour*. Other regional credits include *Much Ado About Nothing* (Shakespeare Santa Cruz), *The Intelligent Design of Jenny Chow* (Portland Center Stage and San Jose Rep), *Romeo and Juliet*, *Macbeth*, and *Julius Caesar* (Chicago Shakespeare), *Love's Labour's Lost* (Next Theatre), *The Tempest* (Southwest Rep), *The American Plan* and *Eloise and Ray* (Roadworks), *Pan and Boone* (Running with Scissors), *Baby With The Bathwater* (Roundhouse Theatre, Berkshire Theatre Festival), *Beckett Shorts* (Berkshire Theatre Festival, Splinter Group's Buckets O'Beckett Festival). She was Associate Director with Michael Mayer and Tour Director of the National Tour of *Angels in America*. Rubinstein is a recipient of the Theatre Communications Group/National Endowment for the Arts directing fellowship and was nominated for the Alan Schneider Directing Award.

Derrick L. Sanders is the Producing Director of the August Wilson Monologue Competition and is on faculty at the University of Illinois at Chicago, USA. The founding Artistic Director of Congo Square Theatre, Sanders has received several Jeff awards for his production of *Seven Guitars*. Chicago credits include *La Clemenza di Tito* (Chicago Summer Opera), *Richard III* and *The Island* (American Players Theatre), and *Topdog/Underdog* (American

Theatre Company). He has also directed at Round House Theatre, Marin Theatre Company, Virginia Stage Company, Signature Theatre, The Kennedy Center, Baltimore Center Stage, Cincinnati Playhouse, and Minneapolis Children's Theatre.

Kimberly Senior is an American freelance director. She made her HBO debut with *Chris Gethard: Career Suicide*, which premiered at the Tribeca Film Festival. Kimberly spent ten years as an administrator and Resident Artist with Steppenwolf Theatre for Young Adults in Chicago. New York credits include *Disgraced* (Broadway), *Chris Gethard: Career Suicide* (Judd Apatow presents), *The Who and the What* and *Disgraced* (Lincoln Center Theater 3). Chicago credits include: *Support Group for Men*, *Disgraced*, and *Rapture, Blister, Burn* (Goodman Theatre), as well as multiple productions with Writers Theatre, Northlight Theatre, Steppenwolf Theatre, and TimeLine Theatre Company.

Leigh Silverman is an Obie Award–winning and Tony Award–nominated director. Her Broadway credits include *Chinglish*, *Violet*, and *Well*. Her off-Broadway credits include *American Hero* and *Danny and the Deep Blue Sea* (Second Stage); *Kung Fu* and *Golden Child* (Signature Theatre); *Go Back to Where You Are* (Obie Award), *Blue Door*, *The (Curious Case of the) Watson Intelligence*, and *The Call* (Playwrights Horizons); *From Up Here* (Drama Desk nomination) and *The Madrid* (Manhattan Theatre Club); *Coraline* (MCC/True Love); *No Place to Go* (Public Theater/Two River Theatre); *In the Wake* (Public Theater/Center Theatre Group/Berkeley Repertory Theatre, Obie Award, Lucille Lortel nomination); *Yellow Face* (Public Theater/Center Theatre Group); and *Well* (Public Theater/Huntington Theatre/American Conservatory Theatre). Silverman has served as the Vice President of the Stage Directors and Choreographers Foundation.

Rebecca Taichman is a freelance American theater director. She received a Tony Award, Obie Award, and Outer Critics Circle Award for Best Direction of a Play for Paula Vogel's *Indecent*. Off-Broadway credits include *School Girls or* The African Mean Girls Play (MCC); *This Flat Earth*, *Familiar*, *Stage Kiss*, *Milk Like Sugar* (Playwrights Horizons); *The Oldest Boy* (Lincoln Center); *The Scene* (Second Stage). Regional credits include work at The Old Globe, La Jolla Playhouse, Oregon Shakespeare Festival, McCarter Theatre, American Conservatory Theater, and Huntington Theatre Company.

Jessica Thebus is the Director of the MFA Directing Program at Northwestern University, USA. She is an associate artist with Chicago's Steppenwolf Theatre, where she has directed *Sex With Strangers*, *Intimate Apparel*, *Dead Man's Cell Phone*, *When the Messenger Is Hot*, and *Sonia Flew*. Among many others, she has also directed *As You Like It* at the Oregon Shakespeare Festival, *The Clean House* and *Stage Kiss* at The Goodman Theatre, *A Civil War Christmas* at The Huntington Theatre, *Harriet Jacobs* at Kansas City Repertory Theatre, and *Jekyll and Hyde*, *Inherit the Wind*, and *Red Herring* at Northlight Theatre. Her favorite projects include the award-winning plays *Pulp* and *Winesburg, Ohio*, at About Face Theatre, as well as the Oregon Shakespeare Festival's world premiere of *Welcome Home, Jenny Sutter*, which then moved to the Kennedy Center in Washington, DC. An artistic associate at the Corn Exchange in Dublin, Ireland, Thebus holds a PhD in performance studies from Northwestern.

Ivo van Hove is the General Director of the Toneelgroep Amsterdam. He made his Broadway debut with *A View From the Bridge* (Tony Award, Best Director). His Broadway production of *The Crucible* was nominated for a Tony Award for Best Revival. For Toneelgroep, Van Hove has directed *The Things that Pass*, *Obsession*, *Diary of the One who Disappeared*, *Mary Stuart*, *The Fountainhead*, *Long Day's Journey into Night*, *Scenes from a Marriage*, *Children of the Sun*, *Othello*, *Teorema*, *Summer Trilogy*, *Antonioni Project*, *Cries and Whispers*, *The Human Voice*, *Rocco and His Brothers*, *Angels in America*, and *Roman Tragedies*. He has staged many internationally acclaimed productions including, in New York, *Alice in Bed*, *More Stately Mansions* (Obie Award), *A Streetcar Named Desire*, *Hedda Gabler* (Obie Award), *The Misanthrope*, *The Little Foxes*, and *Scenes from a Marriage*, all at New York Theatre Workshop; *Roman Tragedies*, *Cries and Whispers*, *Opening Night*, *Angels in America*, and *Antigone* at Brooklyn Academy of Music and *Teorema* at Lincoln Center Festival. Van Hove's opera credits include the premiere of *Brokeback Mountain* at Teatro Real in Madrid, as well as productions of *The Clemency of Titus*,

Idomeneo, Mazeppa, Macbeth, Iolanta, The Makropulos Case, Lulu, and *The Ring Cycle.*

Jorge Arturo Vargas is the Artistic Director of Teatro Línea de Sombra (TLS). After studying under Jerzy Grotowski, he went on to direct *Galería de Moribundos,* which established Vargas's interest in physical and visual theater. Until 2010, he alternated between devising experimental theater and directing plays written by authors such as Roland Schimmelpfennig, Jon Fosse, Anthony Neilson, Neil LaBute, and Lars Noren. The Association of Theater Writers and Critics (UCCCT) twice recognized Vargas and TLS with Best Theatre Group in the Provinces (1982, 1991), and Vargas with two awards for Best Research Theatre Director (2001, 2005). *Amarillo,* the hallmark work by Vargas with TLS, received the Latin ACE Award for Best Foreign Production in New York, in 2012. Other directing credits include *The Forge of the World, Carnaval de Abandonados, Amarillo en la ruta migrante.* Vargas is also the artistic co-director of *Transversales, Encuentro Internacional de Escena Contemporánea,* and also belongs to the National System of Art Creators.

Mark Wing-Davey is the Chair of the Graduate Acting Program at New York University's Tisch School of the Arts in New York City, USA. He first came to prominence in the United States with his highly acclaimed 1992 production of Caryl Churchill's *Mad Forest* at New York Theatre Workshop. Since then he has worked extensively in New York City, for NYTW, Manhattan Theatre Club, Lincoln Center, Playwrights Horizons, LAByrinth, and the Public Theater, directing *Troilus and Cressida* and *Henry V* in Central Park. His acting career extends all the way back to 1974, appearing in TV series such as *A Question of Guilt* and *The Hitchhiker's Guide to the Galaxy.*

Chay Yew was the Artistic Director of Victory Gardens Theatre in Chicago from 2011 to 2020. He has directed world premieres by playwrights Jose Rivera, Naomi Iizuka, Kia Corthron, Julia Cho, David Adjmi, and Jessica Goldberg, and performance artists Rha Goddess, Universes, Alec Mapa, Sandra Tsing Loh, and Brian Freeman. He is the recipient of the London Fringe Award for Best Playwright and Best Play, George and Elisabeth Marton Playwriting Award, GLAAD Media Award, Asian

Pacific Gays and Friends' Community Visibility Award, Made in America Award, AEA/SAG/AFTRA 2004 Diversity Honor, and Robert Chesley Award. As a playwright, Yew's plays have been published in two titles, *The Hyphenated American Plays* and *Porcelain and a Language of Their Own*, by Grove Press.

Madani Younis is the Creative Director of the Southbank Centre, having been the Artistic Director of Bush Theatre, where his directing credits included *Leave Taking*, *The Principles of Cartography*, *Zaida and Aadam*, and the critically acclaimed UK premiere of *The Royale*. He was previously the Artistic Director of Freedom Studios, and worked nationally and internationally as a theatre director, writer and practitioner. Film directing credits include *Ellabellapumpanella*. In 2013 Younis received the Groucho Club Maverick Award for the theatre and was the recipient of the Decibel Award at the South Bank Awards show in 2006. Younis is a member of the Mayor of London's Cultural Board.

Index

action 6–7, 14–16, 49–51, 76, 89–92, 97–98
Alfreds, M. 129; *Different Every Night* 74
Aristotle 5–7

Ball, W. *A Sense of Direction* 89–90
Bogart, A. 24–26, 71–72, 189–190
Brecht, B. 16–21, 194–195
Brook, P. 21–24
Buxbaum Danzig, L. 137, 142–143, 145–147, 156–157, 159–160, 207

Carden, C. 150–153, 160–161, 206
character 8–10, 13–14, 17–19, 24, 45, 62–63, 74–75, 86–88, 98, 154, 180–181
Chavkin, R. 75, 118–119, 206–207
Chekhov, A. 12, 44, 190; *The Seagull* 13, 88–90, 95–96; *Uncle Vanya* 74
Columbus, C. 33–34, 133–134, 207
conflict 14–16, 47, 50, 53, 88, 90–93, 98–99, 186–187

Davis, W. 78, 208
Dean, A. and Carra, L. *Fundamentals of Play Directing* 66–67
DePaul University 10, 15, 35, 43–44, 57, 63–65, 79–80, 88–89
dramaturgy 7, 34, 46, 54, 169, 186

Ellis, S. 45, 91–92, 104, 208

etudes *see* improvisations
event 6, 9, 49–50, 53, 62–63, 87, 95, 147, 149, 169–173, 176

Falls, R. 38–39, 62–63, 73–74, 209
first day address 32–35, 113, 172–173
Fondakowski, L. 148–149, 157–159, 209
Frecknall, R. 36–38, 210

Gaines, B. 114–115, 121–122, 210
Garrett, N. 47–48, 56–57, 74–75, 92–93, 211
given circumstances 10, 13–14, 63, 85, 91–96, 168–169, 180–181, 188
ground plan 68, 186

Hauser, F. and Reich, R. *Notes on Directing* 70, 90, 186

Icke, R. 59–60, 131–132, 211
improvisations 15–16, 25–26, 62–63, 179–180

Jory, J. *Tips: Ideas for Directors* 69–70, 171–172

Kauffman, A. 72, 82, 125–126, 212
Kaufman, M. 138–139
Kramer, D. 76, 212
Krymov, D. 99–100, 213
Kulick, B. 96–98, 129, 132, 213

Luscombe, C. 126–127, 213

Marting, K. 144–145, 154–155, 214
Mitchell, K. *The Director's Craft* 49, 63, 85–86, 168–169
moment chain 171–172, 186, 198–199

new plays 42–43, 51–52, 56–57
Newell, C. 98–99, 214

O'Hara, R. 39–41, 102–103, 127–128, 215

Parson, R. 38, 117, 215
PigPen Theatre Co. 150–153, 160–161
Portes, L. 35–36, 45–46, 106–108, 115–117, 215
Posner, A. 52–54, 80–81, 216

Rauch, B. 43, 96, 216
relationships 15, 74, 86–88, 180–181
Rhoads, J. 142, 145–147, 156–157, 159–160, 216
Rubinstein, K. 52, 61–62, 217
run-throughs 7, 23, 66, 73–74, 99–110, 182–183, 196–197, 200

Sanders, D. 46–47, 86–87, 101–102, 217
Saxe-Meiningen, Duke of 7–11
Senior, K. ix–xi, 66, 76–77, 103–104, 124, 130–131, 133, 196–197, 218

Shakespeare, W. *Hamlet* 9–10, 68, 115, 132; *Macbeth* 39–41, 80–81; *The Merchant of Venice* 8–9; *Othello* 43, 96; *Richard III* 33
Silverman, L. 57, 79, 108, 218
Sinek, S. *Start with Why* 173
Stanislavski, K. 11–16, 89, 93
subtext 81, 85, 91–92

table work 13, 15, 44–53, 55–57, 59, 176–179
Taichman, R. 42, 44–45, 56, 82–83, 218
Tectonic Theater Project 138–139, 148–149
Thebus, J. 32–33, 108–109, 113–114, 119–121, 219

Van Hove, I. 53–54, 105, 122, 219
Vargas, J. 140, 143–144, 220

Williams, T. *The Glass Menagerie* 35–36; *A Streetcar Named Desire* 7, 10, 13–14, 49–50, 52, 54, 64–65, 85, 87–88, 91, 93–95, 98, 168–171, 178, 180, 181, 184–185, 188–189, 198; *Summer and Smoke* 36–38
Wing-Davey, M. 50–51, 60–61, 129–130, 179, 220

Yew, C. 51–52, 78, 84, 220
Younis, M. 141–142, 155–156, 221

Ziegler, A. *Boy* 19–20, 34–35, 109–110

For Product Safety Concerns and Information please contact our EU representative GPSR@taylorandfrancis.com
Taylor & Francis Verlag GmbH, Kaufingerstraße 24, 80331 München, Germany

www.ingramcontent.com/pod-product-compliance
Lightning Source LLC
Chambersburg PA
CBHW070603300426
44113CB00010B/1383